Mckinley Memories

A coming of age memoir of growing up in the
American suburbs of the 1950s and 60s

By

Frank Alan Burr

ISBN-13: 978-1984944146
ISBN-10: 1984944142

Printed in the United States of America

Previous book by Frank Burr:
Common Thoughts -
Poems and Essays
2007 & 2018

Dedicated to my wife, Dale,
son Andrew,
grandsons Tyler, Noah & Sean
brother Bill
and in memory of Mom and Dad

- Frank Alan Burr

Dad, Mom, Brother Bill in back,
Frank (Buddy) in front
Cadwalader Ave., McKinley

Contents

Author's Note

For some time I've felt compelled to put down a modest chronicle of my childhood, growing up in a small American suburban community during the 1950s and 60s. I've tried to create the feel of that unique time through the eyes of a boy slowly maturing into young manhood. These pages include my best recollections, bolstered by memories from certain relatives and friends. How I may have viewed an individual then is what is described, however, in retrospect, as someone with over seven decades under his belt, it may not be how I think of that person now.

It has never been my intent to belittle or embarrass those of whom I refer. There are many inferences, herein, of honest self-deprecation. In many instances I will use a person's full name. If I wish to bestow a modicum of anonymity, I've used only their first name. If a higher level of protection is required, I've chosen a pseudonym with an initial phrase such as "whom I'll call . . . . . ."

May everyone who reads these pages be drawn to the deep feelings of their own childhood.

Foreword

It was in November of 1948 when our family of four made the move from the West Oak Lane section of Philadelphia to a little community called McKinley in the nearby Montgomery County suburbs. A single family three-story frame affair, built around the turn of the century, our new home signified a step up from the residential neighborhood of small row houses. Its detached garage provided more room for the particular wares and supplies of my dad's self-employment, with ample space for his green Chevy panel truck emblazoned with the words, "William C. Burr • Painter & Paperhanger." Laid off from the Frankford Arsenal soon after World War II, Dad had reverted to his old profession as a house painter.

My first memory of McKinley is that of standing next to my mom on the enclosed front porch of our new home on a cool autumn day. She was in quiet conversation with a man who I believe was the real estate agent who'd handled the sale of the property. Being only three years old at the time, I recall little else. However, I do have memories of my earlier childhood on 21st Street in West Oak Lane and playing with our neighbor's son Freddie. Misty images of my crib in the row house's second floor bedroom, and Sunday afternoons in the kitchen after attending church also linger hazily in my mind.

Being so young, I easily adjusted to the move – it was probably less so for brother Bill who, at five years my senior, needed to make the adjustment of meeting new friends and attending the third grade of McKinley Elementary School for the first time.

McKinley is an unincorporated little blip on the map – no post office – no sign telling you that you are entering or leaving the community. The only hint of identification for this little, "insignificant" town was etched in the marble blocks above the entryways of its two main buildings – the fire house and the elementary school. There, one could find the name of the assassinated president that proudly provided the community's identity.

As in many small towns of its ilk, there was an evident, but subtle, strata of society. As I grew up in McKinley in the 1950s and 60s, our family lived in the "town center" area, since the two aforementioned institutions were located on our street. Turn-of-the-century houses, like ours, were evident up and down Cadwalader Avenue. Most breadwinners in this section of town were of the "working class" – blue collar and lower-level white collar. Tacit racial segregation was evident. "The Hill," on the east side of Jenkintown Road was a predominately African-American neighborhood, but some mixture of the races existed on Osceola Avenue, the street behind ours.

North of town center was "the village" – streets lined with modest brick houses owned by the middle class. Farther in the same direction, near Jenkintown, was "the manor" – stately, stone homes occupied by the well-to-do.

The old elementary school was built in 1898 and designed by the famous, Philadelphia-area architect, Horace Trumbaur. This institution stood as the greater community's social equalizer. If the parents, representing various socioeconomic neighborhoods, didn't mingle freely, at least their children did; that is, in the classroom and in the schoolyard. And, occasionally, pick-up games of various sorts took place on the large public playground bordering Jenkintown Road, most notably among children from "town center" and "the hill," after school and on weekends. But children of different races rarely played at each other's homes. That was an unwritten taboo. When sixth grade dance parties were held at the homes of the white families, the affairs remained white by invitation.

Back in the day of stay-at-home moms and single car families, McKinley provided a self-contained and self-sustaining environment. Within a few blocks of our home were the ACME supermarket, and a number of small independent stores and shops: a drugstore, a hardware store, a barbershop, gas stations, two grocery stores, a garment cleaners, a snack shop, and a bakery. Olivet Presbyterian Church was just down the street from us, and St. James Catholic Church wasn't far across Township Line Road in the neighboring community of Elkins Park in Cheltenham Township. We residents of McKinley in Abington Township shared the Elkins Park postal zone with our nearby Cheltenham neighbors and their more upscale community. Thus, we referred to our area as the poor man's Elkins Park.

Public transportation was important in those days, especially when the breadwinner utilized the family's only vehicle to go to work. The Philadelphia Transportation Company's (PTC) "XA" bus had a route stop on a corner near our home. A regular schedule provided access to the city via these noisy and smoke-spewing vehicles. The bus terminus was at Fern Rock Station in the far northern section of the city providing subway train access to the rest of the metropolis. One of the earlier stops on the line, Logan station, was located a few blocks from my great-uncle and aunt's home in that section of the city. We spent many hours visiting them during my childhood.

This provides a basic backdrop of my boyhood town. The details will be provided as we make our journey back together.

Beginnings

The Family Background

I suppose some discussion of my family roots may put things in perspective. Much information concerning my Burr heritage didn't become apparent to me until I was in my mid-fifties. I always imagined that I was somehow related to the controversial Aaron Burr, third vice-president of the United States and the victor of the mortal duel with Alexander Hamilton. That connection turned out to be somewhat fanciful, but at least it gave me some measure of cachet during my childhood.

As it turns out, I'm a direct descendant of Henry Burr, a Quaker who arrived in America in 1682 at the age of 18 on one of William Penn's three voyages to the new world. He eventually settled in Mt. Holly, New Jersey with his wife, Elizabeth Hudson, and built a house in 1725. As the family grew, he built an addition to the structure in 1732. His home, Peachfield Plantation, still stands today and is maintained by the New Jersey chapter of The Colonial Dames of America. Burr descendants continued to live in this residence until the early 1900s.

In my specific genealogical line, Henry's great grandson, Caleb, appears to be the first to leave his Quaker roots behind. The Mt. Holly Monthly Meeting minutes for October 7, 1790 indicate: "Caleb Burr reported for neglecting meetings and marrying out." Evidently his new wife, Martha Jones, was not of the Quaker faith. Nonetheless, Caleb's family continued to attend meeting for a while thereafter, since in 2001 I uncovered his son Benjamin's initials with the year "1801" carved in one of the ancient pews of the Mt. Holly Quaker Meetinghouse. All of Caleb and Martha's eight children were born in Mt. Holly. The next to youngest child, Alexander, who was born in 1807, is my great great-grandfather. At some point in the early 19th century, Caleb made the move across the Delaware River and settled in Philadelphia.

McElroy's Philadelphia Directory for 1843 lists Alexander as a house painter living on Pine Street near Seventh. His son,

William Henry Burr, my great-grandfather, established a painting business on Market Street in West Philadelphia in the 1880s.

Great grandfather William H. Burr
at the West Philadelphia store, 1891

Employees, including family members, supported an evidently thriving business, painting many homes for the well-to-do on the Philadelphia Main Line. When William, a Civil War veteran of the 72nd Pennsylvania Regiment, died on New Year's Day 1915 at the age of 77, his sons – including the youngest, Clarence, my grandfather – subsequently carried on the business. The company, W. H. Burr Son's, thrived until the early 1930s when it fell victim to the Great Depression. My dad continued in the profession as an independent contractor. It would appear that his family background greatly affected his formidable work ethic.

Whereas my father had a reasonably stable childhood with strong family ties, my mother's early years were more fluid and uncertain. My mother, Lucy, was born in Camden, New Jersey in 1914 to Enos and Lucy Shuman Wernett. Enos apparently made a living as a salesman of some sort. Mom's brother, Enos Jr., was born two years later. This scene of seemingly marital family bliss suddenly and tragically ended when Lucy Sr. fell victim to the influenza epidemic in 1918 and died at the tender age of 28. Being only four years old at the time, my mother retained only fleeting memories of her mother's demise. Evidently there was a shortage of caskets for adults because of the great death toll caused by that plague, and mom once told me that they had to break the legs of her mother to fit her body into a smaller youth coffin than, otherwise, would have been used.

It would appear that my mother's maternal grandmother then took charge of her two grandchildren for a few years while her son-in-law continued in his employment. In any case, he remarried in 1920 and, soon after, pursued his career in Kansas City, Missouri, taking son Enos, Jr. with him and leaving young Lucy behind. It is open to speculation by my mother's account that there may have been infidelity on her father's part before his first wife's death. Existing letters from young Lucy's father to her mother's mother unconvincingly convey that it would be best that his daughter be raised by her grandmother. So it was that my mother was estranged from her father for the rest of her life, never meeting him, or desiring to meet him, again. Although she was well cared for by her stern grandmother, it wasn't a particularly happy childhood to this point.

While living with her grandmother, my mother found some solace in a couple of pets. Her favorite was a parrot with a full vocabulary which filled the role of a surrogate sibling and friend. Mom also cared for a duck kept in the dwelling's yard. Tragically the poor bird was dispatched one day by mom's grandmother and subsequently served as a main course for dinner. Mom related that she was heartbroken at the cruelty of her grandmother and could not bring herself to partake of that particular meal.

Upon her grandmother's death at age 65 in 1929, mom, now age 14, briefly lived with a rather malevolent relative in Camden until rescued from the dire situation by her uncle – her mother's brother – who lived with his wife in the Logan section of Philadelphia. Uncle and Auntie, as I knew them, became her surrogate parents until her marriage and provided her with the loving, nurturing support she had never known as a child.

My fraternal grandmother and Auntie were acquaintances, providing the connection that, years later, culminated in my parent's marriage.

The Early Homestead

Our house on Cadwalader Avenue in McKinley was a childhood dream to me. The turn-of-the-century, three-story structure provided ample room for two young brothers to let off excess levels of energy. Earlier photos of the frame house show that it once had wood clapboard siding. By the time our family moved in, it had been replaced with white asbestos shingles. The roof retained its original slate tiles. My father had storm windows added years later, so I suppose the rooms were quite drafty during those early winters. Some years before we arrived, the coal furnace had been replaced with a centralized hot water, fuel-oil heater. I recall that at least one house on the street, owned by the Donahue family, still utilized coal. When a Lyman Coal Company truck made its delivery, one could hear the cacophony of sound caused by the black nuggets streaming down the chute to the neighbor's basement.

An enclosed front porch with tall windows extended partially around the side of our house and faced a large yard. The entrance door had a large glass panel, and the interior French doors were multi-pane. To your right as you walked in, the long staircase with its oak banister led to the second floor. A stained glass window at the base of the stairs over the radiator provided natural light, as did a smaller window with multicolored panes at the top of the landing.

The hallway, straight ahead, took you to the small den where our family, as a whole, spent time together watching TV. To the left of the front hall was the fairly large living room used primarily for entertaining, and the dining room was situated directly behind. Along the length of the rear of the house were the kitchen and a small breakfast nook which included the back door to the yard.

Of the three bedrooms on the second floor, the largest, my parents', was located at the front of the house overlooking Cadwalader Avenue. My brother Bill's room was situated behind that, and a small bathroom separated his room from mine – the smallest bedroom of the three at the back of the house. Parallel to my parents' room was a hallway with one side overlooking the staircase. At the end of the hall sat a Singer sewing machine by the natural light of a front window where my mother did her mending. To the left of the machine was the long stairway to the third floor that proceeded to a small landing and a few more steps to the left.

The third floor consisted of a medium-sized room to the front with a larger room to the rear, and a small storage room adjacent to that which overlooked the side yard. This room contained a small solitary sink with a solid brass faucet. The front room had a double bed which Uncle and Auntie used when they visited and stayed overnight.

The dank basement was divided into two sections with the smaller area toward the back of the house containing the washing machine and tub, and shelves filled with dad's containers of paint, varnish and shellac. Nearby, was an enclosed lone, cold commode with a creaky wooden door surrounded by a wainscot barrier. Populating the basement's large front space was dad's workbench and ample room for storage as well as an electric train platform.

Behind the house was a detached two-car garage, housing a gas-powered reel lawnmower and an adequate supply of garden tools. In the space beside the garage and a cinder block wall that separated our property from a line of garages which were rented by the firehouse was a small garden where my mother grew rhubarb and strawberries. A raspberry bush along the back of the property and a concord grapevine outside the rear kitchen window provided additional fruit. Several wild cherry trees and a large azalea bush lined the border on the opposite side of the yard.

Since the house was situated, essentially, on a double lot, there was plenty of yard space in which to run around and play. A row of rose bushes lined a concrete walkway that ran between the house and the yard. The side of our home next to McKinley firehouse abutted a common driveway between the structures. A privet hedge surrounded all of the property except for the cinder block wall by the vegetable garden.

A homestead, of course, can only provide the physical backdrop for one's childhood. It was the love of family and friends, and the unique ambiance of a modest post-World War II neighborhood, which gave rise to the memories worth sharing.

Our home at 221 Cadwalader Avenue

First Friendship

My preschool memories of living in McKinley reside in a rather hazy corner of my mind. Since we arrived in our new hometown two months after my third birthday, that period would have consisted of only two years. But, during that time, an early and lasting friendship was born.

There were no near neighbors who had children of my age. In West Oak Lane my first friend, Freddie, lived right next door. Here in McKinley the scene was a little different. Sure, I shared many happy moments with my brother Bill at this stage in life, but being five years older, he had already established friendships with older children in the elementary school, so we naturally formed different age-related interests.

As I remember it, a small red tricycle provided my first means of mechanical locomotion. Since McKinley Firehouse was located conveniently next door to our house, its wide concrete driveway apron leading to its garage doors provided an ample, smooth surface for whiling away the hours via my first mode of transportation.

On the other side of the firehouse stood the Hamilton residence. Ray and Frances Hamilton were adult siblings who lived there with their aging father. Brother and sister were both employed. Their retired father could often be observed riding around town in his 1936 Studebaker sedan while sporting a top hat and a prodigious Victorian-era mustache. I'm not sure what Ray's regular job was, but he was actively involved in local Republican politics. I remember his peculiar swinging gait as he strode down Cadwalader Avenue past our house, often craning his neck to see if anyone was sitting on the front porch with whom he could talk and share his opinions. I believe Frances was a secretary. She could be seen in the morning catching the PTC's (Philadelphia Transportation Company's) creme and green "XA" bus at the nearby corner of Cadwalader and Cypress Avenues for a daily jaunt to the city.

In any case, the residents of the Hamilton home evidently needed help with common household chores given their unique demographic situation. Every Friday they received domestic help from Emma Bauerle who lived, perhaps, a half mile away on Forrest Avenue. There, as a single parent, she raised a family of two older girls, and two younger boys. Emma had emigrated to the United States in 1928, escaping the negative effects of the growing upheaval in her home country of Germany. She and her family moved to 363 Forrest Avenue in McKinley in 1936. Her youngest boy, Johnny, was the same age as I. When she came to do her work at the Hamiltons, Johnny was brought along, bringing his tricycle with him.

Clearly we hit it off right from the start, spending many hours playing and riding around in front of the firehouse. Since it was a volunteer station, there was rarely much activity during the day. To the left front of the station stood a brick memorial to deceased McKinley firefighters. Behind glass doors were special grooved boards on which little plastic letters were applied. Most of the departed members' names were displayed in white letters, whereas those of military veterans were posted in gold. I don't believe any active members' names, such as company officers, were displayed.

Johnny and I often played on and around the memorial when not riding our "trikes." We must have been given strict orders as to our boundaries, because we never wandered far from the firehouse area, although I don't believe that our activities were too closely monitored. Our weekly meetings went on happily for two years until kindergarten came between us and pushed me into a lonely, forlorn funk.

My tricycle and I

The McKinley Institutions

It wasn't long after we moved to our new home that my father became a member of McKinley Fire Company No. 1. He surely didn't have to run far to catch a truck when the call went out, with the firehouse right next door. Dad loved physical activity so joining was natural for him. Being a house painter, he found the activity of climbing ladders second nature. A reasonably strong contingent of neighbors enjoyed the comradery of the institution, and the members formed many casual relationships. Volunteers were mainly of the blue collar working class, but individuals such as salesmen also joined. Having flexible work schedules, they were more often available to serve if a call would come during the day.

As far back as I can remember, Henry "Tip" Leary was the fire chief. His tenure may have been interrupted a time or two during my childhood, but he was pretty much the incarnation of the institution. Like many organizations, the politics of membership alliances held sway, and Tip was routinely voted into the chief office year after year. The junior officer positions were more often in flux with a greater degree of rotation in office. Petty arguments would sometimes cause an individual to resign a

McKinley Firehouse on Cadwalader Ave.
Member memorial display at left

position in a huff, his office quickly filled with someone else who maintained favor in the unofficial pecking order.

Dad preferred to be a worker and had no designs on a field officer position, although he served on the board of directors a number of times. As a member of the Odd Fellows Lodge in the Logan area, he had some exposure to administrative positions, having served as Grand Master on several occasions.

The firehouse's siren was located atop a nearby pole. Due to our close proximity, it literally shook the house when it blasted its report. I suppose it was quite startling to me when we first moved there, but I rather quickly became accustomed to the high decibel, undulating roar and slept soundly when it announced a fire call in the middle of the night. The siren also went off every evening at 5:00, a signal to the neighborhood children to come home for dinner.

In the early 1950s, the running equipment consisted of an AutoCar engine and an American La France. The members routinely kept them in beautiful shape, washing and waxing the brilliant red paint finish to preserve the shine, and drying the trucks down after a run in the rain. McKinley routinely garnered trophies during parade celebrations.

Three doors down from the firehouse in the direction of Jenkintown Road was McKinley Elementary School. After playful times of riding my tricycle or accompanying mom to the store during the day as a preschooler, attending kindergarten proved to be quite a shock to my system. Making matters worse, Mrs. Bauerle didn't enroll my friend Johnny in kindergarten since attendance wasn't mandatory and she would have needed someone to look after him for a full day. As I was bashful by nature, the whole situation created a great deal of discomfort for me.

In my early memory of kindergarten, I sat on the sidelines, not participating in any activities, despite the best efforts of our teacher Miss Broomball. The classroom was located in the front, left of the building as you faced it. As you walked up the front steps and inside, you encountered a long hallway, and the entrance door to class was to your immediate left. Those front steps became the annual stage for class photos. Back then, kindergarten was not much more than three hours of day care. Its prominent value was in enabling a child to socialize with others of the same age. I wanted nothing to do with that. Activities consisted mainly of play time, nap time, and snack time. With envy I looked at classmate Denny Fulton who loved playing with the giant hollow wooden blocks. Houses and forts could easily be made with these simple building components, but, because of shyness, I didn't participate.

Evidently I never brought the word home about the daily snack time of milk and cookies. Mom was supposed to provide a nickel for the milk, but she wasn't initially informed, so I sat there like a lump. One day an extra milk carton must have been available and Miss Broomball kindly offered it to me with a couple of Nabisco Buttercup cookies. I gratefully accepted, providing my first meager step toward joining society as an active member. Later a note eventually got home to my mother and from then on I continued to partake of the daily treat.

The first friend that I recall in class was a little Jewish girl named Wendy Rosner. She had such a sweet disposition. We used to often amuse each other by uttering the words "pumpkin pie," with emphasis on the alliterative "P's," thus producing some hilarious spittle. There was little interaction on my part with the other boys.

But, in any case, the ice had been broken, and I was ready to move on.

Hearth and Home

Mom often said that the main reason she married was to have children. Brother Bill was born a year before the United States entered World War II. This evidently provided a deferment to active military service for my father. He supported the war effort on the home front through employment at the Frankford Arsenal in Philadelphia, and in the evening as a neighborhood air raid warden. Because of the uncertainty of the war's outcome and its possible ramifications, I wasn't conceived until the allied victory was nearly assured, and national optimism started to

Mom and I, July 1946

abound. Thus, I was born five days after V-J day on September 7, 1945.

After the war dad was laid off from the arsenal as the government geared down from a military footing. This caused dad to resume his previous profession as a painter and paperhanger. Depending on his workload, he would employ helpers for larger jobs. I recall a man named Jim who occasionally worked with dad, helping him get ready for the day's work, picking the paints to be used for the current job, and loading dad's truck with cans, brushes and ladders.

Mom maintained her daily routine of cleaning the house, doing the laundry, fixing meals, and readying her boys for school. To each day of the week she assigned herself a different household chore. One day may consist of cleaning the second floor bedrooms and bathroom; another the first floor rooms. I believe it was the latter of the two which was deemed "roll, mop and dust" day. On wash day mom would hang the wash on the backyard line, weather-permitting, or if it was too cold or rainy, she hung the clothes on lines strung just below the ceiling of the basement.

On ironing day, mom would set up the board in the kitchen near the refrigerator which had an ivory colored radio on the top of it. A lover of music, mom often sang along with the melodious strains. One of her favorites, which she approached with great vocal gusto, was the novelty song, "Be Kind to Your Web-footed Friends" which was sung to the tune of Sousa's "Stars and Stripes Forever" march. During one of these musical sessions I remember hearing what often is considered the first rock and roll song: "Life is But a Dream," or more commonly known as the "shaboom, shaboom" song.

Often I would sit on a kitchen chair while mom performed her ironing magic. Nothing compared to the sweet warm smell of that steaming metal implement deftly gliding over the clean wash. During these times I felt especially close to her – just she and I in a little corner of the world, protected and loved. Words of wisdom flowed from her lips as she went about her work, sharing stories about her life – even those that she may have felt uncomfortable confiding to adults. Of course she instilled general parental instructions upon me, such as never to get into a car with a stranger, and to always look both ways before crossing a street, and then only at the intersections.

Food shopping was within easy reach at the old Acme supermarket on Township Line Road, not far from the corner with Cadwalader Avenue. I often accompanied mom on food forays through the store. On occasion I would wander off by myself to another aisle and lose track of her. This brought on a terrible fear of being abandoned. But Mom would shortly locate me again, and all would be well. Invariably we would be checked out at the register by the friendly white-haired lady Mrs. Kelly. Later in the 1950s Acme sold their store to McCray and Hunter. Later on the building was converted into a foreign car showroom which sold Lotus and NSU Prinz vehicles.

If mom needed just an item or two, she would go to the Square Deal Market on the northwest corner of Township Line and Cadwalader. This little grocery store was owned by Jewish merchant brothers. Sam, the oldest I suppose, was the driving force. As you approached the cash register with your selections, he would try to interest you in additional items such as fresh produce and the like. A mild mannered relative named Bill was a bit of a "gopher" who was ordered around with abandon by the brothers. As I got older and was awarded more freedom of movement, I would often be sent on a solo mission to pick up a needed item at the store.

When mom had access to our car, and the cupboard was in more dire need of restocking, we would make our way down to the large Baltimore Market on Cheltenham Avenue at the northern terminus of Broad Street. It was the first true supermarket in the Philadelphia area. On top of the building stood a giant neon "B," visible for miles to those traveling up Broad from the city. It later became Best Market, allowing the large "B" to retain its significance. I loved roaming the aisles with mom, and by the time she was done, the cart was stacked with groceries. The treat for me, as we approached the checkout lines, was the rack displaying the comic books. I was allowed to buy one copy each time we shopped there. Back then there were no electric conveyor belts at the checkout on which to place your items. The cashier drew the products on the long counter top closer to the cash register with a simple "L" shaped wooden contraption. One of my sharpest memories during this period, back at home, was that of a short phone conversation that I overheard. I distinctly remember sitting in our den with Mom as Dad happened to be walking through in his painting work clothes when the phone rang. The old black Bakelite instrument sat on the radiator by the window overlooking the side yard. In our geographical area at that time, the phones did not yet have rotary dials. In any case, my dad answered the phone and he seemed somewhat startled by the message on the other end. After he hung up, Mom asked what was the nature of the call. Dad said, "they offered me my job back at the arsenal." Evidently America's entrance into the Korean War created a need for experienced workers.

Dad loved working with his hands and performing the physical labor of his painting job. But mom knew the cyclical nature of the work and the unpredictable nature of steady income that it provided. It didn't take mom long to convince my dad to go back to his old job at the arsenal. For my parents, having lived through the Great Depression, this was not a difficult decision to make.

House painting would always be in dad's blood, and he continued to take on smaller jobs, completing them at night or on weekends. And through the years, he always found other opportunities for moonlighting.

A Second Home

The twin home at 5801 Marvine Street in the Logan section of the city was where my mother, in her mid-teens, took up residence with her maternal uncle, Frank Shuman and his wife Anne Luther Shuman after her maternal grandmother died in 1929. To our family they were simply known as Uncle and Auntie. Auntie gave birth to a stillborn baby years earlier and she remained childless thereafter. Raising my mother would not be a unique experience for her, however, since she had previously provided a temporary home for the two sons of her brother when he was having marital difficulties.

Physically, Uncle was of average height, slightly portly and sporting a bald pate. Although he affected a stern demeanor, he retained a quipping sense of humor. Auntie maintained a somewhat royal, sophisticated appearance similar to that of Queen Elizabeth II of England, although she was down to earth.

My mother was well cared for in her new stable environment. Auntie, although just an aunt by marriage, became a mother to her. After graduating from Olney High School Mom put her formidable typing skills to work as a teletype operator for Western Union. An off again, on again, courtship with my father culminated in their marriage in May of 1938. Mom sensed that dad was a hard worker and would provide a stable home life, something that was lacking in her own childhood. Basically, however, she was a romantic, and said to me from time to time while I was growing up that she married with her head and not her heart. This, I believe, was basically true, but a bit of an exaggeration.

In their early married years my parents lived at the Marvine Street address, and during this period mom gave birth to brother Bill in November 1940 at Hahnemann Hospital in Philadelphia. Bill was an only child till after World War II when I arrived on the scene.

The Marvine Street abode was a warm and inviting homestead. It had an open porch close to the sidewalk. Mature trees lined the thoroughfare, and gas street lamps provided gentle light at night. Uncle's two-tone blue, 40s-something Hudson sedan retained a parking space by the curb. The attached twin was the residence of Dr. J. Stanley Walker, our longtime dentist. I spent many agonizing hours in his office over the years, since there was nary a visit when I didn't have a cavity. On the other side of Auntie's home was a narrow common lawn shared with the neighbor's house. The home's small backyard, bordered by a wrought iron fence, provided an oasis where Uncle displayed his gardening skills.

On the first floor, from front to back, were the living room, dining room, kitchen dining area, and a small kitchen. The refrigerator in the dining area was a model with a large round exposed compressor on top.

Ann Luther Shuman & Frank Shuman
(Auntie & Uncle)

Auntie, Mom, big bro Bill & I

Upstairs was the sitting room with windows overlooking the street. This is where the family relaxed. There was a large console radio by the interior wall where the family listened to programs in the evening, and where Auntie caught her favorite soap operas during the day. Behind the sitting room were a small guest bedroom, the bathroom, and a small room with a writing desk. Along the back of the house was Auntie and Uncle's bedroom, replete with twin beds.

Auntie routinely provided Monday night dinners for our whole family after we had moved to our McKinley address. Sometimes mom would drive us down to Logan after we returned home from school, although often she would arrive by herself midday, and I waited at home after class until Bill returned from school a bit later. Then we walked down to the corner together and caught the XA bus that ferried us to Fernrock Station in far north Philly where we transferred to the Broad Street Subway, and then rode the train to Logan Station.

Uncle worked downtown for the Pennsylvania Railroad where he was employed in the freight accounting office. His job was to keep track of the location of the various freight cars as they made their way to their destinations, and back again to their station of origin.

Often Bill and I walked from Marvine Street up Ruscomb Street to the Logan subway station on Broad Street where we met Uncle as he ascended the stairway to sidewalk level after his workday. Other times I remained at their home during his commute time and waited for Uncle to walk down the pathway to the back door as he tapped on the dining room window along the way to alert me to his imminent arrival. This was a sign for me to hide behind a piece of furniture. As he entered the house he'd say, "Isn't Buddy here?" Then I would wait awhile and jump out from my hiding place, yelling, "Here I am!" He then feigned surprise. The routine never got old.

My Uncle's given name was Frank, and I was named after him. Mom didn't like the other children calling me Frankie, since it sounded too old for a child, so she resorted to the less-objectionable moniker, Buddy, in tribute to her brother, my Uncle Bud, who shared the same nickname.

Continuing the house tour – down in the basement one found two coal bins toward the street – one for the small nuggets and one for the larger. Uncle banked the coal in the furnace on cold nights. I remember watching the warm incandescent glow through the small isinglass window on the furnace's door. Across from the furnace was a walk-in pantry lighted by a single bulb on a pull string. The shelves were lined with jars of jelly and canned goods. In the back of the cellar were the washing machine and a sink. And, in the corner, was a light green, floor model, windup record player with sound louvers on the front, and a place for record storage on the shelves beneath. This is where I busied myself, listening to old 78s while Auntie did the wash.

On overnight visits to the house, I usually slept in Auntie's bed while she slept in the guest room bed. I can still remember the sweet smell of her perfume on the pillow. After dark I became hypnotized as I watched silhouettes dance across the bedroom ceiling caused by the headlights of passing cars, and when the windows were open on summer nights, I was lulled to dreamland by the distant sounds of the city. I was normally asleep by the time Uncle came to bed, and he was up again in the morning before I awoke.

The Marvine Street residence was truly a home away from home.

Auntie on her porch on Marvine Street

Early School Years
&
Neighborhood Doings

First Grade

At the age of six I was ready for first grade at McKinley School, having survived my kindergarten experience. The transition was made easier since I was reunited with my best friend Johnny. However, my group of friends quickly expanded as the year went on. Robby and Billy lived in the village, and like John and me, had a friendly relationship with each other, and we became part of their informal alliance as the year went on. The class was also an introduction to me of our two African-American students, Gary and Joan, who lived up on "the hill."

Our teacher, Miss Russell, was a friendly, patient soul. Back then, first grade was often a child's first encounter with reading. The Dick and Jane series of books was the primary instrument for learning this skill. And evidently they did the job. I quickly absorbed the teachings and eventually made it to the top reading group along the way. The fundamentals of math posed a bigger challenge for me.

Since the classroom was at the back of the building, it provided easy access to the six-seat swing set and the outdoor playground via a concrete staircase. A 15 minute recess each day gave us children the opportunity to let off our pent-up energy. There was much running around on the large swath of grass, which occasionally resulted in head-on collisions, requiring a trip for the unfortunates to the nurse's office, followed by the application of an ice bag on the stricken area. Back then safety was not much of a consideration since the swing set was positioned on an unforgiving blacktop surface. The ringing of the bell in the school tower signaled the end of recess.

Although there was a cafeteria in the front basement of the building, I never partook of it for lunch. Mrs. Hetherington was the long time cook, and ran the operation with great efficiency. As my poor mother could attest, my menu of acceptable culinary delights was extremely limited, so I would always walk home for lunch. One of my staples was a bologna sandwich. Usually Mom was there to prepare lunch for me, but if she happened to be on an errand, the back door was always

Miss Russell's First Grade Class - McKinley Elementary - 1951-52

First Row: Dennis Fulton, Billy Barwig, Robby Holmes, Judy Vance, Frank Burr, Don Sutton, Barbara Quail

Second Row: Paul Trimborne, Wendy Rosner, Mary Eleen Bauer, Jimmy Sauer, Barbara Sillman, Gunther ?, Susan Gretz

Third Row: John Bauerle, Barbara Henry, Jim Sutherland, Beverly Drapp, Ricky Coulston, Tina Shregger

Fourth Row: Richard Deakyne, Barbara Feick, Mark Miller, Susan Palmer, Tom Morrison, Paulette Kulka, Dennis Ralston

unlocked, and my sandwich would be in the refrigerator, neatly wrapped in wax paper. Lunch was usually eaten quickly so I could get back to the school playground and partake of more outside activities with friends before returning to class.

About once each month we would have more structured athletic activities when the traveling Phys. Ed. teacher, Miss Haldeman, would instruct us in competitive activities such as kick-ball. Dodge-ball in the gymnasium was reserved for when the weather turned colder. She was a tall, jovial, sturdy individual with red hair. Her appearance was always preceded with great anticipation.

Musical instruction, however, was another matter. Miss Miller was the itinerary township plier of this discipline. She was a short dour woman with greying hair and spectacles who didn't take kindly to student interruptions or misbehavior. The musical instruments utilized for our instruction were kept in a big box and they consisted mainly of colored wooden sticks, triangles and tambourines – percussion all around. The sticks weren't very popular items, and the kids would scramble for the other instruments first. I don't remember these sessions being much fun for those involved. Maybe that's why I never had an interest in playing a more traditional instrument as I grew older.

I distinctly remember one day when Miss Miller looked at me and said, "have you been sick?" as if I looked like death warmed over. No, I hadn't, but the next day I was, and stayed home from school – oh, the power of suggestion.

A supplement to the appreciation of music was the use of the record player with its ample library of 78s. The ditties played upon it were often instructive like the refrain: "Let the ball roll, let the ball roll, no matter where it may go." That was intended to keep the children from running out in the street after an errant orb and becoming human road kill.

Along the way during that seminal year, a sweet little female classmate, Barbara Sillman, caught my eye and I was smitten. We talked quite a bit when we had a chance, and when school was dismissed around 3:00 in the afternoon, we would play for a while behind the building. One day we commandeered sticks of chalk somewhere, and we happily drew pictures on the sidewalk. I have no idea where she lived, and she didn't return to class in second grade. But, after all these years, she still stares at me with her bashful smile from the class photo taken on the school steps.

A Spiritual Bedrock

In many ways Auntie was the spiritual bedrock of our family. Her loving spirit tended to permeate all who knew her, and many of these qualities were instilled in my mother after she came to live with Auntie in her teens.

The basis for Auntie's religious principles was found in her study of Christian Science. As a younger woman she became acquainted with the religion through a friend when Auntie was struggling with a painful physical condition for which she could get little relief despite the best effort of the doctors. When she was healed of the malady through spiritual means and reliance on God, she turned wholeheartedly to the religion, and became a member of Second Church of Christ, Scientist in Germantown. Although the metaphysical aspects of the religion, as they applied to physical healing, were of great importance to her, the truths she learned, such as the Golden Rule, provided her with a spiritual outlook on life which she lovingly reflected. Uncle would attend services with Auntie, but never became a member of the church himself.

It was natural, therefore, that my mother started attending church with Auntie and began to live by the same precepts, but not regularly till after my brother was born and had been baptized in a church of a different denomination. I, on the other hand, was raised in Christian Science from the beginning. So, at the age of three, I began attending Sunday School regularly at the Germantown church. This instilled, in me, a sense of a spiritual relationship with God which was taught by the loving teachers.

Nearly every Sunday our family would put on our sartorial best and make our way down to the church in Germantown where we would meet Auntie and Uncle. While the adults went to the service in the large auditorium, Bill and I would attend Sunday School in the back of the building. Often Auntie and Uncle would drive back to our house in McKinley after the service and spend the afternoon with us. During the nice weather, Uncle would be out in the garden actively planting and weeding, taking advantage of a much bigger growing area than was afforded by his small backyard in Logan.

Dad had bought a television early in the 1950s, so if there was a Phillies or A's baseball game being televised on Sunday afternoon, he, Uncle and brother Bill would sit and watch it on the 10-inch screen of the RCA set. Baseball didn't interest me very much in my early childhood.

Mom and Auntie would usually attend the Wednesday evening testimony meetings at church as well. And Auntie would often come back to our house after the service. Normally dad would have put me to bed before their arrival, but I would invariably wake up (if I had gone to sleep at all) as Auntie made her way through the front door. She always took the time to come up and sit by my bed for a while and tell me a short, impromptu children's story – often about Tarzan and his monkey companion Cheetah – before I drifted off to sleep. I remember, in particular, a dark-blue dress that she wore. It had small white globes on it which seemed to magically glow in the dreamy darkness. A great feeling of protective love would come over me during these encounters.

Because of the teachings of the religion I never became a smoker or drank alcoholic beverages, and never had a desire to. During my early years I remember that dad was a rather heavy smoker of Pall Mall cigarettes. I suppose it was what I was learning in Sunday School which, in turn, encouraged me to ask him to stop smoking, which he did, cold turkey. And I never saw him or mom touch an alcoholic drink.

Of course any religious and moral beliefs, however noble, must be practiced to be effective. And taking the straight and narrow path is always a challenge during the formative stages of one's life, and beyond.

Fear of Miss Perkins

Having survived Kindergarten and first grade at McKinley Elementary, I began to gain a bit more self esteem as I mingled more freely with my classmates and accepted the precepts being taught by the teachers. The young mind is nurtured in those early school years by caring professionals teaching the rudiments of life – without losing sight of the youngster's childlike nature. For me this blissful view of youth came to an abrupt end in the second grade.

Second grade in many ways is a rite of passage. Gone are the thick pencils and crayons with which we learned to write and draw. Reading skills have accelerated to the point where children are segregated into various groups based on their ability and propensity for learning. Math workbooks appear with perforated pages that were torn out and submitted to the teacher as each lesson is completed. Everything is becoming more structured and less simple.

Demands were tough enough in second grade, but Miss Perkins made the situation almost intolerable.

I, and most of my fellow students, lived in fear of Miss Perkins. I've decided not to use her real name to protect the innocent and not-so-innocent. "Toothy Perkins" was a character in a children's book I had at home at the time. The name fit my teacher well, because she had a distinct over-bite which served to add to her menacing visage.

Miss Perkins had a way of making a small person feel smaller, embarrassing you in front of the class for any real or supposed transgression. If you were found doing anything disruptive, such as whispering to your neighbor at the improper time, she would call your name and summarily lead you out into the hall and devastate you with a harsh diatribe, thus reducing you to tears. When your eyes were sufficiently red, she would march you back into the classroom, thereby completing your embarrassment and simultaneously serving a warning to the rest of the class.

I was a victim of this verbal harassment several times. My best friend John had a knack for avoiding detection – except in one instance. I don't recall his infraction, but I do remember my barely concealed sense of glee when he finally got caught instead of me. My mirth was short-lived. When he returned to the room from his auditory shellacking, tears streaming down his cheeks, he pointed an accusatory finger toward me, citing me for some unremembered, but totally unfounded, violation. Out the door I went with the fuming Miss Perkins close behind me.

To this day I haven't totally forgiven John for that one.

Creativity was also frowned upon – at least as it pertained to mathematics. During a routine math lesson a classmate named Ricky thought that the figure for the number one (a vertical line) was rather plain-looking. In a display of imagination Ricky affixed a small triangle at the top of the number making the digit look like a pennant atop a staff. Pretty neat, I thought, but not so Miss Perkins. She commanded Ricky to the front of the room and had him scrawl his unauthorized version of the digit on the blackboard. In a booming voice, she scolded that she never wanted to see anyone take such liberties with the sacred principles of mathematics again.

Ricky slunk back into his seat.

Perhaps the most pernicious punishment was the "opportunity" to play teacher. Shame on you if you had the audacity to turn ahead a page or two while Miss Perkins was reviewing material from one of the textbooks. Such an act would evoke a reprimand: "If you think that you are privileged enough that you can read ahead, then you can come up front and teach the class." This sentence sent trembles through the accused. Standing up unsteadily, head bowed, it was impossible to utter a word. After a few interminable seconds followed the growl, "If you have nothing to say, then sit down and don't you ever do that again."

To every tyrant, however, comes a challenge. In this case it was embodied in the person of Marc Fischer. If my recollections are correct, he joined the class sometime during midterm, and departed before the end of the school year. Marc was very quiet and didn't seem to associate much with his classmates. I suppose that his family moved about quite a bit, and he was reluctant to make friends. Perhaps it was this transitory nature that allowed him to do what he did.

An elementary school tradition was The Weekly Reader. Current events and short stories graced the few pages of this publication. As was the custom, Miss Perkins would hand out the latest copy of the periodical in class, and we would review pertinent articles in the exact order prescribed by her. One day, while she was reviewing a particular item with the class, Miss Perkins' ever-watchful eye caught Marc turning the page of his Weekly Reader – unfazed by the threat of the coming storm.

Marc's desk was directly to the right of mine. Being that close to the focal point of her tirade was quite uncomfortable.

"Mr. Fischer, if you think that you are so privileged that you can read ahead, then you can come to the front of the room and teach the class," she exhorted. Without hesitation, and with a self-assured swagger, Marc marched to the head of the room.

The class collectively sank into their seats and sighed an audible groan. This act of defiance was unprecedented.

"Class," Marc intoned, "please turn to page two of your Weekly Reader." He then began discussing the article on strawberry-growing in California. We sat in awe.

Miss Perkin's face flushed a bright crimson. She was momentarily nonplused. In a barely controlled rage she indicated that would surely be enough and commanded Marc to return to his seat. Marc had made his point, returning dutifully to his desk, but with a slight smirk that only his classmates could see.

I don't recall much else about Marc, but that single act made the remainder of the school term more tolerable. Miss Perkins never seemed quite as threatening, her vulnerability having been exposed.

Miss Perkins, despite, or because of, her stern demeanor and belittling methods, had somehow heightened my sensibilities, and a slight lad named Marc Fischer showed me the power of peaceful defiance.

Every Tuesday at Two

At the time it seemed like an unwelcome, imposed respite. Every Tuesday from 2:00 till 2:15 p.m. our second grade class was required, collectively, to put their heads on their desks. Miss Perkins would then turn the knob on the brown plastic radio which sat on the window sill, and we would be forced to listen to a program consisting of music played on the "Betsy Ross Spinet."

Quiet interludes such as these may have been appropriate in kindergarten, but the energy level of the typical seven-year-old resists being harnessed for the interminable period of fifteen minutes: fifteen minutes without the creak of ancient floor boards under itchy feet; no squirming in the chair; no waving of frantic hands accompanied by, "Miss Perkins, Miss Perkins, I know, I know!" – just unnatural quiet – except for the melancholy ethereal strains of a small piano transmitted through the small speaker on the brown plastic radio.

But, as usual, despite mental protestations on my part, I was invariably drawn into a misty-hued trance of contemplation – eyes drawn to the radio on the windowsill – the paint-chipped windowsill with the small pots of seedlings stretching toward the light – the wide windowsill above the cast iron radiators with their womb-like warmth – the windowsill with its glass of water whose level diminished daily through the magic of evaporation.

And above the sill – wavy panes of glass through which unrestricted views of the young world could be glimpsed – where trees beyond the playground swayed in the autumn wind – yellow maple leaves silently dancing in the air – windowpanes; witness to the changing seasons with the swirl of snow through naked trees; dancing with the rising and falling notes of the piano.

And beyond the trees on a chill spring day, the billowed sculpture of changing cloud formations – drawn with the wind and the clouds to some unknown beyond with its uncertain future – drawn to that outer limit – but held – held for the present in that communal warmth of the classroom – behind the cast iron radiators – below the windowsill – this side of the wavy panes of glass – in the warmth.

Every Tuesday at two.

Near Neighbors

As I previously mentioned, I only lived within the Philadelphia city limits during the first three years of my life. The suburbs offered the post World War II public a new option for expanding one's horizons, both physically and emotionally. Many families began to feel that it was a divine right – a scaled-down manifest destiny – to pull up stakes from the relative confinement of row house living and move to an area of expanding horizons.

Living in a detached house on a more-than-modest tract of land brought out a bit of the pioneering spirit. In the previous West Oak Lane community, it was difficult to ignore neighbors, even if you wanted to, because of the close proximity. The suburbs offered your family more self-expression in the way you maintained your house and yard, as well as providing a more comfortable distance from your neighbors.

As I recall, our interaction with most near neighbors was cordial and friendly, but it was not a situation where neighboring adults visited each other freely, or where housewives got together to sip coffee and gossip. Despite this yearning for a measure of privacy, there was still a great sense of community among the people of McKinley. In warmer months, when individuals were more apt to be working outside, greetings and a bit of idle conversation would often ensue. Most members of the community walked to the local stores to shop, which provided ample opportunity for chance meetings. And the firehouse brought together the local male volunteers so they could interact in a testosterone-laden environment. Many wives of the firemen – my mother not included – belonged to the institution's ladies' auxiliary which helped to coordinate social events including the traditional Fourth of July activities.

Our near neighbors represented a cross-section of middle class families employed in blue and white collar jobs. The firehouse, being our next door neighbor, was a casual hangout for men during periods between the activity of fighting fires. Mom and dad often spoke with the various firemen over the side privet hedge when the opportunity arose. As a volunteer fireman himself, dad attended member meetings and fire school activities on a regular basis.

On the other side of our house, separated by a fairly large side yard, was an Italian-American family. Ralph and his wife Diehl lived there with their daughter Madeline, who was several years younger than I, and also little Ralphie, her brother, who was born during the mid-1950s. Madeline, I believe, had a bit of a crush on me, but, being a rather bashful individual, I limited most social contact. Father Ralph looked a bit like the director Carlo Ponti. Diehl was a fairly large woman with light hair pulled straight up into a pleasing bouffant of some sort. Tallie, another family member – Diehl's sister I believe – had dark straight hair of medium length which she wore loosely. Tallie, though very friendly, seemed to maintain an eternal frown as if the weight of the world was on her shoulders. And the matriarch of the family, Mama Mia, rarely was seen outside of the house, but spent many hours in her room on the second floor.

Mama Mia, apparently, had few teeth, and she didn't speak any English that I'm aware of, but she was a sweet old woman. At times, when I was playing in the yard, I would hear a call from her second story aerie, beckoning me to come over into their yard. With a smile, and words of greeting that I didn't understand, she would ceremoniously toss me a packet of Italian candy wrapped in a napkin, and tied with a ribbon. I would gleefully retrieve the gift accompanied with a word of thanks. Mama Mia would smile and disappear into her room.

My most delicious memory, however, was the occasional Sunday afternoon when we would hear a call from either Diehl or Tallie. Standing on the other side of the hedge separating our properties, one of the sisters would offer us a piping hot plate overflowing with spaghetti and meatballs. That would become our Sunday evening dinner. In my mind I can still taste those deliciously seasoned meatballs, the flavor of which I have never found equaled in the years since.

Directly across the street from us lived the Mutschler family: Nels and Ginny, and their children Jean and Walter – the daughter being several years older than I, and the son several younger. Weekend and summer evenings would be filled with the clank of friendly horseshoe tournaments, between family members and acquaintances, taking place on their side yard. I don't think that our family ever participated in that activity. On one occasion Nels and Walter joined dad, Bill and I for a jaunt down to a Phillies game at Connie Mack stadium.

To the left of the Mutschler's, in a small brick abode, lived the jovial Mamie Plunkett, a short, stout middle-aged woman. I believed that she worked downtown at the Wanamaker's store. She had a rather whining, high-pitched voice which could be heard for great distances. In nice weather, at the break of day, she would often work outside, puttering around her house. During these sessions, Mamie had a tendency to play rather loud radio music through an open window. My mother, trying to get some sleep, would, at times, disguise her voice in a ventriloquist's manner, and yell from her bedroom window: "Mamie, turn it down!"

The house to the right of the Mutschler's home belonged to the Geigers, Jim and Dot, with a daughter, Irene, the oldest child, and two sons; Jimmy, the eldest boy, and Bobby. Dot's parents also lived in the house, as did Jim's younger brother Bernie for a time. Irene was older than I, and the boys, younger. I believe Jim worked in a factory of some sort.

Directly behind our property were two homes on Osceola Avenue owned by African-American families. In our early years in McKinley, a little girl my age, Dee Dee, lived in one house. There were tall hedges, perhaps eight feet tall, lining the back of our property, so our interaction with these neighbors was minimal. Next door to Dee Dee's house was a black man who, I believe, lived alone. He kept a vegetable garden in his back yard of which he was very proud. My mother later told a story of an event that occurred shortly after we moved into our McKinley home. I was playing in our back yard adjacent to the man's garden, and my mother was nearby. Evidently the neighbor was tending his garden, and I spotted him. Innocently I said to my mother, "look mom, a black man." Having never seen a person of color in West Oak Lane, I suppose I was surprised. The man turned away in anger. It was years before the man acknowledged us again, and that was when he thanked my father for cutting our property's bordering hedge to a lower height, permitting more sunlight to shine on his garden.

Dee Dee's other neighbor on Osceola toward Jenkintown Road was a white family, the Hartmanns: Carl and Eleanore, and their two sons Bobby (several years older than I) and Tom (a.k.a. Tuck) who was a year older than I. Bill and I had much interaction with Bobby and Tuck over the years. Carl had a roofing and heating business which he took over from his father. Later he bought Abington Cab service, partnering with Fred Wahl who owned the tavern on the corner of Cadwalader and Township Line across from the Square Deal Market. Carl bought out Fred's interest in the business one year later. Eventually an office was set up in the basement of the Hartmann home, replete with a two-way radio system to dispatch the taxis. In 1960 Carl was short cab drivers so he marched his youngest son to the local notary to obtain a license, thus Tuck became an illegal driver at age 15.

Easy access to the Hartmann home from ours was provided by a cinder block wall at the end of the firehouse property which had several rows of block missing. This provided a convenient passageway for us boys to visit each other or gain ready access to Osceola Avenue.

It's worth noting that my parents became rather good friends with the fire chief Tip Leary and his wife Dot over the years. Tip served in the Korean War and married some time after his return. At one time they rented an apartment over Davis' Drug Store located at Township Line Rd. near Cadwalader Ave. I remember visiting with my mother several times and playing with toys on the floor with son Jimmy who was a year or two my junior. In 1959 the Learys moved to a home on Jenkintown Rd. near Tulpehocken Ave. which had a storefront that became Leary's Grocery Store. Tip also was a house painter on the side.

So, that was the immediate neighborhood mix of families with whom we interacted.

Any Old Rags

In the suburbs of the 1950s much of the commercial business was transacted door to door. There was hardly a house that didn't receive a morning delivery from the Harbison or Sealtest milkman. Fresh bottles of milk were placed on the front door step, and the spent bottles taken away. One had to be aware of the weather conditions. If it was a particularly cold morning, there was a chance that the milk would freeze and break the bottle or pop the lid. On a hot summer day, the milk needed to be put in the refrigerator before the contents spoiled. Since deliveries were made early in the morning, I rarely saw the milkman other than on collection day.

Mom also had bread delivered by the Freihoffer truck for a short time. But it was too tempting to buy nonessential items on the day the bread man collected. He'd bring a tray of baked goods to the door and ask if you were interested in buying some sweet treats. I particularly remember the round, pink coconut, marshmallow iced cakes sitting conspicuously on the top of his display tray. Rather than being tempted by these costly, sugary temptations, mom would instead make a short trip to the Square Deal market when bread was needed.

Once or twice a year the Fuller Brush man would make a stop at the house, leaving a catalog for perusal. I remember the American Grand Prix driver, Phil Hill, being the featured pitch man in one catalog. Mom would, at times, buy an item or two, but nothing expensive.

Every summer we would listen for the ringing bells of the Good Humor man who drew the neighborhood children to his truck in Pied Piper fashion. First you would have to cajole a dime or two out of mom before the driver rounded the corner. On a good day for the traveling merchant, kids would form a long line for their treats as he reached into the side door to search for an individual's selection. I loved those frozen raspberry confection containing the tart fruit's seeds which would lodge between your teeth.

Every month or so the relatively quiet suburban environment would be interrupted by the cry of, "any old rags?" emanating from the driver of a beaten old pickup truck, slowing making its way down the street. Somehow he kept his vehicle on course with the driver's side door open, and with his body half hanging out of the truck. It was the classic trash picker on wheels, trying to make a subsistence-level living.

There also were itinerant merchants who would knock discreetly at the back door, figuring, I suppose, that the woman of the house would be in the kitchen. There was an elderly man who would knock and present an opened wooden box full of sewing needles and colorful spools of thread. And there was a similar merchant that would offer to sharpen your knives for a price.

One particular incident has stuck in my mind after all these years. We had a delivery of some sort on a hot summer day. The cargo must have been rather heavy and the black laborer was sweating profusely at his toil. When the task was completed, mom offered him a cold glass of water which he kindly accepted and quickly drained. Shortly after the man left, she placed the glass in the sink and ran it under hot water for a few minutes. It was an example of a good Samaritan moment tainted by a measure of muted racial prejudice – witness to the evolving perceptions in society.

Unrequited

Second grade class at McKinley Elementary was not a particularly happy time for me, thanks to our teacher, Miss Perkins. As previously described, she could be rather acrimonious to any of her young students if she felt that her authority in any way was being breeched. However, there was one individual, in particular, who never had to be worried about being disciplined. Little Susie, whether she sought the benevolent attention or not, filled the role of teacher's pet. She could do no wrong, while the rest of us students (especially the boys), always had to tread carefully. Whereas I lived a rather monastic existence in kindergarten, and started to tentatively come out of my shell in first grade, by second grade I started to interact to a fault. I had the habit of talking to other students during class when I should have been listening to the instruction from the front of the classroom. Miss Perkins dubbed me "Chatterbox," which happened to be a character in one of our reading books. When I got a bit out of hand, she would use that moniker in a derisive manner to get my attention.

But second grade did have its redemptive moments, thanks to the bevy of female classmates. One little girl, Barbara Quail, caught my eye for a period of time. She was a rather giggly, bouncy, curly-tressed blond. I found that it was easy for me to make her laugh, which somehow fed my youthful ego. However, Barbara was a little bit flighty, and, with no warning, would burst into song, pertly uttering the lyrics of "Billy Boy, Billy Boy" in Shirley Temple fashion. Maybe it wouldn't have been so annoying if my name had been Billy.

It wasn't long thereafter that all of my attention focused on a new member of our class that year – stately Jane. To me she was the most beautiful being that ever walked the halls of McKinley. I suppose that I wasn't the only boy that felt that way. My friend John, for example, followed suit in a similar affection toward her. She carried herself in a refined manner and was an excellent student. Her home being in the manor, she naturally reflected the refined, but unpretentious style of her station in life. It was difficult for me to even speak to her. But we were both in the first reading group which provided me with some degree of access. I would feebly break the ice at times with some attempt at humor to get her attention.

There was one time during February of that year which provided me a measure of hope in regard to finding a bit of space in the young girl's heart. We poor unsuspecting urchins of both sexes were being subjected to the annual ritual of Valentine's Day. One had to be duly prepared for the impending stress which this holiday embodied. In preparation, a trip with mom to Woolworth's 5 & 10 in Jenkintown was required so I could pick out a package of low-cost Valentine cards for distribution to classmates. My eyes fell upon a cellophane-wrapped pack with a beautiful grownup-looking card on top. Of course that was the only worthwhile card in the bunch, because hidden beneath it was a slew of goofy non-folding cards with pictures of silly animals on them, spouting inane sentiments.

I, of course, picked that special card to be the one that I would bestow on Jane, and let the perceived lesser lights of the opposite sex deal with the remaining trite epistles of affection.

The manner in which the cards were distributed in class, I cannot recall. But after everyone had a chance to open their personal hoard, Miss Perkins instructed everyone to hold up their favorite card for all to see. She'd do most anything to cause embarrassment in her young charges. Of course I fumbled for the unspectacular card which Jane had addressed to me, and sheepishly held it up. I looked toward her as she quickly flashed a fancy card that I thought may have been the one I addressed to her. But it all happened so quickly, that I couldn't be sure. It goes without explanation that I never could quite conjure up the nerve to ask her outright about her selection.

Well, Jane became my obsession throughout elementary school. And my affection for her remained basically unrequited until a brief moment of hope which appeared far into the future during sixth grade.

Summer Guest

During the summers of the early 1950s, I spent a good deal of time at my Aunt and Uncle's house in Logan, staying overnight on many occasions. A special guest named Paula made several extended visits during those years.

Auntie's nephew, Allison, lived in Erie, Pennsylvania. Allison was the son of Auntie's brother Adam, or Uncle Ad to me, who in earlier years experienced marital difficulties and separation from his first wife. Auntie, during that period, served as a surrogate parent to Allison, therefore they remained close over the years. Paula was the only child of the union of Mary and Allison Luther. Although not formally trained, Paula's dad was probably a near genius in the field of electronics, although he had trouble holding down a regular job. When he made money,

Dad, Mom, I, and Paula
Erie, PA 1950

he was apt to spend it on expensive equipment, building his own devices. In Erie he had a makeshift studio where he could record sound directly to 78 rpm discs. He had an electronic organ that he fashioned himself, and the musical talent to play it well. And he understood the science behind color television, but never had the means to build one himself.

It was against this backdrop of an eccentric father that Paula grew up. When she came to visit Auntie she experienced a greater degree of love and affection than she experienced at home in Erie. Paula was about four years older than I, but we got along famously. The closest thing I ever had to a big sister, she was a pretty girl with dark hair and possessed Tom Boy tendencies which suited me fine. We spent much time in the Logan home playing games orchestrated by Paula. In particular, I remember us mimicking a popular TV show of the period, Private Secretary, starring Ann Sothern. Paula, of course, acted out the antics of Sothern's character, the secretary, Miss McNamara, while I stood in for her boss Peter Sands, who was played by Don Porter. The desk in Auntie's guest room provided the centerpiece for our office scenes.

One summer day in 1952, Paula was entrusted to take me to see a movie playing at the Logan theater on Broad Street. Before our excursion Auntie cautioned her to look both ways, and only cross the major streets when there was a green light. Heeding those instructions, we successfully made a safe trip down Ruscomb Street to the movie house and enjoyed watching Hans Christian Andersen starring Danny Kaye. The musical strains of "Inch Worm" and "The Ugly Duckling" stay fixed in my memory to this day.

Paula also stayed a week or two at our McKinley home where she slept in the extra bedroom on the third floor. I can't recall if our family ever took her down to the Pleasantville, New Jersey cottage. In any case, she was very close to my mother who treated her like a daughter. My mother had a great sense of humor and would often kid around with us. Paula, due to her home environment, wasn't used to this type of attention and could be a little thin-skinned, thinking she was being made fun of when we were all just having a good time. On several occasions she would retreat to her room and cry her eyes out. But, by the end of her visit with us, mom had brought her around, and she was able to join in the frivolity without any ill effects.

During several summers we visited Paula's family in Erie, Pennsylvania as well – going on picnics and bathing in local creeks, and visiting the Admiral Farragut flagship on Lake Erie near Presque Isle.

On one visit Allison recorded the voices of brother Bill and me to disc in his home studio. He also gave us records that he made while playing popular music on his electronic organ. Paula's dad liked animals, and prior to one of our stays at their home a litter of puppies was born. At night I can remember sleeping on a makeshift bed on the livingroom floor as the little restless canines crawled over Bill and me during the night. I feared that one of the puppies, in a nocturnal call to nature, would relieve itself on me. It surely wasn't like home, but having Paula to pal around with made it all worthwhile.

Reading and Writing

Third grade was another transitional year. Our class moved to the opposite side of the elementary school building. No longer did students have a view of the playground that we enjoyed while in kindergarten through second grade. But it was great getting out from under the authoritarian regime of Miss Perkins. Our new teacher, Miss Hamell, was a God-send in comparison. It wasn't that Miss Hamell didn't invoke discipline when required, it's just that she did it in a manner that wasn't meant to humiliate or embarrass you.

Reading was not a problem for me, and I did well in those annual California Achievement Tests which were meant to test your skills in a variety of areas, and to provide a rudimentary measure of your IQ. However, penmanship, i.e., the mechanical art of putting pencil to paper, was not a discipline in which I excelled. Somewhere along the line, the Abington school district replaced the Palmer Method of cursive instruction with that of the Petersen Method. An ever-present guide in which to help facilitate the transition from blocked letters was the placement of green rectangular posters above the blackboards. Each poster depicted two letters of the alphabet, longhand style, in both upper and lowercase. Every student had a Petersen workbook. An exercise would include a new letter outlined in dots which one would connect to form the letter. Then you would move on to create that same letter in a freehand manner – over and over and over. Although my letters were fairly legible, they usually did not meet the standard of good penmanship. Through my elementary school years, I often was instructed to redo some of my class work in a fruitless effort to help me improve. It didn't help much.

—

It was also in third grade that I had the first recollection of participating in reading a selection from The Bible at the start of the class day. There must have been a schedule that let each student know when it was his or her time to perform the task. I looked forward to the assignment with dread, mainly because I rarely prepared in advance. The selected verses had to come from the Old Testament in deference to Jewish students. On one occasion, when it was my turn, I opened the book randomly and started to read. It started off well, but then I came across the passages that described a hereditary line, whereas it was "so and so," the son of "this and that," and on it went – one unpronounceable name after another. At least I didn't pick the Song of Solomon. When my face started turning red and I could take no more, I lead the class in the Lord's Prayer, being comforted somewhat by hearing someone else's voice rather than my own.

I remember one particular occasion when the class bully, Steven, had the daily readings. He was well prepared. He knew exactly what he was going to read. The verses that he chose contained the word "ass," meaning of course the beast of burden, and not a person's posterior. When some of his compatriots started to chuckle uncontrollably, Miss Hamell sternly warned him not to make a mockery of the Scripture. I have a feeling that she was laughing on the inside though.

May Day at McKinley School - 1955
Miss Hamell with Dale Morrish (a girl who would come into my
life many years later)

Miss Hamell continued to keep the class in tow. There was one instance when I was casually disciplined by her when she observed me placing what I'll delicately call "nose refuse" under my chair. I never did that again.

"Show and tell" became a regular part of class activity. On one occasion a student brought in a number of silver coins that had been fashioned into jewelry in an American Indian style. After the items were shown and explained, they were placed on a table where they would be displayed for a few days. One morning someone noticed that the 50-cent piece was missing. Miss Hamell explained that if anyone took it or found it, it should be brought back, no questions asked. Several days later, my friend John announced from the cloak room that he had found the coin on an upper shelf, and then returned it. As I was told many years later, John was actually set up to find the coin by another class member who was the actual culprit. What I do remember is that later in the school year, Miss Hamell once admonished John, saying, "to my face you're an angel, but behind my back you're a devil." Of course I was shocked, but secretly pleased, that my best friend was reprimanded rather than I for some unknown misdeed.

After the school year there was a realignment of classes, sending some of McKinley's students to the elementary school on Cedar Rd. in Huntingdon Valley. Steven, the bully, whose father happened to be the manager of the Hiway movie theater in Jenkintown, was among them. I didn't miss his departure. Among the other students that departed were Paul, Frank, Mark, and Paulette.

In any case, Miss Hamell was a gem of a teacher, sufficiently preparing us for the years ahead.

Eats and Treats

In a world virtually without fast food restaurants, the residents of McKinley were somehow able to manage sufficiently. There were no McDonald's, but there was the Snack Shop on Jenkintown Road. This small establishment, with its food counter and swivel chairs, was located next to the McKinley firehouse at the intersection with Cadwalader Avenue. The firehouse had moved from its old location on mid-Cadwalader Avenue in 1954. The earliest proprietors of the snack shop, which I remember, were the Pearces.

I was a finicky eater as a child and still am today, but I often had a hunger for hamburgers and french fries. At times when my mom didn't feel like cooking something up for me, and to quiet my moaning, she would give me a bit of money and send me on my way. Hamburgers, as I recall, were 25 cents. I don't remember the price of the fries which were served in a paper cup. The grade of the ground beef surely wasn't premium, but the sandwich was generally a tasty treat for me. However, I do remember that, on occasion, I'd bite into a small gritty chunk of gristle which would induce a fit of gagging. But that was a small price to pay.

Later on Mr. and Mrs. Tucker managed the Snack Shop. John and I visited the establishment frequently. They had a gum ball machine that dispensed a substantial variety of little plastic toys as well as the sweet spheres. Another globed wonder spewed forth bright red pistachios upon receiving the appropriate coin. Relief from the summertime heat came in the form of ground ice from a noisy machine deposited into paper cones. Your favorite flavor would be added from a colorful bottle. When the shaved ice became depleted, Mrs. Tucker would alight a small stool and put large ice chunks in the top of the metal cylinder to be chewed up by the appliance. Often a drop or two of sweat would cascade off of her nose into the mix as well, at no additional cost to the patrons.

Doc Davis' Drug Store on Township Line had a soda fountain, a counter, and a line of swivel seats that you could hoist yourself upon and order up your favorite treats. Old Doc was a gruff little balding man with glasses. He tolerated us children as long as we made a purchase of some sort. During the summer, my friend John would spend most of the daytime at my house, and we'd wander down to Doc's for something tasty. Fountain sodas such as cherry or vanilla Cokes for a dime were always refreshing on a hot day. Lime or grape Rickys were served in a tall thin, frosted glass, and cost an extra five cents. Sometimes we'd order a strawberry root beer soda, with the main intent of hearing old Doc repeat our request in his Yiddish accent – "strawbeery vootbeeeer!" One had to be careful if you asked for a roll of Lifesavers because he'd invariably slap them down on the counter with a force adequate to break those fragile little circles into pieces. Three Musketeer candy bars were among our favorites. Back then they were big enough that you could easily break them into three pieces along lines depressed in the chocolate. I can also remember on summer days when Uncle was up from Logan to work in our garden. Often he'd take me down to Davis' to buy me a large five-cent Charms lollipop – raspberry being my favorite flavor.

Whole milk was the primary choice of a beverage for me on the home front, but every now and then – especially in the summer – mom would announce that she felt like something fizzy. She'd send me down to Davis' to buy a large bottle of Canada Dry Ginger Ale for a quarter. On occasion I'd buy a bottle of 7up instead. Before embarking on the errand mom would admonish me not to run while carrying the bottle home. The empty bottles could later be returned to obtain the five-cent deposit.

Another summer treat was ice cream. Back then the freezer section of our Coldspot refrigerator was only large enough to hold little more than a couple of ice cube trays. Therefore, a dairy treat had to be purchased in such a size that it could be consumed in one sitting. Dolly Madison was usually the brand of choice, and the drug store had an ample supply. Other favorite frigid items included Mr. Big ice cream cones wrapped in a paper cover, and the ubiquitous Popsicles in sundry flavors.

When Johnny was at our house during the days in the summer, mom would often give us both a few cents so we could make purchases of penny candy at Jack Steven's General Store on Cypress Ave. Jack and his wife Isabel nicknamed me "smiley" because of my sober demeanor. I was basically just bashful.

Under a glass counter was displayed a multitude of goodies. One could buy little wax bottles of Nik-L-Nips containing various fruit-flavored syrups. One would just bite off the top and sip it down. Also, in the realm of wax treats, were red lips, buck teeth, and black mustaches. After wearing them as a disguise for a while, you'd chew them like gum to extract the sweet flavor.

Wampum beads were always favorites – long strips of paper with pastel colored candy dots that you would bite off, invariably taking a little paper with it. For one cent you could buy half of a strip, or a whole strip for two cents. Other sugary penny treats included Mike & Ike's, Mary Janes and Good & Plenties.

Good old Jack later went on to become a janitor at Abington High School, and his establishment closed after his change in employment. During his tenure with the school, another janitor was electrocuted in a horrible accident.

A Rude Awakening

The summer of 1954 was rather cataclysmic in some respects. The routine order of home life would be permanently changed. All began in a normal carefree manner for me. Mom and I were staying at Auntie's house in Logan. Uncle had been sick for a week or so, and mom decided to stay at their house to help out. Brother Bill, being five years older at 13, stayed home and managed to take care of himself during the day while dad was at work.

Uncle had retired from his job at the Pennsylvania Rail Road barely a year prior. We happened to be at their Logan residence on his final work day when he made his last trek from the Broad Street Subway station, down Ruscomb St. to their Marvine St. home. I remember Uncle slowly coming in the back door, making his way to the living room, and slouching in an arm chair – not even taking time to shed his overcoat. In a melancholy manner he began to recount his last workday, telling of all his associates that came by to wish him well in his upcoming retirement.

In recent years prior to this summer, I recall a telling sign – its full impact not occurring, as yet, to my youthful mind. When Uncle climbed the long flight of stairs at our home, or in his

Logan abode, I would hear a low lament being uttered. No other family members were around during these instances, and, I suppose, I was amply out of sight. One time when he was slowly, methodically walking up the long staircase at our house, I surreptitiously drew closer. Then I heard his exact words being rhythmically muttered with each step: "Oh me, oh my. Oh me, oh my." I sensed something ominous, but I suppose that I was in denial.

Getting back to the summer visit in 1954, I recall that I was in need of something to amuse me. At some point during the day, mom took me to a toy store on Broad Street to make a purchase. For quite awhile I had my eye on a large toy boat which was displayed in the window. Mom broke down and made the purchase with the promise that I could float the new toy in Auntie's bath tub on the following day.

That evening Auntie, mom and I were relaxing in the second floor sitting room at the front of the house watching television. It was a second-hand TV purchased from their dentist neighbor, and friend, Dr. Stanley Walker. The TV had a 10-inch screen which was viewed through a large blue magnifying glass. In any case, Uncle, being under the weather, was in bed at the rear of the house. At one point during the evening, Uncle called out: "Did Buddy leave his peanut butter crackers on the mantel?" He evidently had been dreaming, since I hadn't partaken of any snacks. Auntie stopped back to assure him that all was well.

It must have been a very active day for me because I fell asleep quickly in the spare bedroom and slept uninterrupted through the night. It was in the late morning that I awoke to the morning light, and the uncontrollable sobs coming from the first floor. Uncle had passed away during the night and Auntie was grieving terribly.

I had slept through it all. Mom had ascertained Uncle's sad demise when she checked for his pulse, and the funeral home had removed Uncle's body before I awoke.

During the day I tried to keep on the sidelines, not knowing how to handle such a situation. I loved Uncle, but, somehow, I didn't feel a great sense of remorse. Maybe all was happening too fast, and I didn't know how to react to my youthful emotions. Later in the day, when things had settled down a bit, I insensitively asked Auntie if I could float my new toy boat in the bath tub as mom had promised the day before. She quietly said, "Not today Buddy. Not today." The love of her life was gone.

On the days following this sad event, neighbors and friends would stop by to express their condolences and to bring baked goods to Auntie. After the welcomes and the hugs, Auntie would start crying all over again.

—

Kirk & Nice, the country's oldest funeral home, which was located in Germantown, handled the arrangements for the funeral. Prior to the service, someone (probably mom) led me past the casket where Uncle was laid out. I had never seen a departed individual before, and it was a bit disconcerting to me. I quickly glanced at the body and walked away. Following the service, I rode in the main limousine with Auntie and the family – I sitting on one of those little fold-down seats. The First Reader of our Christian Science church, who presided over the memorial service, sat facing me. He talked to us along the way to the cemetery and was very consoling and loving in his manner. I don't recall anything of the ceremony at the grave site.

—

It was obvious that Auntie wasn't going to be able to live alone in her home on Marvine St. for any length of time. During the remainder of that summer I stayed with Auntie by myself for a two-week period. Mom would drive down from McKinley a couple of times a week to check on the situation and help with meals, but she needed to attend to the normal chores at home and feed dad and brother Bill. During this period I remember being quite homesick.

Somewhere along the line it was decided that Auntie's brother, Ad, and his wife, Emma, would move from their apartment in the Olney section of Philadelphia and take up residence with Auntie. This arrangement didn't last for more that a few months, I believe. There were too many personality incompatibilities.

At some point it was obvious that Auntie was destined to move into our home. I was too young to know how the preparatory discussions went, and if my dad had any problem with the situation. However, he was usually quite adaptable.

To allow for our new tenant, space would have to be provided for Auntie. As it turned out, two of the vacant rooms on the third floor would become the bedrooms for Bill and me. He, being the older brother, had sway in the selection. To my amazement he chose the smaller front room, while I got the large back room. Bill evidently liked the view from his aerie, especially when the young girls walked by on the sidewalk below. I was quite happy with my new digs. Bill's old bedroom would become Auntie's bedroom, and my old bedroom her sitting room, replete with her secretary desk and two easy chairs. Thus was set the new structure for our home, physically and emotionally, for the remainder of my days living there.

Settling in

She was a sweet saint, rarely raising here voice at her students. Every teacher has their own way of communicating and making an impression on their young charges. I suppose that Miss Dunmire never pushed us too hard academically, but we managed just fine, and discipline was never a problem.

Our fourth grade classroom at McKinley was situated midway in the building at the high end of the sloping central hall. At the low end of the hallway was a wing housing the first and sixth grade classes as well as the principal's office.

Most academic activity entailed expanding the skills learned in previous years, especially in the area of long hand, or cursive, writing. In the arena of mathematics, multiplication and dreaded division were making themselves known. For the first time we had two alternating student teachers which helped Miss Dunmire in her chores. One in particular had a significant degree of musical talent, and she tickled the keys of the upright piano when it was time to burst into song – my favorite ditty being "Ashem Was a Tootin' Turk."

Our class was also introduced to playing music on our own. The vehicle for this discipline was the amazing Tonette, a black plastic piccolo-type affair that we were forced to buy for the hefty sum of 50 cents. Along with the instrument came a book of songs with notes accompanied by numbers which corresponded to the finger holes along the shaft of the playing piece. I was totally intimidated by the notes on the printed scales despite being instructed that the four spaces between the lines in the measure represented the notes "FACE," while the lines were "EGBDF," or Every Good Boy Does Fine. These mnemonics didn't help me a bit, and I totally relied on the numbers.

Evidently Miss Dunmire couldn't read music either, because she allowed us to use the number system much to the chagrin of the itinerant and bad-humored township music instructor, Miss Miller. On one of her scheduled visits, she upbraided Miss Dunmire in front of our class for not instilling more discipline in our musical instruction. The most that I accomplished was playing "Hot Cross Buns" – not exactly a ticket to the Curtis Institute.

—

Being the ever-fussy eater, I headed home each day for lunch, walking the short distance from the school rather than partake of a meal in the cafeteria. The back door leading to the kitchen was always unlocked. I suppose I mainly lived on bologna sandwiches offered by mom personally, or left in the refrigerator if she and Auntie were out gallivanting in Auntie's 1953 Dodge four-door sedan with Fluid Drive. Actually Auntie never learned to drive, but gave it a noble try after the death of her husband. In any case, I would eat my lunch in front of the TV in the den. My favorite program was the game show "Who Do You Trust" with Johnny Carson as the emcee. He broke me up when he looked at the camera with his signature smirk when responding silently to a contestant's funny remarks during his interviews. The game was simply a vehicle for his antics.

After lunch I would rush down to the school yard to take up position as pitcher for the midday kick ball game, or "movin's up," as it was called. The field would begin to fill up with players as they ascended from the cafeteria. The game was played on a rudimentary baseball diamond. Home plate was located under the shade of the trees that lined the school property along Cadwalader Avenue. The "batters" would kick the large rubber ball which was rolled to the plate by the pitcher. The batter would make an out either by being hit by a thrown ball by a fielder when running between bases, or if the ball was caught in the air. A fielder catching a ball for an out would then trade places with the batter. Other players making outs on the base paths were replaced one by one, starting with the pitcher's position to that of an outfielder. Anyway, the game was addictive, but ended promptly when the school bell rang.

—

Back to fourth grade, I can only remember one time when Miss Dunmire lost her cool. On one occasion during class, Johnny and I were entrusted to carry correspondence of some sort to the principal's office which was located near the lower end of the sloping hall from our classroom. All classes were in session so completing our mission in silence was assumed by our teacher. As it was, the hallway was fairly narrow and bordered by a wall of windows. The unique acoustics created by this space allowed for a significant echo when words were uttered. On our way back to the classroom I decided to take advantage of this environment by loudly singing the beginning lyrics from a popular song of the day, "Dance with Me Henry." Johnny chimed in along with me in exuberant fashion: "Dance with me Henry. All right baby. Dance with me Henry. I don't mean maybe. Dance with me Henn-nnry, you gotta dance while the music rolls on." We were unfortunately limited to singing one verse as Miss Dunmire burst out of the classroom door and scolded us, her eyes on fire. Johnny and I meekly slunk into the room, our singing careers abruptly ended.

Of course, the last thing that I wanted to do was to upset my special teacher. All was forgiven in short order and the school year progressed in good fashion. It was a peaceful academic interlude before the more challenging environment of fifth grade.

A Monthly Routine

In the early days of our McKinley years, mom would accompany brother Bill and me on a short walk to the corner of Tulpehocken Avenue and Jenkintown Road for our monthly encounter with Frank Cook, the local barber. Not long after this routine was established, Bill was entrusted with my care on this local journey.

Mr. Cook was a rather short middle-aged Italian-American with a heavy accent. He wore glasses and looked a lot like a portly Harry Truman. The shop had three barber chairs, but only one was utilized since he was the only barber for most of the early years; a young barber named Mike joined him in the mid-1960s. Mr. Cook utilized the chair closest to the door where he could keep an eye on the town's movements through two large plate glass windows.

Along the far wall of his shop were shelves containing various products such as overpriced men's socks which he would try to cajole adult customers into buying to help supplement his income. To the left of that wall was a doorway into his family's living space. Mrs. Cook would appear at times to say hello to the customers and to sweep up the hair clippings off of the floor. She, too, wore glasses and had a conspicuous cascade of gray-flecked dark hair that flowed all the way to her hips.

Mr. Cook's business flourished well enough since it was the only game in town. Finesse was not a quality of his, since he went after your tresses with gusto, twisting your ear when necessary to get to the hair behind that impediment. In the early years I believe that he charged the going rate of one buck which he eventually raised to $1.25. Our mom never gave us money for tips.

As the summer months approached, mom would make a guest trip with us to the barbershop to make sure that old Frank gave us a close-cropped crew cut for the season. She felt that boys shouldn't have long hair during the summer – too hot.

At some point around the time of my junior high years, Mr. Cook underwent cataract surgery. This did not deter him in his profession, however. He now relied on glasses with Coke bottle lenses to view his customers at close range. Around this time, as I matured, I was shocked when he brought out the straight blade to use on me for the first time. There was nary a session after that one where I didn't leave the shop without a nick or two on my neck. But, overall, he was a jovial decent fellow who served his community well.

I remember that when I returned to get a haircut for the first time after my two-year hitch in the army, another customer paid for my haircut in gratitude for my service.

Sometime in the late 60s or early 70s after I left town, Mr. Cook and his wife went out for a walk one day and began crossing Jenkintown Road at the corner of his shop. A speeding car approached and Frank pushed his wife out of the way of the oncoming vehicle, but it hit him, full-force, killing him. A McKinley icon was gone.

Summer Doings

My childhood summers look idyllic in retrospect. They often took a leisurely pace in the sultry days before home air conditioning was prevalent. Mom used to say that my friend Johnny practically lived at our house during those months, and she didn't care a bit, even providing lunch for John and me every day. Every morning I'd wait in anticipation for him to arrive on his bike, parking it by our back porch, hopping up the back steps and peering through the screen door. John's cycling skills were much more superior to mine at first because I was a slow learner. My first bike was a used 24-inch model which dad purchased for me from Crofty's Cycle Shop on Jenkintown Road. Now having wheels of my own, John and I were greatly able to expand our horizons.

Each year, during the first week after classes ended, the summer program at McKinley school began. Every morning from 9:00 to noon the doors to the gymnasium at the back of the

It is I (Buddy) with best friend
Johnny Bauerle in the backyard of our home

building would swing open. Two adult teachers from the Abington School District would oversee the programs every day. It was a way for them to make extra money in the summer when schools were out of session. One year Miss Hamell performed this roll. Games, arts and crafts were available in addition to other organized activities. The first couple of weeks I'd have to fend for myself since John attended vacation Bible school during that period.

Since the summer program was open to all community children, it was a time when we were able to mingle with the Catholic school kids as well. I remember playing some spirited games of badminton with Allan Gargan, a local boy who attended St. James during the school year. His sister, Anne, would go on to marry my brother years later.

Most of the children that attended, however, were local. Rarely did one see a child from the village or manor show up. My brother, although five years older than I, liked to participate as well, usually helping the adult coordinators with the organized activities such as softball and basketball. One year he was secretly enamored with an attractive young female teacher who was helping with the program.

One of my significant accomplishments during this period was learning how to play chess. I can't recall who taught me, but I do remember playing a number of times with Bruce Hall, an African-American classmate of mine. On the "artsy" side, I made several baskets out of popsicle sticks.

The summer program would terminate around the end of July when it was celebrated on the last day with school district-supplied watermelons which fed the assembled gang of urchins.

—

Two of the favorite summer haunts for John and me were the playground and Craig's Woods. The playground was located, as it is today, across Jenkintown Road between Cadwalader and Osceola Avenues. Jenkintown Road was a moderately busy thoroughfare and one had to be careful when crossing. I remember nearly getting hit as a car slammed on its brakes and stopped inches from me, thanks to my inattention.

At the top of the playground was the softball diamond and beyond that was the open field where pickup games of football were played. At the far end of the field there was outdoor gym equipment such as the sliding board, swings, and monkey bars. My favorite was the merry-go-round which could be spun at amazing speeds. You would grab onto a side bar on the perimeter and run as fast as you could before hopping on and taking a seat on a wooden plank. Occasionally a girl would participate, and it was the young man's duty to push the contraption fast enough to scare the wits out of her.

Past the play area was the creek, or crick as we called it. It was just a shallow, slow-moving body of water, but it provided hours of entertainment for John and me. We had fun damming the currents to make little pools, looking under rocks for crayfish, and watching the small minnows darting about. The crick ran under a bridge that crossed Osceola Avenue and meandered in the undeveloped area known as Craig's Woods. Entrance to the woods was provided by the hulk of a long dead tree on which you could traverse on your way into the sylvan cathedral.

The woods ran all the way to Cedar Road and were probably a part of an old farm property that faced Jenkintown Road where a deteriorating main house – which we were told was haunted – was surrounded by several out buildings. On windy days an errant door to an old chicken coup would creakily swing and clap in an eery manner. I can only remember entering the main house once under the protection of my big brother. Magazines and papers from transient visitors were strewn across the floor.

In the middle of the woods was a small ravine which we often explored. John and I would pretend that we were stalking enemies. At times we would arm ourselves with water pistols which we would reload with water from the crick. I remember a memorable incident during one of our forays. One afternoon John and I were near the water's edge in an area that was rather thick with bushes and bramble. Suddenly, feeling a presence of another human being, we looked up and saw a silhouette through high grass above the far bank. It appeared to be an old man in a straw hat who growled, "get out of here!" As a rush of adrenalin flowed through our systems we jumped up and took off. But John slipped on a wet stone and fell in the crick, soaking his pants. Well, on that occasion our expedition into the wild came to a sudden end and John had to retreat to the real world of his home to get dried out, and probably receive a tongue-lashing from his mom.

Craig's Woods also became the location for my brother's war games. He fancied himself a military leader and enjoyed leading his "men" into battle. Naturally he made himself a general. His next two commanders in rank were the Hogg brothers who lived on High School Road. Richard was in my brother's school grade and was the next in command with an officer's commission. Sammy was two years older than I and may have been deemed a sergeant. John and I were lowly privates. I believe that I was ceremoniously promoted to the rank of corporal during one of our military maneuvers. In any case, there was a particular incident concerning this elite military group which sticks in my mind. Actually I believe that it occurred in early spring while some of the trees were beginning to show early signs of light green foliage.

Evidently Sergeant Sammy committed some unremembered offense and was summarily court marshaled by Richard and my brother. His punishment was to have his leg tied by a rope to a discarded Christmas tree that was found in the woods. Poor Sam was left behind to fend for himself in the woods as the military party took off through the wilderness to pursue other adventures. His survival skills evidently intact, about a half of an hour later or so we spied Sammy in the distance through the trees, making his way through the underbrush, unencumbered by any obvious impediment, with his father by his side, steadily advancing to our party's position. Our unit took off as fast as it could, exiting from the woods somewhere along the way. We lost Sam and his dad, but poor Richard had to pay the piper when he went home later that day.

—

Almost every summer dad planned an automobile trip. This was in addition to our usual one week at the Pleasantville shore shack. Months ahead, in preparation, dad would unfold and spread out maps on the diningroom table, marking the course we would take. In the early to mid 50s we traveled to New England several times, as well as trips to the southern climbs.

Dad loved to drive and could do it for hours without end. Bill and I would, of course, let him know when we were getting hungry and when it was time to take a necessary break. But dad knew how many miles he had to drive in a day to keep us on schedule. I remember going to Niagra Falls, Plymouth Rock and Lost River, New Hampshire where we walked up and down precarious metal steps on the walls of the picturesque chasm. Our mode of transportation in those early years was a 1947 Chrysler New Yorker sedan. Going across a narrow bridge one day, our car sideswiped another vehicle which was approaching us. There was minor damage – maybe the loss of a chrome strip on the driver's side.

In the period before fast food restaurants, finding a place to eat was always a challenge, especially when the family had a picky eater like me to contend with. I probably lived on hamburgers during these excursions. One day in New England we stopped at a diner called Smiley's for lunch. We sat at the counter and waited and waited for service. We sensed that the waitress knew that we were not locals, so we went to the end of the queue. We finally left after we realized it was going to be a long time, if ever, before we were going to be served. After leaving we acknowledged the irony of the restaurant's name, since we didn't encounter any smiling faces. This became an ongoing joke during our trip.

On one of our southern trips we took the Skyline Drive through the Great Smokey Mountains, and visited Williamsburg, Virginia where we stayed at a lodge overnight. Back in those days, tourist cabins were more prevalent than motels. One could find a cozy, but non-ostentatious, cottage for a few bucks a night. There was one cabin in New England that was situated on a stream, where Bill and I could test our balance walking on the exposed rocks. Morning breakfast was served by mom on the screened-in porch overlooking the water.

Summer travel vacations were always happily anticipated. One year was the exception when, instead, dad renovated our bathroom at home at a considerable expense. When I asked mom where we were going on vacation that year, she facetiously retorted that I'd have to spend it in the bathroom.

—

As previously mentioned, we lost our next door neighbor in 1954 when the McKinley Firehouse expanded and moved down the street to the corner of Cadwalader Avenue and Jenkintown Road. Prior to this period block parties were held in front of the old building during the summer. It was a festive event with neighbors milling around under the colored lights which were strung on wires across the street. There were all kinds of games of skill and chance set up, all in an effort to raise money to defray the firehouse's expenses. My favorite was penny pitch where you tossed a copper cent onto a mat and hoped to land your circular missile in an area designated with a higher denomination. Landing on the bull's eye earned you a dollar. I first tasted birch beer at one of these annual events. It was dispensed from a stainless steel keg by my friend John's big brother, Freddy. I once asked mom for a nickel so I could purchase a cup of the treat. Having none, she gave me a quarter which, she tried to explain to me, was equal to five nickels. That concept was too complicated for me. She finally relented and unearthed a nickel somewhere.

—

Among all the summer activities, there was still time for introspection. In some instances just being alone had special significance. For example, I usually didn't see John on Sundays, so I'd occasionally walk down to the playground by myself in the early evening. With no other humans around, I'd sit on a swing and let my mind wander, taking in the expanse of the playing field before me as I rhythmically glided back and forth with the air whistling sweetly by my ears. Expectation of an unknown future, near and far, would fill my young mind – a combination of wonder and melancholy. How would it all unfold?

The In-between Years

Transition

What I most remember about the summer of 1955 is my growing interest in professional baseball. In previous years I would buy football bubble gum trading cards at Davis' Drug Store, and had a simple knowledge of that game, watching the older kids compete in pickup contests down at the playground. But the Phillies were starting to gain my attention. The Bowman "TV" trading cards were very popular that summer, depicting players and umpires in full color photos with a border which resembled the screen of a console television set. John and I would garner a nickel from here or there and make our way to Davis' on our bicycles, buying the latest series of cards. Consecutive individual series of cards, in total numbering four or five, would be issued throughout the summer. Duplicates of players that you had already collected would start to pile up as you reached the end of the buying season for a particular series. I suppose that future hall-of-fame pitcher Robin Roberts was my first hero. Despite his formidable prowess on the mound, the Phillies lingered in the depths of the second division most of the season.

About the time that Labor Day approached, I was informed of an upcoming event that I didn't anticipate and couldn't fully grasp. I remember mom and Auntie sitting at the kitchen table and calling me from the den where I was playing. Mom, with an angelic countenance, told me that in a few months I'd have a baby brother or sister.

What? Are you kidding me? Talk about throwing a wrench in your life.

I just stood there stunned, not knowing what to say. Here I was, just turning 10 and the world was about to be turned upside down. The whole fabric of the nuclear family was going to be torn asunder, and I didn't have any voice in the planning. But, most of all, I just couldn't understand how this was happening. Mom was nearly 41, although she looked happy, now being two months into her term. I wasn't happy. I didn't know how to respond to this new revelation. It was easy for me to sublimate this new found knowledge until mom started to show.

The annual shock of starting a new school year diverted most of my attention. Although summertime was great fun, eventual boredom made one secretly yearn for classes to begin again.

Our fifth grade classroom was subterranean, occupying the previous space of the school library which moved upstairs a year or so prior. Natural light was limited to a line of high narrow windows which were at sidewalk level overlooking the school playground. Our new teacher was Mrs. Whitely, a young attractive woman with alabaster skin. She conducted class in an easy and fair manner. If you needed to be disciplined, you got to sit on her lap for a few minutes until you professed that you would correct the alleged wrong. I suppose that this trial was supposed to embarrass you, but it wasn't an unpleasant situation if you were a boy.

This lap-sitting punishment began to abate, however, when the lap in question started to shrink. Mrs. Whitely was obviously progressing through a pregnancy of her own. My life was being buffeted on all sides as a result of shenanigans going on behind closed doors. She left on leave fairly early in the school term and was replaced by a substitute teacher for two weeks while a full time teacher was being selected. Our substitute was a tall pretty woman whose name I can't remember, but her image will be forever ingrained in my memory since she posed with her students on the school's front steps for our annual class photo.

The whole tenor of teacher/student relations was about to change with the arrival of Mrs. Hartmeyer. She was a slightly rotund middle-aged woman with streaks of grey in her pageboy-styled hair. Rather austere in nature, she rarely cracked a smile. Her major method of discipline was to take the offender in hand and squeeze his cheek into submission between her able thumb and index finger.

I was still madly in love with fellow classmate Jane, but she of the manor-born showed little interest in me, and my shy demeanor surely didn't help matters. But there were moments where we could interact since we were both in the top reading group, and she did comment once that I had a nice singing voice which I displayed for her while singing the rounds of "Now the Day is Over."

Banking and commerce first made its way into the classroom during fifth grade. The Philadelphia Savings Fund Society (PSFS) had a program where they established student passbook savings accounts for those interested in creating a nest egg at an early age. I'm not sure if I volunteered or was selected to be a school banking officer, but I happily assumed the position. Once a week students were encouraged to bring in their spare change and deposit it in their accounts. I and others, acting as tellers, accepted the deposits and recorded the transactions on spreadsheets. This record, along with the individual passbooks, was packaged up and forwarded to PSFS where the deposits were recorded in the individual books and returned again to the students for next week's activity. Once a month PSFS would record any accrued interest in the passbooks as well. That account became the basis for my college tuition years later.

On a social level several of the students who lived in the village and the manor held after-school parties at their homes. For the most part the events consisted of not much more than games, refreshments and favors dispensed by the host parents. What was notable was the fact that no African-American children were invited. Whether this was a decision by the host parents or their children, I do not know.

Amidst the daily sameness of our classroom activities came a new female student who remained with us for just a few months. I suppose that her parents were living with relatives for a time before they found permanent residence elsewhere. Her name, Pam Mayhew, sticks in my mind for some reason. I can remember what she looked like although I have no photo record of her. She had a pageboy hairdo, was tall for her age, and could have easily passed for a sixth or seventh-grader. Pam was unique in that her family had what no other student's family possessed – a color TV. I don't think any of the other students were fortunate to view her magical television themselves, but we knew that she was going to be watching it the night of the elaborate production of Peter Pan starring Mary Martin. So it was that the following day, many students questioned Pam as to the costume colors worn by the various actors and what were the varied hues of the stage set. She sat there supremely and answered every question thrown her way.

Brotherly Alliances

As always, best friend John and I were practically inseparable, forming that lifelong bond. However, there was also another important male duo in our class during our McKinley years. Robby Holmes and Billy Barwig had a similar alliance. Robby lived on Huron Avenue in the village and Billy not far away on Forrest Avenue at the informal border with the manor. That placed them on a slightly higher social stratum than John and I. As I remember, Robby's dad was a graduate of Penn State while my immediate family had no college graduates. Robby's older sister Wendy and my brother Bill were in the same grade when they attended McKinley.

Physically, Robby and John shared a similar, sturdy build, while Billy and I were both thin and wiry. All four of us tended to interact in class and on the playground during recess, but after hours we usually went back to our separate pairings. Occasionally, however, I would meet with Robby after school for some play time, as did John and Billy. During the Christmas recess I made it a habit of going to Robby's house during the daytime where we would share and play with our newest toys. One year Mr. Potato Head was the popular gift and Robby and I would spend hours creating various characters with vegetables and fruit provided by the attractive Mrs. Holmes who reminded me a bit of Betty Crocker. Each day she would offer me lunch, but since I had such a phobia of being offered food that wasn't included in my limited menu, I would courteously, but shyly, decline her offer and run home to have a quick lunch prepared by mom – hopefully some left over Christmas turkey between two slices of bread.

Billy and I would also meet after school hours at times. Back in those days tent caterpillar nests could be spotted in trees all over the neighborhood in the spring. When the furry little critters emerged, they would be seen crawling all over the streets and sidewalks. On occasion, Billy and I would meet behind the McKinley Elementary gymnasium and conduct caterpillar races up the stucco exterior of the rear wall.

Robby, in the school environment, was more of a natural born leader, taking the initiative when playing games on the playground or in the gymnasium. He was always self-assured and consistently maintained that unique air about him without being a snob.

There was one occasion when all four of us went on a mission. I'm not sure from what location we started, but we made our way down to Elkins Park near the intersection of Church and York Roads. One of the four of us – surely not I – felt that we should engage in a bit of mountain climbing. There's a fairly high cliff to the right of York Road as it travels south and cuts into the intersection. Beyond this outcropping of rock were the Yorktown Inn and Yorktown movie theater. Our Alpine party began to ascend this promontory at street level. There seemed to be enough rocks and ledges to get a handhold and foothold during our ascent. I was last in the party and followed the path of the others. As far as I was concerned it seemed to be a perilous journey as the route took us far above York Road, busy with traffic. As we approached the summit, my three fellow climbers made the successful climb to the top. Trailing behind by about six feet or so, I couldn't find anything substantial to hold onto. I took a peek down below and saw the traffic whizzing by. Looking up I could see the silhouette of Robby's head through some tall grass. He asked if I was all right. I froze, and possibly said a prayer or two to myself. Something told me to reach to the right where an outcropping of weeds was securely rooted behind a rock. I grasped it, and it held, and I was able to make my way safely to the top. I had nightmares about that event for years hence.

—

Of course I had interactions with other fellow students as well. On occasions, I'd play at Ricky Coulston's house in the manor. He had a magnificently large bedroom with his brother Van overlooking a wooded back lot, and he had an assortment of model airplanes hanging from the ceiling. Van was a year older than Ricky and rather athletic, playing quarterback on the elementary school team.

The highest academic achiever in our class was Tommy Morrison who would eventually graduate at the top of his class at an Ivy League University. Of the girls, Judy Ashton, Jane Sullivan, and Barbara Feick were the academic stars. Dee Dee Nelson and Beverly Woodly joined that informal elite group when they became class members in sixth grade. Jane and Barbara were practically inseparable as friends. I continued my ways as an underachiever. During the period of the 1950s, Abington Township elementary schools utilized a unique, limited grading system for their students with the categories of High, Medium, and Low, rather than the conventional A, B, C, D and F which were used in junior high and above. My grades were usually weighted equally between Highs and Mediums – Mr. Mediocre.

———

Joy Then Grief

The school year slipped into the spring of 1956, the beginning of another presidential election campaign. We were a Republican family, so, naturally, mom, dad, and Auntie backed Eisenhower for a second term over Adlai Stevenson. But the real attention was on mom who was nearing term in her pregnancy.

Easter fell on April 1 that year – April Fool's Day. The newspapers made a lot out of it. Brother Bill and I received our festive baskets, as we did each year, filled with marshmallow chicks, chocolate bunnies, and coconut creme eggs, but I'm sure that mom's mind was on other important matters.

I can't remember if it was the following Friday or Saturday, but the time had come and dad drove mom to Germantown Hospital to give birth. On the afternoon of Saturday, April 7 dad called from the hospital to announce that my baby sister, Ann Victoria Burr, had been born. I was in the den at the time whittling a figure of a small deer out of a block of pine wood with an x-acto knife. My hand had slipped performing this chore a day earlier and it put a nice size gash in my left ring finger. Anyway, Auntie took the call and made the announcement. The gravity of the situation finally occurred to me and I let out an ecstatic yelp.

The weekend went by in anticipation of little Ann coming home. Monday morning I bounded off to school. I remember walking down the steps to our fifth grade classroom in the morning with Robby Holmes and telling him that I was no longer the youngest member of our family, and he congratulated me. I don't think that I had told any of my classmates previously, except Johnny, that my mother was expecting. When lunchtime rolled around, I walked home as usual to have a sandwich. I never ate at the cafeteria. After finishing lunch I walked through the interior door to our front porch. Auntie had been sitting on the side porch, and dad, with his back to me, had just come from the hospital and was speaking with Auntie. I said something to dad, but he seemed distracted and didn't respond to me. I proceeded out the front door and made the short walk to school to take part in the lunchtime kick ball game.

That evening I was informed of the sad news; my newborn baby sister had died. It stemmed from the fact that mom and dad had incompatible blood types with the
Rh-factor which usually caused complications with the third baby born to such a couple. As the second child it affected me to some extent when I was born. I had jaundice and didn't cry right away when the doctor spanked me. This condition can now be remedied, but there was no known treatment in the 1950s. I was devastated, as was brother Bill, but the adverse effect that it must have had on mom was unimaginable. I didn't know what to say to her when she came home, trying to go about my normal daily activities as best as possible without trying to cause her any distress. I think my brother was even more devastated than I since he better sensed the gravity of the situation.

That afternoon I walked down to the school playground feeling unbearably depressed. Neighborhood children were happy and playing and I just wandered around as if in a trance not interacting with anyone.

It was many weeks before mom began to approach her normal level of joviality, and I know that she never really got over the whole situation for the rest of her life. The house still displayed lingering reminders of the event, such as the gifts received during baby showers, which provided a haunting unreality for our household. The items were given away or disposed of in a relatively short period of time.

I didn't have the strength or courage to tell any of my classmates of the loss, not even my best friend John. He eventually confronted me a week or so later with the news that he had heard from a member of his family. I was in denial.

The Ventriloquist

As the spring of 1956 moved on, so did the challenges of fifth grade. One exception to the trials and tribulations was a unique picnic lunch held at one of my classmate's home. It was held in the village, and I believe that it was put together by the mother of a fellow student, Beverly Drapp. On that day we all walked together for the short trip from the school to the host home. I can't remember what was on the menu, but evidently it was something that was acceptable to my limited palate. As Mrs. Hartmeyer relaxed in the back yard, I was shocked to see her light up a cigarette. This seemed unimaginable to me. I should have known better, I suppose, since the teachers' break room, located off the main hall back at the school, would produce a cloud of smoke when the door was opened.

Back in the classroom environment, Mrs. Hartmeyer didn't make many changes in the scholastic rankings established by her predecessor; therefore, I was still firmly ensconced in the first reading group. I could smugly sit with others of my ilk in that special corner of the room and actually read and speak all those important words which contained multiple syllables. Sure, there was a certain status in not being associated with those two "other" reading groups, but by the same token there was more expected of you.

Actually, the best part of being in the first reading group was the supreme honor of sharing its membership with Jane Sullivan, my perennial, unrequited love. Just to sit there and watch her form each precious word with those pretty lips was enough to make my aching heart flutter. It was, however, one of Jane's little acts of kindness that did me in.

In preparation for an upcoming assembly in the auditorium, our reading group was selected to put on a play for the benefit of all the elementary school's students. I can't remember if parents were invited to attend. That detail has been blocked out of my memory. In any event, the play selected by Miss Hartmeyer had to do with trees – trees that stood around in some city park (what else could they do with those roots) and talked to each other. About which they spoke, I don't recall. What I do recall is that the Sassafras tree had some really funny lines.

Now, I always considered myself a bit of a class comedian. I suppose that I took on this role to deal with some of my insecurities including a bashful nature. Making somebody laugh was a way of gaining acceptance. So I sat there with eager anticipation when the various deciduous roles were handed out. As expected, Jane got the lead role as the Maple tree. The Maple tree had the most lines, and, most assuredly, the most boring lines. When it came to selecting the individual for the Sassafras role, I had no doubt that Mrs. Hartmeyer had no one in mind but me. Let's face it. I was a natural.

But then something awful happened. She picked some unfunny classmate. In a state of shock, I couldn't contain myself. Tears started running uncontrollably down my cheeks. This was very embarrassing, having my usually-hidden sensitive nature laid bare before my peers. However, dear Jane came to the rescue – so she thought – by offering her Maple tree role to me. The tears stopped quickly, but not because of relief, but because of fear. Of course I couldn't say "no" to the girl of my dreams and hurt her feelings. But how was I going to learn all those lines for that very boring part.

In preparation, I can remember pacing back and forth on our back porch, book in hand, trying to remember all of those inane Maple tree lines. Over and over I would say them in my head. Over and over I would try to say them out loud without looking at the book. It wasn't looking good.

The moment of truth finally came. The big day arrived. There I was, shaking in my bark; waiting for the curtain to part so my inadequacies could be displayed to all of the world.

I stood conspicuously in the middle of the stage. Before me lay a sea of faces waiting to be entertained. Well, they got their wish.

I believe that I had the first line. My mouth opened but nothing came out. I couldn't remember a word, as hard as I tried. Mrs. Hartmeyer sat in front of the stage, book in hand, relaying one word to me at a time. I became Knuckle Head Smiff to her Edgar Bergen, as if she were remotely controlling my lips. Her face became increasingly flushed in concert with her anger. She was figuratively pinching my cheek and shaking it in a vigorous manner.

Mercifully the play eventually ended, and I unceremoniously marched my little trunk off the stage – trying to avoid Mrs. Hartmeyer with all my being.

In later years I pretty much mastered my fear of performing before audiences, doing little stand-up comedy routines at goodbye lunches for work mates preparing to change jobs. But sometimes – just sometimes – while peering into the crowd, I'd imagine that round, red face looking straight at me. It's enough to start my leaves shaking all over again.

West Philly Visits

They lived in a narrow West Philadelphia row home located on 5113 Walton Avenue. It had a postage stamp-sized backyard surrounded by a wrought iron fence. The first floor layout from front to back was: living room; dining room; kitchen. Several times a year on the weekends we'd travel in from the hinterlands of the suburbs and visit my father's parents.

My grandfather was a mild, easy-going man with a quiet sense of humor who loosely resembled Jimmy Durante – nose and all. Nana, a small rather flat-faced woman, was attentive, talkative and a bit peculiar.

My Grandparents (1955)
Clarence Burr (Pop Pop) & Katherine Batdorf Burr (Nan)

Great Uncle Frank Burr
in his younger days

Pop Pop, as we called my grandfather, continued to work as a house painter after the family paint business went belly-up in the depression. By the 1950s he had taken up part time jobs such as pushing a trash dolly through daily cleanup rounds at the Strawbridge and Clothier department store in center city. He didn't have a pension and probably collected a minimal amount from Social Security.

On sunny Sunday afternoons we "men" would walk to a nearby city park and fortify ourselves with roasted peanuts from a vendor, but most of the time was spent in the confines of the living room. Nan would take my mom upstairs to the front bedroom and show her the collection of cloth material that she planned to use in sewing projects, although I can't remember seeing any finished work.

On many occasions my Aunt Helen, her husband Clarence, and my cousins Sid, Gerry, and Jimmy would also stop by for a visit. Jimmy was the offspring of Aunt Helen's second marriage and was, therefore, a half brother to Sid and Gerry. Jimmy was two years older than I, while Sid was my senior by 13 years and Gerry by eight years.

The visits that I relished most, however, were when it was just my parents and I making a visit, because then I would have Uncle Frank all to myself. At the top of the staircase to the second floor was the entrance of a small gloomy room. Upon approval from my parents I would shyly ascend the steps and pause outside the doorway. An invitation to enter the darkness was readily forthcoming.

In the corner sat Uncle Frank. As my eyes adjusted to the meager light of the hall lamp, his features would appear – most notably a perpetually smiling squint which portended mischief. To the right of his chair was his bed. What space remained in the dim confines was filled with small cabinets and tables containing the examples and tools of his trade.

Uncle Frank was my grandfather's older brother and was his senior by fourteen years. He was seventy-five when I was born. How he came to live with my grandparents I'm not sure, but I think his pension check had something to do with it. Nana got a cut of the proceeds for tolerating his presence in her home, although I'm sure that he was as unobtrusive as he could be under the circumstances. Uncle Frank never married, his fiancee sadly dying years before, shortly prior to their proposed wedding date.

In the many visits to my grandparents' house I never remember seeing Uncle Frank outside his room. Grandma, I'm sure, made him stay in his place like an unwanted pet. I vaguely remember him coming to our house one Christmas day with my grandparents. He was always invited, but, I assume, not allowed to come, save that one instance. So for all practical purposes our personal encounters were confined to those dreary, but fascinating, surroundings. It was just the two of us, and I would listen intently to his stories, although I forget many of the details today. I do remember him telling me how, as a young man, he saw Teddy Roosevelt while serving in the National Guard.

What intrigued me as much as his witty stories were his wood carvings. As a young artisan he carved elaborate horses for carrousels. The surviving examples of his profession were those which could fit into the limited space in his room. On the wall above his bed hung "The Moon Shiners," a framed scene of surly-looking men working at a whiskey still, carved on a thin piece of rectangular hardwood. One of my favorite pieces was the figure of an elk fashioned in mahogany. That treasured work is in my possession today.

His passion for woodcarving helped him to survive his "confinement" I suppose. And, although his advancing years lessened his ability to duplicate the intricate craftsmanship of his youth, his later works were more special because some were created especially for me.

Sitting on the desk in front of me as I write this essay is a rather crude, cartoon-like carving of a four and a half inch tall man with a top hat – no small feat, considering that Uncle Frank worked in virtual darkness without eyeglasses. I can remember when he presented it to me more than sixty years ago, and how I gazed at it in wonder. The project wasn't complete on that particular visit, however, since the Lilliputian still required arms. Those stiff appendages would be added before my next visit.

Those times alone with Uncle Frank were very special – an old man sharing memories with his favorite grandnephew. I always felt sorry for him sitting in solitary confinement although he never seemed unhappy. My assumption is that he was allowed out by grandma after our family departed – at least to eat or get an occasional hair cut.

As mentioned in the previous chapter, at the age of ten, in an effort to emulate my grand uncle, I carved a small figure of a deer using an X-Acto knife. This minor work (sans one leg) has survived the last five decades and occupies the shelf above one of my desks. I remember taking my handiwork to Uncle Frank for his inspection during my next visit. He properly congratulated me on my effort. So it was over time, through my teen years, that I made an effort to visit him and continue our special bond.

Summer of 1956

As usual, the normal summer routine set in. John and I were glad to be out of school for a few months of leisurely diversion. Our family made its annual trip to Pleasantville, New Jersey to spend a week at the ramshackle abode at 303 East Edgewater Avenue. Daily trips to the beach at Ventor were routine while nights were often spent on the boardwalk at Atlantic City or Ocean City.

Unfortunately the national pastime, as far as Philadelphia was concerned, was more of the same. The woeful Phillies continued their annual, futile quest to win a pennant in the National League. The last time that they achieved that honor was in 1950, but I was too young to remember. John and I continued to collect our baseball cards with frequent purchases at Davis' Drug Store. Brother Bill made things interesting for us by devising a dice game which we played using the cards, dividing them into teams – John playing the American League, and I the National League. Many sultry days were spent in my third floor bedroom with us sitting on the floor, rolling dice and filling out box scores for our imaginary league.

Although the real Phillies finished the season in fifth place, 22 games out of first, there were some individual player highlights. My hero, catcher Stan Lopata, hit 32 home runs while utilizing his squat-like crouch at the plate. That was a lot of round-trippers for a Phillies player. He also drove in 95 runs, as did left fielder Del Ennis who connected on 26 long balls. It was to be the last year for Del in Philadelphia since he was traded to the Cardinals in the upcoming off-season. Despite his consistent productive performance over the years, he became the target of Philadelphia's famous boo birds. On the pitching front, Robin Roberts had 19 wins, but 18 losses, and lefty Curt Simmons finished with a record of 15-10. The Brooklyn Dodgers, in their last year in New York, lost to the Yankees in the World Series which was highlighted by the perfect game pitched by Yank Don Larson.

At some point during the summer dad was working on a project of some sort in the backyard. He had some extra scrap wood piled behind the garage which he didn't plan to use. Utilizing this supply, I laid two of the boards on the ground, parallel to each other, and started to nail horizontal pieces onto them. Before long I had created a wall that Johnny and I subsequently used to build a clubhouse in the area behind the outdoor fireplace. It was a project which took us several weeks to complete. Nails were a fairly cheap commodity and we made quite a few trips down to JAX, a hardware store on Township Line, to pick up an adequate supply. We built a roof and covered it with old shingles that dad provided. The one small window that we fashioned on one wall projected an inadequate amount of light, but there were enough gaps between the odds-and-end wall boards for the sun to penetrate. This makeshift building would become the "B - B" clubhouse, which was identified as such by a sign hanging over the entrance door. Many hours were spent in our private enclave.

As August turned into September, anticipation grew as the school year approached. It was rumored that there would be a new sixth grade teacher, and we students would be the kings and queens of the castle upon reaching our last year at McKinley elementary.

An Adult Male Presence in School

This was a real novelty – a male teacher. Back in the 1950s male teachers in elementary schools were a rarity, except, possibly, at the sixth grade level. James Morrell, fresh out of college and a hitch in the military, was about to embark on his first full-time teaching assignment, and we boy students were excited. And the girls probably felt a bit of a tug on their heartstrings since they surely classified him as "cute."

Mr. Morrell had evident athletic ability and had previously tried out for the Philadelphia Phillies' minor league team, but was deemed too short for the job. As a result of his competitive zeal it was natural that he got our class involved in sports, including football, soccer and basketball. As the year progressed our teams would play those of other elementary schools in the Abington School District.

Adding a bit of excitement to the coming year was the influx of new students – including two sets of twins. The Weiner sisters, Rosalind and Kathy, lived on Beaver Hollow Road in a new housing development of predominately Jewish families. The enclave was bordered by Forrest Avenue and Jenkintown Roads. The Thrift brothers, Marc and Rene, lived at the Old York Road Country Club where, I believe, their father was employed. And from The Hill section of McKinley were Beverly Woodley who lived on Osceola Avenue and Dee Dee Nelson who resided on Douglass Avenue. Charlotte Waetjen, with a home on Jenkintown Road, was also new to our class and had transferred from a school in the city.

During the initial fall period, Mr. Morrell wasted no time in getting the male students involved in "tails" football. Each player had a strip of material, or tail, stuck in the back of his belt. The ball carrier was "tackled" when a defensive player successfully pulled off the dangling tail from his opponent. I was assigned the position of tackle for most of the season despite my meager physical presence. Once I was relegated to fourth string quarterback. I suppose that set my standing slightly above the fifth-graders on the team in status. I'm not sure who was the first string quarterback, but it was probably Robby Holmes.

Our football practices were held on a regular basis after school. Mr. Morrell identified the different offensive plays with a number. I believe that it was play number four that we were scrimmaging one day when I ran a designed route after the ball was snapped. A fifth-grader, Jeffery Roach, on the opposing team, crashed into me head-to-head while coming across the line in the opposite direction. The point of impact on me was the bone above my left eye socket. His was a less vulnerable spot on his forehead. With the blood being spilled, it was obvious that both of us needed attention. Mr. Morrell abruptly ended practice and swooped us into his car for a trip to the emergency room of Abington Hospital, not having time to contact our parents first.

Well, having been brought up as a Christian Scientist, I didn't have much contact with doctors and medical procedures, save my small pox vaccination at a young age. So, as one may imagine, it was quite a traumatic experience for me. As it turned out, Jeff only needed one or two stitches, but I required about four. I was petrified during the whole process. When all of the sewing was completed, they coated the wound with some new type of plastic fluid which hardened over the affected area. No bandages were used. It made me look a bit like Frankenstein.

A few weeks later, it was time to get the stitches removed. Since we didn't have a regular primary care doctor, my mother took me to the office of a physician in Germantown, Dr. Hartung, who delivered my short-lived sister a year before. He was a kindly older gentleman. After the procedure, Mom reminded him that he had never billed her for the birth, and, as it turned out, he never did.

Of course football practice continued as before, but it was sullied again by another injury. Bobby Hicks, a fifth grade student, went out for a pass and ran straight into a metal pole near the end zone, wounding his forehead. Poor Mr. Morrell had to make another trip to the emergency room.

As I recall, it was on the same day of the latest incident, or thereabouts, when Robby Holmes got a new puppy. Since Bobby received stitches and was given a traditional head bandage after his accident, Robby called his dog Stitches in tribute.

McKinley's Finest

There was a local McKinley presence in the Abington Police corps, since three officers lived in the nearby community. It always behooved the neighborhood children to behave because the streets were being patrolled regularly by these individuals who ranged in demeanor from good cop to bad cop.

Andy Harkins was the oldest of the lot, and probably wasn't far from retirement age. I believe that he lived on Osceola Avenue on the white fringe of The Hill. Grandfather-like old Andy was as friendly as could be with a continuous smile on his face. When I was quite young, before attending grade school, he was called to our house to take away our dog Happy, which was probably suffering from distemper. When I came downstairs in the morning I arrived in the kitchen after the deed was done, and there sat Mom in the corner near the dog's bed crying her eyes out.

Andy was also assigned crossing guard duty from time to time, before and after school, at the corner of Cadwalader Avenue and Jenkintown Road at the locale of Waxy's Texaco Station. As a member of the school safety patrol, I occasionally pulled duty on the same corner. He always conversed with me in a friendly way. A slightly deranged black man, named Leon, would occasionally walk by and utter some gibberish to Andy who would always respond in a kindly manner.

Officer Mainwaring, who lived nearby at the corner of Cadwalader and Cypress avenues, represented a more authoritarian approach. I remember him yelling at me from his patrol car one day because I was bouncing off the hedge by the sidewalk of our family's property. Obviously it was something that I shouldn't have been doing. However, that reprimand was nothing compared to the fear that could be instilled into a youngster by Officer Jim Grimes.

"Grimesy," as he was called, was a thin, manic policeman with a constant malevolent countenance. I remember an incident down by Olivet Presbyterian church, catercorner from the

Mainwaring residence. One afternoon Billy Zimmer (a year or so my junior and a fellow Cadwalader Avenue resident) and I were observing Billy Williams and another youth whom I can't remember, throwing a rubber ball against the side of the church. Williams was around my brother's age and attended Catholic parochial school. Anyway, it so happened that in trying to bounce the ball off of the church wall, a window got in the way and noisily shattered. This prompted a nearby resident to call the police.

In a flash, Grimesy arrived on the scene, and commanded the four of us into his squad car – Billy Williams being placed in the front seat. Grimsey turned in his seat and looked straight at Billy Zimmerman and me and began yelling at us, hoping to extract a confession to the dastard deed from the youngest offenders. Tears immediately started flowing down my face. Williams cooly informed Grimesy that we were merely observers, and we were subsequently released from captivity.

Some years later I saw a less threatening side of Jim Grimes when he was part of a small group of us who went to see a stock car race at the Hatfield Speedway. Along with Dad and brother Bill, we accompanied Tip Leary and Grimesy to the races. We all took up position in the infield rather than sitting in the stands. Old Grimesy ran back and forth like a man possessed following the progress of his favorite car, and when there was a crash he nearly jumped out of his shoes in excitement as he scurried toward the site of the mishap.

—

A police state, on a smaller scale, existed during class days at school. Being part of the Keystone Safety Patrol was quite an honor. Boy students who were chosen for the corps wore a white woven cloth strap around the waist and over one shoulder with a rectangular aluminum badge over the chest strap which identified the individual as one of the elite. Girl safeties had to settle for a less conspicuous adornment which consisted of a round metal badge which was worn on the upper arm. Each week the boy safeties were assigned to a post for morning, lunchtime, and afternoon duty at strategic intersections to guide coming-and-going students across the street. In those days, students were allowed to go home for lunch. Girl safeties policed the playground during recess to make sure students behaved well. They also had the supreme duty of ringing the school bell in the lofty tower to signal when recess was over, and it was time to get back to class.

A platinum-haired fourth-grade teacher, Mrs. Gallagher, managed the safety corps with an iron fist. At the beginning of the school year, and at the midpoint, three officers were chosen from among the troops – one captain, and two lieutenants. The captain's badge had a red keystone insignia and lettering to identify the office, and the lieutenants were identified with the color blue. I suppose the selection of the officers was a bit of a popularity contest. For the first half of the school year Robby Holmes was elected Captain, and Bobby Hicks and I were awarded the lieutenant positions. So, I suppose I was held in some regard by others. Billy Barwig became Captain and Johnny Bauerle, and another unremembered student, served as lieutenants for the second half of the term. I believe Jane Sullivan and Barbara Feick were chosen from the female contingent to serve as captains.

One of the main duties of the male officers was to check the various crossing spots to make sure that the regular safeties were at their posts on time. To facilitate getting to the outlying areas, a bicycle was utilized. Since I walked to school, I borrowed Billy Barwig's bike which was quite speedy. Its lack of fenders, however, did provide a bit of a problem on rainy days.

Every week of so, Mrs. Gallagher held a disciplinary court, where students identified by safeties as committing an infraction – such as crossing an intersection before being told to do so – were brought before the court and summarily chastised. Nonetheless, I remember no cases of police brutality.

This year was an important one in the emergence of the Elvis Presley phenomena and his unique effect on the youth of the day. Presley first appeared on the Ed Sullivan show that September and the craze hit the students of McKinley. A small, but important incident, related to The King occurred during the first day back to school after the Christmas break. I was pulling safety duty at the corner of Jenkintown Road and Osceola Avenue. A thin girl with glasses made her way down Jenkintown

Road from her home on High School Road. She was a fifth grade student and I wasn't really acquainted with her, but she caught my attention by a round badge she was wearing on her jacket. Its white letters on a blue background announced "I Like Elvis," except that the word "Like" was written on a piece of paper taped to the badge. It was actually an "I Hate Elvis" pin that had been altered to display the girl's true sentiment. Her dad had bought the item for her as a joke at Christmas. I commented on it, since I was also an Elvis fan, and we both laughed. This young lady, whose name was Dale, would fill a significant spot in my life, years hence.

A Boy's Best Friend

Brother Bill and I campaigned for years, leaving little notes around the house stating, "I want a kob!" Now, as a matter of explanation, "kob" was the word for "dog" in the zube-zob language. Over the years, Bill and I devised this alien vocabulary, adding words as we went along. Over a half of a century later, "kob" is the only word in our devised language that I remember. But all of this is neither here nor there; we just wanted a dog as a companion.

Years earlier we had a black cocker spaniel named Gypsy. She wasn't the friendliest dog in the world. I did get her to sit up on her hind legs, and she would stay there as long as I pointed at her face, but she would be uttering a low growl the whole time. Gypsy loved to eat and eat, which turned out to be her downfall. She succumbed to a heart problem at the age of three.

Sometime during the 1956-57 school year, a mongrel puppy became available to us, and my mother, being finally worn down by our constant requests, relented. My memory is that the little guy belonged to a friend of our dentist, and he was the last of the litter. We named him "Teddy" after Theodore Roosevelt. Teddy's coat had various shades of brown and he resembled a hound of some sort.

As a condition of having a pet, several restrictions were put in place by mom. Teddy had to stay on the first floor of the house, and he wasn't allowed on the furniture. He quickly

My Best Friend, Teddy

learned his limitations. Of course I really wanted him to sleep with me in my bed on the third floor.

Teddy enjoyed our large side yard, and Bill and I played games with him quite frequently. He had a small rubber football that he liked to run with. Games were devised where we kicked off to him and he would try to run past us with the ball securely entrapped in his jaws. With his serpentine movements, he almost always eluded us and scored a touchdown.

Of course my brother and I were supposed to assume the responsibility of feeding and walking Teddy, and letting him out to do his business. Well, we did let him out. He was never good on a leash, always straining at his collar, taking you for a walk. Mom did try to keep him close to home by tying him to a pole in the backyard. But he looked so forlorn in that situation that it didn't last for long. Teddy loved his freedom, and he was usually let out the back door when it was time for him to succumb to nature's call. Unfortunately, nature's call also included encounters with the opposite sex.

Although it was against the law in Abington for a dog to roam the streets, we didn't heed that restriction for the most part. Teddy would disappear for hours gallivanting throughout McKinley, usually returning when it was time for his supper. Occasionally, however, when a neighborhood female dog was in heat, he would camp out overnight near the residence of his amour.

A neighbor a few doors down, on the other side of Cadwalader Avenue, had two pedigree Spitz dogs, one of whom was sending out hormonal signals. In Lady and the Tramp fashion, Teddy didn't allow social mores to interfere with his base desires. In due time a litter was born with all of the puppies resembling our vagabond canine.

One time Teddy went missing for a day or two when we finally received a call from my classmate Dee Dee Nelson who, at that time, lived in The Hill district. Her dog was in heat and she wasn't too happy with Teddy hanging around her property overnight, waiting for his opportunity. I dutifully went to her house and retrieved Teddy. He looked like he had been on an all-night binge.

Unfortunately Teddy wasn't very adept at crossing the street safely. I once witnessed him being hit by a car upon his crossing Cadwalader Avenue in front of our house. He saw me, and just took off. My heart stopped. Fortunately it was a glancing blow, but Teddy received a slight gash on his head. This did not dissuade him from new adventures, however.

In retrospect it would appear that our family wasn't very responsible in restricting Teddy's movements, but, to be fair, many dogs roamed the streets in the 50s and 60s. My mother renewed Teddy's license every year, and it was always fastened to his collar. When Teddy went missing, we usually called the township dog pound, and there we would find him in confinement. He was an easily-captured perpetrator, always coming right up to the patrolling dog catcher when called.

Having a dog license did reduce the fine for each occurrence to five dollars.

Old Teddy would continue to be my best buddy through my junior and high school years – a bond like no other.

———

Dance Parties

The 1956-57 school year was seminal in many respects. For one, rock and roll was becoming the musical mainstay among the youth of the nation. It was revolutionary and much more suggestive than songs such as "How Much is That Doggy in the Window" performed by Patti Page. In the music industry it was almost as cataclysmic as going from silent movies to talkies. Many parents resisted the new irresistible wave, but appearances by Elvis Presley and other rock stars on mainstream variety shows, like Ed Sullivan, placed a measure of legitimacy on the new trend. Ricky Nelson would use the forum of the "Ozzie and Nelson" TV show to strut his stuff.

Our female classmates were, of course, in the vanguard of the rock and roll movement. Inexpensive 45 rpm record players were pervasive, and the girls snapped up the latest hits in the stores, playing their favorite artists in the confines of their bedrooms or in the basement, far from the prying ears of parents. Dick Clark's American Bandstand television show was aired every weekday afternoon from the studio in West Philadelphia. All of the latest dance crazes could be observed as the teens who swarmed across the studio floor put energy into motion. The girls in our sixth grade class picked up the new steps quickly and displayed them around the school's outdoor swing set during recess.

I'm not quite sure how it happened, but during one of those recess interludes, dear Jane invited me to jitterbug. Now, I had gyrated to Elvis on my own in front of the dining room mirror at home, but I had never danced. First of all, I was shocked that Jane would even invite me to partake of her time. Before long, however, she was showing me how to cup my right hand and place it in her right hand – her soft right hand. In concert with her, after a few lessons, I was twirling, bending and swaying to imagined music. I was smitten.

I believe I was invited to our first dance party in commemoration of Halloween. It may have been hosted by Beverly Drapp's mother – I can't be sure – and the event was held in the basement of their home in The Village. Who compiled the invitation list, I don't know, but it was apparent that none of our black classmates were in attendance. And, I suppose, some of the children who may have been considered nerds (before that word was in vogue) were left out as well. Unnatural selection was taking place, but I didn't dwell on the consequences for long.

Before the dancing began on that eventful night, I was introduced to kissing games: spin the bottle and post office. One of the girls directed all participants to squat on the floor forming a circle. A milk bottle was placed in the center, and somehow I was elected to make the first spin. As soon as I gave it a vigorous twirl, I had a premonition of when it would stop and to whom it would point. Let me just say that it was not the prettiest girl in class. Superficial selection criteria ruled the day in those prepubescent times. I could not bring myself to kiss the poor girl, embarrassing myself, and even her more. Finally that hurdle was overcome, and before long everybody was participating, including me – spinning and kissing, kissing and spinning. Of course kisses were only being planted on receptive cheeks with one exception. When we moved onto the more selective game of post office, I found that Charlotte, to my surprise, preferred to make herself known lips to lips.

In playing post office, each individual was secretly assigned a unique number; then one participant would go to a more private out-of-sight location and call out a number randomly. The person whose number was called would join the caller in that special location and exchange a kiss with the other player. As the game wore on, you'd start to identify each individual by number, remembering those which matched the person with whom you wanted to make the sweet exchange. When Jane called out my number, I couldn't really believe that I had arrived. What did she see in me?

As the evening wore on, classmates began to dance to fast and slow dances, the music being chosen primarily by the girls. As the school year marched on, I remember several more dance parties, they being thrown in succession at the homes of Sue Palmer, Barbara Feick, Ricky Coulston, and Veronica Knapp.

I believe that it was on the Saturday after the first party – a Halloween get-together – that John and I rode our bikes past Jane's house on Evergreen Road in the Manor. Lo and behold, she and Barbara Feick were out front. We joined them and relived the previous, glorious evening. A bit of dancing without music even ensued. It was a magical day

As the school year wore on, however, my relationship with Jane would change.

—

Sometime during the autumn of 1956, after the Halloween party, I was on morning safety duty at the corner of Jenkintown Rd. and Tulpehocken Ave. at the location of Frank Cook's Barbershop. John, on his way to school from his home on Forrest Ave., stopped by to talk. John and I had previously discussed the possibility of asking Jane and Barbara to go to the movies at the Hiway Theater in Jenkintown. Of course this required someone asking one of the two girls if they would be interested. One of Mom's adages was: "There are those who make the snowballs, and those who throw them." I was of the former category. In other words, my friend John would become the John Alden to my Miles Standish. It so happened that Barbara Feick passed that intersection on her way to school, so everything was set in place.

As she arrived at the intersection, John simply asked Barbara if she thought that she and Jane would consider going to the movies with us. Barbara smiled and said that she would ask Jane.

A week or so passed and Barbara approached John and me in the classroom during a break. She said, "Do you remember what you asked me about Jane and me going to the movies with you?" In an instant, in an obvious moment of

idiocy and pique, I replied, "We've changed our minds since then." Barbara walked away crestfallen. It didn't really occur to me at the time what a bonehead thing I had just done. I can't remember John's reaction. Heck, why didn't I let him speak for the two of us as I did before? Maybe I was afraid that Barbara was going to tell us that they weren't interested in a movie date, and I wanted to beat her to the punch. But, in any case, it was one of the most stupid things that I did in my life up to that point.

Some days later a fellow classmate informed me that Jane hated me the most, and then John, second. Suddenly it occurred to me that Jane had truly liked me first and was showing me her contempt by hating me the most. My chance of having Jane as an elementary school girlfriend had passed forever.

Going to Camp

A sixth grade tradition at McKinley School was to go on a camping trip during the late spring. To help finance this event, each student was given a supply of flower and vegetable seeds to sell to the public. For every 20 packs of seeds sold, you would win an unspecified prize. I was never the salesman type, being a rather bashful child when it came to activities like this. Nonetheless, I managed to get up the courage and sell seeds door to door in the Crosswicks development which was located off of Forrest Avenue outside of McKinley. Most of my sales, however, came from the effort of my father who took advantage of fellow office workers. In all, 40 packs were sold, earning me two prizes – identical plastic pencil boxes, each with a sliding times table gadget on the top. Big deal!

There was a lot of activity on the morning of the trip. A panel truck pulled up to the rear steps of the school on the sixth grade side of the building. Our janitor, Mr. Hetherington had the unenviable job of loading the truck with all of the sixth grade baggage. It was a three-day outing with two overnight stays. I can't remember what I packed.

We would be staying in cabins at the campsite, so several days prior to the trip, Mr. Morrell assigned four students to each dwelling. I was made the leader of our cabin which included my friend John and Gary Adams. The name of the fourth student escapes me. As leader, I was given the responsibility of coming up with a creative name for our temporary abode. My best shot was "Lincoln's Cabin." John derided me on that uninspired label.

Outdoor activities in the beautiful late spring weather were supervised by Mr. Morrell, though the specifics, for the most part, elude me. Our principal, Miss Garrison, accompanied the trip as well, and probably another teacher or two. She tended to be a bit of a disciplinarian while Mr. Morrell was easygoing.

Meals were held in a big cafeteria and each student was assigned a chore. My duty was to help wash the dishes after breakfast one morning. Not knowing what I should use to scrub the soiled plates, I asked Mr. Morrell. He handed me a brush that was located nearby. It was not too long into my scrubbing chores that Miss Garrison let out with a loud shriek and grabbed the brush from my nimble fingers. "You're cleaning dishes with the toilet brush," she exclaimed. Along with the obvious humiliation, I was instantly relieved of my duties, and Mr. Morrell didn't offer any words of explanation despite my staring at him longingly, waiting for an utterance concerning his complicity. Nothing was forthcoming. Could you blame him? I would be moving onto junior high soon and be long forgotten, he had to continue working with Miss Garrison in the coming year.

On our final evening at camp, we attended a square dance at a faux castle at a nearby location where sixth-graders from another school were spending their weekend. We all dosey-doed throughout the evening. The following morning we headed home.

Our Principal, Miss Garrison

The Great Adventure

I have no recollection of my final days at McKinley Elementary School, my second home for seven years. A special bond and familiarity were formed from associating with the same classmates for more than seven years. There was a consistency in the friends with whom one would associate when each new school year began. But, with the end of the sixth grade, there was a sinking feeling that all of this would change. There was much apprehension in my thought concerning the transition to junior high in the fall. My fellow elementary school students would be scattered into separate categories and rosters, and friendships would change forever. But I was happy to sublimate these concerns during the 1957 summer recess as I contemplated our family's upcoming great adventure.

Dad had been preparing for months. This would be a trip like no other, although it would be a reprise in some degree of his previous expedition west with two friends in a Model "A" Ford during the summer after his high school graduation. In preparation for our journey, maps were laid out on the dining room table in the preceding weeks as he determined the optimum route which would take in a number of national parks and other historic sites. A primary destination in my mind, however, was Disneyland.

Our mode of transportation for this grand event would be our light-blue 1955 Plymouth equipped with manual transmission. Dad employed a roof rack, normally used for ladders, to hold the folded, borrowed tent which would be our temporary home at campsites along the way. Other camping paraphernalia, including lanterns and a cook stove, was purchased from a huge discount warehouse in Philadelphia. This trip would cost dad three weeks of vacation from the Frankford Arsenal.

Another important purchase was that of a Kodak Brownie f/1.9 lens, 8mm movie camera – the "1.9" denoting a special low-light aperture setting. My father was no Cecil B. DeMille, but we would have a running record of our vacation nonetheless, including an excess of sunsets and jumpy landscapes.

I was looking forward to this event with great anticipation. For brother Bill it instilled mixed emotions. He would be entering his senior year of high school in the fall, and he was beginning to develop a great interest in those of the opposite sex – most notably Grace Mainwaring, daughter of the police officer, who lived down the street in McKinley. So, although he was looking forward to this grand road trip, he would be away from his semi-girlfriend for a whole month. A month is an especially long time to a teenager in the throws of intense puppy love.

Auntie would be holding down the home fort, and several lady friends would be staying with her, off and on, during the summer. However, watching our dog Teddy in our absence was too much to ask of her. So my friend John's family agreed to take in my furry friend for the duration.

—

Excitement was high as we got ready to begin our trip early on Saturday morning, July 13. Dad recorded the proceedings with the new movie camera. The Plymouth sat in the driveway all packed up and ready to go. I appear as an adolescent – not quite 12. Brother Bill had already maxed out at six feet of height and towered over me. Even with the distance of five years in age between us, we would be good companions on our journey. Having recently acquired his driver's license, Bill would get the opportunity to drive at various times along the way.

After pulling out of the driveway, Dad made his way down Jenkintown Road as I watched the trees of the Rosenwald Estate pass by, as well as other familiar landmarks along the way such as the Old York Road Country Club. Before long we were on the Pennsylvania Turnpike heading west. It was only several miles before we witnessed the aftermath of a serious accident with the bodies of the injured or dead lying on the median strip and the mangled automobiles nearby. It surely tempered the glee during the early stages of our adventure.

One wonders now at how unsafe vehicular traffic was in 1957 as compared to today. There were no seatbelts, no shoulder straps, no air bags. I can distinctly recall how I was thrown from the rear seat to the back of the front seat when dad had to stop suddenly in traffic. In addition, there were the infamous three lane highways with the common middle lane – often called the suicide lane – reserved for passing.

Dad loved to drive, and he usually set a goal for each day of the trip, and he especially wanted to cover many miles that first day. After all, it was a trip to the West, so he wanted to leave the East as soon as possible. So he drove and drove that first day – almost six hundred miles, entering Toledo, Ohio around 5:30 in the afternoon. The second day we went through Indiana and wound through Chicago and Lake Michigan in the early afternoon. By late afternoon we made it into Iowa and spent the night in Guttenberg. One may ask how I remember all of these details. I don't, but the trip log kept by mom on a steno pad contains much detail. Despite the fatigue of driving, we all had the desire to try out that borrowed tent as soon as possible.

On the fourth day after breakfast at Clermont, dad reached Minnesota in the early afternoon and Mitchell, South Dakota at 3:50. We stopped at random at a small business or residence, and dad asked the owner if we could set up our tent for the first time on an open space on his ample lawn. The owner agreed, and I think that dad gave him five dollars for the privilege. Well, somehow we all made it through a fitful night of sleep on those uncomfortable air mattresses. The home movies of the excursion show dad and I crossing the highway back to the tent the next morning, having relieved ourselves in a nearby gas station restroom.

South Dakota was our first meaningful destination from a tourist's standpoint. Mt. Rushmore, with the heads of four famous presidents, was a wonder to behold. Then there was the Corn Palace in Mitchell, South Dakota – the exterior walls having a veneer of multicolored ears of corn – where we watched a stage show put on by American Indians. As we traveled through the state, roadside signs advertising Wall's Drug Store lined the highway. It was a huge store with many interesting products and oddities like a stuffed two-headed goat. We wandered through the aisles for quite a while.

Our visit to The Badlands was on a rather hot day. The area got its name based on 19th century outlaws using the landscape of rocky formations to hide from lawmen in their pursuit. We walked on a number of trails and came across a married couple by the wayside. The wife had nearly passed out from the heat and was unable to walk. My dad, having been a gymnast in his youth, and despite his five feet, six inch height, volunteered to carry the woman back to the parking lot. He did so, and she and her husband were most grateful. She quickly revived in the shade and took some water to drink.

I will not bore you with all of the detailed accounts of this phase of the trip, but the highlights on the march to the west coast included stops at the following national parks: Glacier (where we tossed snowballs), Yellowstone (had to see Old Faithful), Zion, Crater Lake, and Bryce Canyon. We camped at a couple of the parks along the way, but setting up and tearing down that tent was beginning to get rather tiresome for a family of suburbanites.

When we hit Washington state, we visited the massive Grand Coulee Dam on the Columbia River before heading down the coast to Anaheim and Disneyland. Having watched Micky Mouse Club on TV at home almost every weeknight during the school year, I couldn't wait to experience the park in all of its glory, thoroughly enjoying Fantasy Land, Adventure Land, Frontier Land, and Tomorrow Land. Main Street captured small town life at the turn of the 20th century. We were surprised to spot actor Don Defore sitting at a table in his Silver Banjo restaurant in Frontier Land. Footage of the scene was captured on the trusty Brownie.

It would be hard to surpass Walt Disney's wonder, but Knott's Berry Farm came quite close on the following day. It captured the essence of an old western town with an active steam locomotive. On the old movie reel of the trip Dad was shown sitting on a bench in front of the town tavern. A seated statue of a dance girl was next to him and Dad had his hand placed firmly on her knee.

—

As the trip progressed there seemed to be a more than subtle change in relations between my father and me. Maybe it was just my late prepubescent personality emerging. And maybe being in the presence of dad for one whole month, around the clock, had something to do with it. There could also have been the underlying stress of dad managing the trip and carrying it out on a day by day basis. Worrying about the expense of the vacation as it progressed was probably also a factor. Before the trip I had saved a whopping 20 dollars to spend, and entrusted the sum to my father's keeping. I probably only spent half of the amount during the trip, but I never got my change back.

In any case, we seemed to be at odds a number of times with me not always wanting to follow his instructions, or just moaning about some perceived injustice. I suppose that when I was a year or two younger I looked up to dad with adulation, hoping I'd be like him when I grew up. At almost the age of 12, I was starting to see things more in black and white. It was just a part of my growing up as my identity developed.

—

The Grand Canyon in Arizona was a magnificent site. We camped there overnight and had interesting conversations with an elderly couple from an adjoining campsite. During the night we heard a commotion outside, but didn't give it too much thought. In the morning we discovered that the supply trailer of a fellow camper had been torn open by a marauding black bear looking for something tasty to eat.

One seasoned tourist told us of an out-of-the-way area at the North Rim of the canyon. It was called Point Sublime, and it was located at the end of a 17-mile long dirt road. Dad was up for the challenge, but we all wondered if it was worth it as the old '55 Plymouth rumbled slowly through the dust and heat to the destination. However, when we finally arrived, the view was stunning. No one else was around. Dad stood on a rock outcropping looking straight down at the abyss, while Bill and I kept our distance. Dad's previous occupation as a house painter evidently exempted him from a fear of heights.

Dad's maternal aunt, Laura Stone, lived in Phoenix, Arizona where she had moved with her husband and adopted daughter Sandra, some years before, from Harrison Valley, Pennsylvania. It was thought that the dry heat would be better for the health of Uncle Huber, her arthritic husband, who was confined to a wheelchair.

What stands out most in my mind was Aunt Laura's nasty little wild Chihuahua. You couldn't walk across the room without it snapping at your feet. It made for a tense night's sleep in their bungalow. It attacked Dad on one occasion, but he dispatched it with a swift kick. Aunt Laura wasn't present at the time.

Aunt Laura put dad to work in the daytime, digging up or moving a shrub in the backyard. The temperature was in excess of 110 degrees, but that didn't seem to bother dad. He loved physical work. He and I took a short walk through the community in the afternoon, but the heat was unbearable and the sidewalks were empty.

Daughter Sandy was a pretty brunette, teenage girl who bonded quickly with my mother. She may have been a year older than Bill, and I think that she tended to remind him fondly of Gracie back home.

On the day that we said our goodbyes to their family, mom went to kiss Aunt Laura on the cheek. The malevolent Chihuahua was firmly under Aunt Laura's arm, but that didn't stop the little beast from lunging forward at that moment and biting my mom on the lip. It was a painful way to say goodbye, physically and emotionally.

—

The remainder of the trip was rather uneventful since the vacation was approaching the end of its three-week allotted time – uneventful except for the fact that dad earned two traffic tickets in three days: one in Globe, Arizona and the other near El Paso, Texas. As I remember, neither ticket was really warranted, but more the product of the local police taking advantage of an out-of-state driver.

As was our custom, when returning from long road trips, we all burst into the college fight song in full voice: "Pennsylvania, Pennsylvania, yea, yea, yea, yea!" as we passed over the state line.

Summer vacation trips were always fun, but arriving back in old McKinley was something special. I couldn't wait to go to Johnny's house and pick up our dog Teddy. I remember walking into his living room as our poor mutt slowly came out from behind a couch and greeted me, his tail beginning to wag when he realized whom I was. Teddy had a bare spot near the base of his tail caused by some fungus that he contracted from lying in the grass, but John's sister Helen was alert to the situation and had taken our pup to the local vet for treatment. Teddy had grown in size in our absence. He was happy to get back to his old digs.

The big adventure was over, and now I could start worrying about the new school year and the prospect of my first job.

First Job
and the
Junior High School Years

One, Two Punch

Handling the shock of junior high was bad enough, but now I had a job on top of that. Having attained the ripe old age of 12 on September 7, I was now eligible to become a Bulletin paperboy. Mom wouldn't let that opportunity slip by unfulfilled. She thought that beginning work as soon as possible was essential for my brother and me. He had already put in his time slinging newspapers; now it was my turn.

One Saturday in the late summer of 1957, mom marched me down to the local Philadelphia Bulletin newspaper carrier branch to visit its manager, Joe Tangye. Mr. Tangye, in hindsight, looked a bit like a middle-aged Joe Paterno, long time coach of the Penn State football team. The branch was located in a side room of the barn/garage of an old McKinley home on the southeast corner of the Jenkintown Road and Cadwalader Avenue intersection. At that time it was an investment property of McKinley Fire Company which was located right across the street. It was rented out to a young black tenant named Mario who pretty much kept to himself, but occasionally interacted in conversation with the paper carriers.

As luck would have it, a paper route position opened close to our home. Route 9 was roughly bounded by Jenkintown Road, West Avenue, Township Line, and Haines Avenue. Included, also, was High School Road which paralleled West and Haines. This would become my theater of operation for the next six years. During this period the average number of my customers was about 48.

My friend John didn't avoid this fate either. He inherited my brother's old Route 21 which encompassed the hills of The Manor – quite a challenge for anyone on a one-speed bicycle.

As for my bike – the sporty metallic red Roadmaster that I received as a gift the previous Christmas – it would now become a mode of commercial transportation. An outlay of $2.98, or so, at Croft's Cycle Shop, bought me a clunky, but durable, wire basket which, when attached to the bike, would be situated over the front wheel. I was all set. Lucky me! Good old Bob Croft would become one of my customers.

My after-school routine was set during the week. I'd only have two days off per year: Christmas and Independence Day. After getting off of the school bus behind McKinley Elementary after a long day at Huntingdon Junior High School, I'd make it home, change my clothes and then ride my bike the short distance to the branch. My allotment of newspapers would have been counted out previously by the Branch Captain, Bob Niesen, and placed in a separate pile on the dingy room's floor with those of the other 13 or so paperboys. In addition to being the captain, Bob also had a paper route of his own. But the Branch Captain also pulled in a weekly salary of 50 cents for each paperboy under his charge.

I earned my money by how many newspapers I delivered: roughly based on two thirds the retail price of each edition. So, for charging the customer 30 cents per week for six days of the daily paper, I'd receive 10 cents. I'd get 6 ½ cents for each 20-cent copy of the Sunday edition.

The day before I started delivering, I rode the route with the outgoing paperboy, Skippy Yates, who was getting older and ready to move on. He had a ruddy complexion and curly reddish-blond hair. In short order I was ready to go solo.

The whole enterprise became routine before long. It wasn't bad duty in the fall, but as the season progressed into winter, one had to deal with the cold and the elements. Most of the houses on my route had open front porches, so I made sure that the newspaper was deposited in the vicinity of each customer's front step. Other paperboys in the branch would hang around before delivery and wrap each paper with a rubber band so they could be thrown as they rode along. As for me, I utilized the old method of folding each newspaper as I approached each house by holding the edition flat upon my knee, placing a hand on each side, and inserting the right side of the paper into the individual section folds on the left side, and then bending the paper slightly over the knee till you felt a slight "crinch." If it was done correctly, you could throw the newspaper from the curb to the porch without it disastrously flying apart in the air.

However, the above approach did not always work on two particular days of the week. The Tuesday edition of The

Evening Bulletin, which included many advertisements, was the thickest weekday paper – usually bulking out to approximately 92 pages. Thursday's edition came in second in that department. In contrast, Saturday's paper was the smallest, coming in at about 20 pages. I used to pay Auntie 10 cents to wrap all of my Saturday papers with rubber bands. She'd happily sit at the kitchen table completing her chore. Well, at least she did it happily for a number of years until she requested an increase of five cents in her wages which I refused to pay. Neither one of us would give in, so eventually I had to fold my own Saturday papers. Maybe it had something to do with us both being stubborn Virgos.

Saturday was the busiest day, since collections would have to be made in the morning. I wore a metal coin changer on my belt which was previously used by my brother. The comic section of Sunday's paper along with the myriad advertisements was also delivered at that time to the subscribers of that edition. After collections were made, each paperboy would go back to the branch before noon to pay his bill to Mr. Tangye. If you weren't able to collect enough to pay the requisite amount, you'd have to make up the difference from your own pocket. There were some customers that I knew were home at times during the collection process, but they would act like they weren't, and not answer their doors. If all was going well, I'd receive about five dollars in profit per week. However, I was notoriously remiss at keeping accurate records of who paid and who didn't, and lost money because of it.

When I started, most of the other paperboys were older than I. I recall a soft-spoken, tall black boy named Dennis Raleigh. As I remember, he was a high school senior and quit soon after I was employed. He had served for more than five years, I believe.

The Sunday Bulletin wasn't as popular in the Philadelphia area as the Inquirer, which had more advertising, so I only had about 25 customers subscribing to that edition. That number was plenty for me, though, when I delivered that version of the paper on cold winter Sunday mornings. I didn't have long underwear, but I tried to bundle up as well as possible. I wore a hand-me-down leather hat with ear flaps to keep my head warm, and a scarf that covered my nose and mouth. Inside my front shirt pocket, I would place a metal hand warmer that was fueled with lighter fluid. There were times when I returned home from my Sunday morning deliveries when my hands and toes had almost no feeling, and it was agony as the digits thawed out.

There were two times, I believe, during my years of delivery, where the Bulletin truck drivers, or other union production workers, went on strike, giving us boys unanticipated vacations. The newspaper was still printed by management employees during these strikes. Several industrious paperboys, who were old enough to drive, would make their way down to the Bulletin plant in West Philadelphia and buy a bundle of papers, bring them back to the suburbs, and hawk them on corners where there was heavy traffic, such as the intersection of Cadwalader and Township Line. Charging twice the normal price, they'd make quite a profit.

—

Huntingdon Junior High School would be my home away from home for the next three years. The building, located on Susquehanna Road between York Road and Huntingdon Road, previously housed Abington High School which had just recently opened their new state-of-the-art facility in the Baederwood section of the township. Gone were the cozy confines of the one room class of the old elementary school. Room 207 would be my home room where the same core of individual students would meet every morning to hear school prayer and announcements. Mrs. Wrigley, a young, slight, rather pretty woman, was our home room teacher. Her husband was a distant heir to the Wrigley family of chewing gum fame. She would take role call daily and then prepare us for our dispersal throughout the large facility at the whim of our disparate roster schedules. All would meet again at the end of the school day where we could receive additional announcements and begin our homework.

I was placed in seventh grade roster number four, or simply 7-4. Roster designations could be likened to putting a brand on your forehead, suggesting where you happened to be ranked between prime rib and ground beef on the scholastic menu. Rosters ranged from 7-1 to 7-10 if I remember correctly. In any case, if you were in 7-1, you were probably a future Mensa candidate. If you were in 7-10 – God forbid.

In 1957 there were three junior highs in Abington School District. The other two were Abington Jr. (near the new high school) and Glenside-Weldon. So Huntingdon took in the students from the elementary school students which were closest in proximity.

As I recall, Ricky Coulston was the only student from my sixth grade class who was in my roster, so I had to make a number of new friends. Being a rather bashful individual, especially in a new setting, this would be quite a challenge. In elementary school I could do fairly well with little effort, but now everything would be a greater challenge. Our survey of languages class was taught by Mr. Schneider whose specialty was Spanish, so that's what we learned. His wife taught our roster's social studies/English class. He was easy going with a wry sense of humor. Those qualities did not appear to be present in the missus. Grade-wise, I barely squeaked by in Spanish and social studies. However, as a saving grace there was the pretty dark-haired Marilyn Eckert who sat behind me in Mrs. Schneider's class. We often discussed the trials and tribulations of the latest Spin and Marty episode which was appearing on the nightly Micky Mouse Club TV show.

Our math class was taught by Mrs. Yoland who had red hair and possessed a slightly nasal voice. There wasn't too much of a challenge there academically, although I remember her giving our class a giant assignment over the Christmas holiday week. In typical fashion I put off completing the work until New Year's evening, causing me great stress. Like Mrs. Wrigley, she managed to get pregnant as well during the year.

Miss Harris taught science, and she didn't have a great sense of humor. I sat in a front row seat next to the sweet and attractive Cindy Amberg who was quite well-endowed for a seventh grader. We had a nice friendly relationship. As I became more acclimated to my new environment, I became quite chatty, once eliciting a "Shut up!" from Miss Harris. She also admonished me at one point for having dirty hands. I suppose I was going through a male adolescent grubby stage. In addition, she listed "indolent" as one of my outstanding qualities on my report card. I surely wasn't headed for the honor roll.

The introduction of music class in our seventh grade curriculum was almost too much for one to bare. I thought that learning to play the Tonette in fourth grade was tough enough. The testy Mr. Foster ruled this musical roost in the spacious confines of the auditorium. There must have been 40 to 50 students assembled for this punishment. Each of us had to fashion our own piano keyboard facsimiles out of construction paper and then learn all of the notes. I couldn't identify one note of a piano key today. Although, I must proudly say, I can tell the difference between an eighth note and a whole note on sheet music. I'm sure that I could still point out a moveable "C" cleft, but I haven't seen one since that class.

During the second half of the year, musical study moved to a classroom setting. I remember fellow classmate Jay Staats and I doing our best impressions of Bing Crosby's "White Christmas" to the chagrin of Mr. Foster. Our bespeckled teacher also led the school chorus, but had difficulty enlisting members for that assignment. We often were allowed to make selections from the standard song book to sing in class as Foster clinked away on the keyboard. One student selected the song "Blow the Man Down" which elicited giggles from some of the male students and a stern admonishment from the teacher. I was too naive at the time to realize the significance of the uproar.

It must have been determined in the higher echelons of the school administration in the 1950s that each student should be introduced to training that would provide skills that were vocational in nature in addition to those which were merely scholastic. For male students it was shop class, and for the girls it was home economics, or simply home-ec. My classes were split between wood shop and graphic arts. Taking a liking to working with wood, I produced a plaque of the Huntingdon Jr. Bulldog mascot (now long gone) and a two-tiered shelf. Mom proudly had my shelf placed on the wall of our den at home. It is now situated above the desk in my home office after all these years.

In Bob Cratchit style, students sat on high stools in front of slanted draftsman tables in graphic arts class. Our teacher, Mr. Blythe, had a military bearing about him; humorless in nature he strode through the aisles assessing the skills of his charges. A prominent scar adorned his temple and cheek. If you made one little mistake on your work at hand, the project would be marked down accordingly. Somehow I eked out a grade of "C." It was inspiring, however, to see how one could represent three-dimensional objects on two-dimensional paper.

Gym class was a shock for me. First of all, I wasn't accustomed to dressing and undressing before a bunch of guys that I hardly knew. Wearing a jock strap for the first time was a unique experience, especially when I put it on backwards. Fellow student Jimmy Connors, among a phalanx of laughs, instructed me on the proper way to wear the protective attire. Gym teachers Metzger, Garvin and Charters made sure that we kept appropriately active.

—

Thanks, or no thanks, to my daily chore of delivering newspapers, I couldn't participate in extracurricular activities, and my friend John was in the same boat. But that didn't keep us from attending monthly school dances on Friday nights. On those occasions, dad would drive us up to the cavernous school gymnasium and deposit us at the main door on Huntingdon Road. I wish that I could say that I freely interacted with the opposite sex in romantic slow dancing and wild jitterbugging. I was usually frozen in a bashful stupor, wanting to dance with a number of girls, but not having the nerve to ask them. Often John and I would spend most of the night parked on the bleacher benches waiting for some miracle to happen, like having a girl ask one of us when a turnabout dance was announced. For the most part we didn't interact with the girls from our old elementary school class, since most had moved onto cliques of their own. However, I do remember one time when I danced quite often with an old school classmate, Veronica Knapp. On another occasion I finally got up the nerve to ask the pretty Marilyn Eckert from my 7-4 roster to dance with me. She had been spending most of the night dancing with older boys from the 8th and 9th grade. When I asked her, she smiled and we took a few tentative steps when suddenly I realized that the song was already reaching completion. How embarrassing!

WIBG was the radio station of choice during this period. The latest rock music by Elvis Presley, Buddy Holly, Duane Eddy and others was the mainstay of musicians being featured. One of WIBG's disc jockeys, Harvey Miller, was a guest at one of our school dances, and he kept the students hopping all night long. Coca Cola sponsored the event.

—

While I was diddling around seventh grade and navigating its unique social complexities, brother Bill was a senior at Abington High. As big brother, he allowed me to tag along for a couple of special events hosted at the high school. One in particular stands out – a teacher vs. sports celebrity basketball game. Featured, was one of my favorite Philadelphia Phillies, ace pitcher Robin Roberts. Having been a standout basketball star at Michigan State, he lit up the court with his accurate shots. Another famous participant was Jim Pollard, a gifted player for Stanford and a member of their 1942 championship team. As a professional player and forward for the Minneapolis Lakers, he helped lead his team to five basketball titles from the late 1940s into the 1950s. He also had a three-year stint as head basketball coach for the La Salle College Explorers. I managed to get his autograph after the game, but no longer have it in my possession.

I often wonder how much the professional stars got paid to participate. An exhibition like that would never occur today. Roberts was still an active baseball player who could have risked injury. Today's contracts would preclude such activities.

"Professional" wrestling provided another special event in the high school gymnasium which included a best-out-of-three match between Argentina Rocca and Professor Roy Shire. I suppose that I was too naive at the time to realize that these so-called matches were orchestrated, but that didn't matter even if they were. Rocca was the nice guy athlete of short but muscular stature while the rather flabby Shire took on the villain's role, often using questionable and unsportsmanlike means to achieve victory. In any case, they were both my ring favorites despite their opposite personas.

Shire had long flowing platinum hair and strutted around the mat like an electrified rooster. Of course he won the first round by nefarious means, thus putting Rocca in the unenviable position of taking the two remaining contests to win the match. Equal to the task, Argentina utilized a variety of flying drop kicks and hammer locks to dispose of his opponent to the cheers of the crowd. I obtained Rocca's autograph as well, but it, too, has been lost to posterity.

—

I did pick up one new friend from my roster that year. Russell Becker was a tall boy with a bit of a hawk nose. He and his younger brother once biked their way down from their home in Roslyn to play catch with me at the McKinley Elementary school ground – quite a trip on the one-speed bikes of the day. On another occasion he invited me to attend a Phillies game on his birthday. Another of his classmate friends, Chuck "Chick" Lischer, also came along. After graduation from high school, Lischer became an accomplished airplane pilot who became a nationally known air show performer. Tragically he died in an air crash in 2006 at age 61 while flying an experimental jet aircraft during a classified military radar test in the skies over the Ocean City, Maryland area.

—

The 1957-58 school year assumed a rhythm: get the bus in the morning; go to classes; come home on the bus; change clothes; go pick up newspapers at the branch; deliver the papers; return home for supper; do homework; watch a little TV; and go to bed.

Meeting the other paperboys at the branch provided the opportunity to interact with individuals from the area other than schoolmates, save my friend John. As the holidays approached, I looked forward to seeing how I'd make out with Christmas tips. As I recall, I pulled in about $28 that first year. It was an amount that would grow in coming years as I became established, but it still seemed like a windfall to me.

Almost every Saturday, after I had delivered the afternoon newspapers, I'd ride my cherry red Roadmaster up to Jenkintown (often with John) to visit the Hobby Shop. For $1.50 of my hard earned money, I'd buy an AMT or Johan friction car – a 1/24 scale model of a current Detroit automobile – most often a Chrysler product. As I built my collection, I'd house them in a book shelf in my bedroom. I also raced the vehicles across the living room and dining room floors to the consternation of our dog Teddy who would try to intercept them and then jump out of the way at the last moment.

On our way to the Hobby Shop during the autumn, John and I would stop at Scarborough DeSoto-Plymouth dealer to look for evidence of the new 1958 car lines. Back then the car manufacturers would guard the secrecy of the upcoming model year designs until, on a specified date often advertised on TV, the new lines were revealed with great fanfare. As far as Chrysler vehicles were concerned, there was little change from the previous year. High fins were still being displayed and the lower-priced Plymouth now sported duel headlights – a recent innovation. Since John's brother Fred had a '51 Ford, his allegiance fell with that manufacturer. With the '57 model year, the new Ford had a more extreme make-over with a less stodgy, longer, lower look than its predecessor. As it was, any boy worth his salt could rattle off the make, model and year of all the American steeds plying the roads.

Home for the Holidays

During my childhood and adolescence, the Christmas season was a magical time. In the early years – 1953 and before – much holiday time was shared between our home in McKinley and that of Auntie and Uncle's in the Logan section of Philadelphia. As I recall, Thanksgiving was routinely held at Auntie's house, while Christmas was always celebrated at our home in McKinley.

While Uncle was still alive, he and Auntie would celebrate Christmas Eve with us and spend the night, sleeping in the front bedroom on the third floor. Brother Bill and I would have trouble falling to sleep, although, being older, he wasn't quite as excited as I. In any case we usually made our way downstairs before the sun arose and then scampered in the stillness to the den at the end of the hall. When we turned on the lights, an array of toys would be magically revealed. Mom never wrapped the gifts, so we would just be overwhelmed with the abundance before us. Toys would be strategically placed on the chaise lounge and the floor.

The large Marx play sets were always special. They would come in large flat cardboard boxes. One year, when I was quite small, Bill received a Marx army set with scores of soldiers, weapons, and military vehicles. The command post building had to be assembled from enameled sheet metal. The sheets had to be bent at appropriate points to fashion the walls, roof and base. Little metal tabs on the edges would be placed through related slots, and then bent down to hold the assemblage together. A year or so later, Bill received the Roy Rogers Mineral City set with sundry plastic cowboy figures and horses. Roy's wife, Dale Evans, was represented, but was considered rather matronly and not too attractive. A shapely, slim cowgirl figure was "popular" with her male cowboy counterparts, and could be counted on to sashay (as best as we could replicate such behavior in small scale) around the ranch to the delight of the ranch hands.

In a subsequent year, I received a Tom Corbett Space Cadet set. Old Tom (played by Frankie Thomas, Jr.) had his own TV show on various networks from 1950 through 1955, participating in a variety of adventures throughout the solar system. My favorite toy figures were three aliens that looked like a cross between a gremlin and Mickey Mouse.

Brother Bill received a chemistry set one year. Inside a wooden box, which opened like a book, were vials of exotic substances. An alcohol, or Bunson, burner was included. Used to heat the various compounds in test tubes, one could observe chemical reactions. I remember my brother using the burner to bend a glass stick – quite amazing. When he graduated to more "grownup" toys in later years, I'd utilize the set myself. Glycerine was my favorite chemical. Heating a bit of it in a test tube produced an audible pop, sending gooey projectile to the bedroom ceiling. I suppose that the necessary chemicals to produce nitroglycerine weren't included in the set. With today's safety restrictions in place, a toy such as this would never be marketed. One wonders what is more dangerous – violent video games of today or hands-on chemistry sets of yesteryear.

One of my favorite toys was Robert the Robot. Tethered to Robert was a cable similar to that used for speedometers. A manual hand control on the end allowed you to move old Robby forward and to turn him. I think that the cable broke after only a few days of use, but he was still able to talk by turning a small crank on his back. In a metallic voice he would utter, "I'm Robert the Robot mechanical man. Drive me and steer me wherever you can."

Another favorite toy which I received during my seventh grade Christmas was based on a popular TV show, "The Rifleman." Chuck Connors starred in the show, playing Lucas McCain. Johnny Crawford of former Mouseketeer fame played his son. My gift toy rifle mimicked the real weapon used by Lucas in the series. His rifle was modified in such a way that it could be pumped quickly using a metal loop below the trigger, firing the weapon in machine gun fashion. The toy was similar, allowing you to go through a roll of 50 caps in short order.

—

During the 1950s into the early 1960s, the celebration of Christmas at our house remained essentially the same. There was a perennial comfort in the routine. Dad would drive to North Philly on Christmas eve and pick up Aunt Emma and Uncle Ad to spend the evening with us. While brother Bill and I trimmed the tree in the living room, Christmas music would be played on the record player, reducing Uncle Ad to sentimental tears. As it got later in the evening, Dad would ferry them back home, then retrieve them again the next morning for Christmas day celebration.

Ever the taxi service, Dad would also pick up Nan and Pop Pop in West Philly and bring them home for dinner as well. While Uncle (Auntie's husband) was still alive, much of the day was spent by Dad, Uncle and Uncle Ad in playing cut throat, three-handed pinochle. After Uncle passed away in the summer of 1954, brother Bill was instructed in the art of the game and became Uncle's replacement in the annual ritual. Above the fragrant smells of turkey and filling were the pungent wafts of cigar smoke emanating from Uncle Ad's "el ropo" Phillies-brand cigars.

Stormy Weather

As mentioned earlier, there was a mostly amiable, but tenuous, relationship between the races in McKinley. Although there were no African-American families on our block of Cadwalader Avenue, there was a mixture of black and white families on the section of Cadwalader on the other side of Jenkintown Road as well as on Osceola Avenue which was located behind our street.

Black and white children often interacted at the school ground and the playground, riding on swings together; talking; riding around on bikes; playing pickup games of football. Billy Wilson, a black boy who was a year or two younger than I, lived on Cypress Avenue as I recollect. His dad worked with my father at times in the evening at the Sunoco station on Township Line Road. Billy had a nice friendly nature and we got along well together whenever we would meet by happenstance in the community. However, Billy would hang out with another black boy, who I'll call Harry, who lived on Tulpehocken Avenue toward the Hill section of McKinley. Harry's older brother, James, was a friendly, studious, easy-going guy, but Harry tended to be an unpredictable bully.

So it was that one late Saturday afternoon in the winter, after the sun had already set, that John and I made our way home along Jenkintown Road after a visit to the Hobby Shop or Woolworth's in Jenkintown. Somewhere along the route Billy and Harry emerged. In one of his bullying moods, Harry took it upon himself to taunt me and bodily handle me along the way, pushing me and throwing me into bushes. John, as I indicated before, had grown physically in stature during the summer before seventh grade, but I was still a typical, skinny, pre-adolescent kid. So Harry vented no malice upon my friend. Billy, to his credit, didn't participate in the untoward behavior; he just continued walking along at a distance.

As we neared McKinley, John either left the group at Forrest Avenue to proceed home, or waited till we got to my house, and left immediately on his bicycle since it was approaching dinnertime. Although I had a few scratches from being thrown into the bushes during our trip home, most of the damage was emotional. Maintaining my composure the best that I could during the ongoing torturous journey, as soon as I got inside our house, I burst into tears. My dad, who had just come home from a weekend painting job, asked what was the matter. When I reluctantly told him, he said, "Where are they?" I told him that they were walking down Cadwalader toward Billy's house.

Dad flew out the door in a contained rage. In a matter of moments he brought the two boys back to our house and onto our enclosed front porch, holding them both by their collars. Now, you have to realize that my dad stood only about five feet, six inches tall, and he was probably no taller than Henry, but he was muscular, having been a gymnast. In Dad's grasp, they stood there trembling before me. Dad asked me, "Are these the boys?" I answered lowly, "Yes." Billy with fear outlining his face uttered pleadingly, "I didn't hurt you, did I?" I answered, "No." Dad turned to Henry and told him to apologize and never to touch me again. He muttered an apology. Dad, with fire in his eyes, ushered them out the door. I had never seen Dad respond that way previously or after, but I was so proud of him and felt so protected.

A year or so before this incident, Henry encountered me down by the playground along Jenkintown Road. In his bullying manner he whirled me around and threw me against the embankment near the outdoor water fountain. I put out my arm to break the fall and my hand landed on a sharp shard of a broken bottle. It put a one inch gash in the palm of my right hand. I rushed home and mom put a bandage on it. I never got stitches. I told her that it was simply an accident. In any case, after Henry's encounter with my father, he never bothered me again. The scar is barely visible today.

—

Another area where we white schoolchildren interacted, to some extent, with our African-American neighbors was at the school bus stop every morning prior to our trip to Huntingdon Junior High, and later Abington High. The stop was located at the entrance of McKinley Elementary School's gymnasium on Osceola Avenue. While all the students waited for the arrival of the bus, clutches of individuals would form by race. After the bus signaled its presence with the screech of air brakes, the doors would unfold with a clap and everyone climbed aboard. The black kids moved to the back rows of the bus, not because it was mandated as in the South, but because it was a territorial statement of sorts.

Most mornings there would be a good bit of laughter from the rear of the bus, and on many occasions the black students would all break into spontaneous song. I remember, particularly, the singing of their version of "Stormy Weather" – a popular 1930s-era standard by Harold Arlen and Ted Koehler – in flawless and uplifting two-part harmony:

> "Don't know why,
> Don't know why;
> There's no sun up in the sky,
> Stormy weather,
> stormy wea-ea-ea-eather, ah-ah hoooo,
> Since my baby and I ain't together,
> ain't toge-e-e-ether; ah-ah hoooo,
> All-l-l-l-l the time,
> all-the-time, all-the-time, all-the tii--me, ahhh-hooo;
> All the tiii--me."

I wondered when or where all the participants practiced that rendition of the song with such precision. To this day it still echoes in my mind, and I give it my feeble interpretation at times during my morning shower.

Metamorphosis

When I look back and compare my class photo of seventh grade to that of eighth grade, it's obvious that a change was taking place. The former likeness is one of a cute pre-adolescent schoolboy with perfect skin. The latter is one of a more mature, full-faced individual with the subtle appearance of facial irruptions common to young teenagers. Since school photos were usually taken at the beginning of the school year, I assume that I had begun slipping into the subtle grip of puberty during the previous summer – the summer of 1958.

In any case, there was a strange difference in how I felt about the opposite sex. Previously, only a pretty sweet lass would attract my attention. Now, I felt a stronger magnetic pull to certain girls even if they didn't possess starlet-like beauty. Hey, I still had a great affection for Annette Funicello and Cheryl Holdridge of Mickey Mouse Club, but I was able to imperceptibly settle for less in the real world. Please don't get me wrong. I was no Elvis Presley by any means. And I was still generally bashful when it came to interaction with those of the opposite sex in whom I had an interest. But more about this later in the chapter. Let's take a look at eighth grade first.

As the school year started, I continued in my role as underachiever, doing what I had to do to get by. Testaments to this trend were my activities in English class. Our teacher was a tall, well-built, fair-complected individual named Mr. Edelman. He was an even-tempered man with a deep voice and the traces of facial, acne scars. In his younger days, Mr. Edelman must have been moderately athletic because he claimed that he played minor league baseball with future hall-of-famer, Hank Aaron. He used Aaron as an object lesson in the need for acquiring adequate skills with the written word of the English language because the great athlete evidently lacked that ability – by Edleman's account – to express himself well in writing. So, the story went: Hank Aaron became quite successful, but the chance of us peons having the skills of highly-paid athletes was practically nil. Therefore it would be wise to put our collective noses to the grindstone and learn how to read and write adequately if we were going to make a sustainable living in our school afterlife.

When it came to reading books, I was pretty much a sluggard. It was our charge to read literature of our choosing during the school year and to periodically write book reports to show our ability to adequately express ourselves and provide a sufficient measure of our comprehension. All book reports, however, were written during a class period. Since it was rare that I had actually read a book in the first place, I would have to improvise. Other than a blank pad of lined paper and a pencil, we were only provided with a dictionary. Invariably I'd go to the biographical section in the back of that reference book and look up a famous character like John Paul Jones. I'd then conjure up an imaginative book title and author such as John Paul Jones by Frederick Morris, pluck a birth date out of the biographical sketch and then conjure up a story about old JPJ. Somehow it worked, and I never got caught: not something to be proud of. I can't recall my grades as a result of these haphazard efforts.

The number designation for eighth grade rosters was based on the foreign language the student selected to be taught. Our roster was 8-8, and Spanish was chosen to be my area of study. I became friends with Richard Roth, one of my fellow students in this roster. Rich had previously lived in the Olney section of Philadelphia and displayed a bit of an urban swagger which appealed to my rather pedestrian, suburban run-of-the-mill temperament. We normally sat close together if possible in the classroom and cut up with each other when the teacher wasn't looking. Our math teacher was Mr. Lorhrig – an amiable and humorous man with a deep nasal voice. He'd tell comical stories about his escapades in the military, for example, in between explaining principles of mathematics such as simple algebra.

Rich, however, had a knack for getting under Mr. Lorhrig's skin since he was rather outspoken at times. Back in his prior urban environment, Rich hung around with a gang of friends which evidently smoked cigarettes to bolster their manly egos. One day in class while Mr. Lorhrig stepped out into the hall for a minute, Rich lit a match for a second. When Lorhrig returned to the classroom he picked up the sulphur scent right away and demanded to know who lit the match. Rich somehow avoided detection and the class continued.

That year, by lot I suppose, I was assigned to metal shop which was taught by Mr. Joachin who was a tall grey-haired fellow who appeared to be past his retirement years. Each student was to complete a project during the term. But first, in order to improve skills in metal working, a select few, including me, were given a small bar of iron and tasked to form it with a sloping edge at one end by utilizing a rotary bench grinder. As one progressed, you measured the slope on a gauge to see if it matched the precise angle required. Try as I might, week after week, I could not get the proper match. As the term was nearing the end, I hadn't even started my shop project. I saw a big failure notice coming my way. In response, I pilfered a small sheet of brass from the shop and took it home. In dad's basement workshop I was able to fashion a reasonable letter opener out of the purloined metal and receive a "B-" for my efforts – another academic tragedy avoided.

Social Studies was taught by Mr. Vernon. He was notable for eating caramels during class, although we students weren't able to partake of such pleasures. I did find him quite interesting, however. Unfortunately I was wrongly accused in one instance of shooting paper wads around the classroom with rubber bands. I didn't participate in this malfeasance, but a projectile inadvertently landed on my desk, and as I picked it up, Mr. Vernon spotted me and commanded me to come to his room after class to be disciplined. So, during his home room session at the end of day, I entered his class to get what was coming to me although I did nothing wrong. As he began his diatribe, I burst into tears. He then became more embarrassed than I. I was summarily dismissed with little fanfare.

Adjoining Mr. Vernon's room was that of Mr. Schmid's. A door with a glass panel separated the two classrooms. One day when Mr. Vernon was admonishing our students for some misbehavior, Mr. Schmid stood behind the glass door making funny faces, unbeknownst to our teacher. As our class broke up in uproarious laughter, Mr. Vernon would become more irrate, his face turning increasingly scarlet. This went on for several minutes with Vernon becoming more and more exasperated. Slyly walking away from the door, Mr. Schmid returned to teaching his class as Mr. Vernon stood wondering how he possibly lost control of his students. Evidently Schmid had some administrative ability because he became school principal some years later.

My eighth grade science teacher, Mr. Steltzer, was one of my favorites. Like Mr. Wizard (Don Herbert) of 1950s television fame, he made the subject interesting. I can remember being amazed by Mr. Steltzer as he mixed alkaline and acidic solutions (baking soda and vinegar I believe) in a beaker, culminating in the eruption of a frothing black foam that enthralled the class. We were introduced to the "periodic table" which listed the atomic weight of elements. In explaining how new, synthetic elements were often named after famous people, he regretted to inform me (in jest) that I didn't have a chance since there were already a Francium and a Barium.

My friend John also had Mr. Steltzer for science, but in a different class. However, we were allowed to collaborate on our science project. I envisioned creating a model of our solar system, so we agreed to give it a try. Using an astronomy book that I used as a reference we began fashioning each planet, I formed the spheres, in appropriate relative sizes, out of wood dough, and John meticulously painted each orb to match the Illustrations in the book. Before the wood dough hardened we ran a thin wire through each planet. Later we utilized several cardboard boxes, spray painting the interior a dark blue and then accenting with silver points to suggest stars. Using a string of white Christmas lights below a partition on the back wall of the structure, indirect lighting was provided to give an otherworldly glow. Each planet was strung between the top and bottom of the box in their appropriate position around the sun which was the largest sphere and covered in aluminum foil. One could view the whole scene through a Saran Wrap front window. We pulled an "A" on the project.

—

I'm a bit hazy on the exact time – probably early spring of 1959 – when John and I became interested more intimately in the opposite sex, although it probably wasn't much more than advanced puppy love. In any case, we used to prowl around the environs close to my house, often riding our bikes around the school yard or sitting by the front steps of the edifice which faced Cadwalader Ave. Two Catholic schoolgirl friends from the area would often walk down that thoroughfare toward Davis' drugstore on Township Line. Joanne lived on Tulpehocken Ave. and would meet up with Rita who lived across from the school. Rita was the same girl who owned the Spitz dog who allegedly gave birth to the puppies fathered by my family's wayward Romeo, Teddy, our mixed breed canine.

At some point in time, as the days grew longer, the four of us engaged in conversation and began a loose relationship of hanging around together. I suppose one of Darwin's theories had something to do with the match-ups. Rita gravitated toward John, and Joanne toward me. As was most often the case in these early relationships, the girls chose the boys. Rita was a shapely blonde who had, shall we say, a colorful command of the English language. A girl with freckles, and more reserved in nature, Joanne was low-key and suited my sensibilities. Interaction among the four of us would occur usually by chance on the weekends during school, and in a more freeform manor during the summer. We'd usually meet and talk by the elementary school or down by the swings at the playground. On several occasions we'd meet at the front steps of either Joanne's home or Rita's. Both of their homes were twin houses. Rita's adjoined neighbor was the prolific Donahue family of eight children, six girls and two boys in the following descending order by age: Jean, Ronnie, Maureen, Paul, Denise, Tommy, Kathy, and Donna. One of Joanne's neighbors on Tulpehocken was the lively Marion of the same age who had designs on other boys.

As the summer of 1959 wore on, the relationships became more fluid and a bit weaker. A kiss or two on the cheek would be interchanged from time to time, but that was the extent of it. There was one occasion, on a hot summer day, where I was alone with Joanne on a bench at the playground. The wooden seat with concrete supports was located in the shade of a large tree at the base of a steep hill. We talked quite a bit, and I gave her a peck on the cheek. But that was pretty much the end of it by then. However, I remember one early summer evening when I was sitting on Rita's front porch. Joanne was nowhere in sight, but her friend Marion was in attendance. I sat on one side of her and Steve Alaverde sat on the other. Steve was more a "man" of the world and a couple of years older than I. Marion, being a bit flirtatious, was trying to egg Steve on. She'd give him a kiss or two, then suddenly, plant one right on my lips. Of course I was smitten and thrilled at the attention. She carried on this little bit of folly for several iterations. Of course I was too naive to realize I was primarily being used as bait to make Steve a bit jealous. I wasn't complaining though.

So, the summer melted into fall, and by that time most all of the bonds between the parties had been broken. So John and I continued our daily routines which included serving The Evening and Sunday Bulletin – earning money for purchases at the drugstore or hardware store. John would ride his bike from his home every morning during the week and we'd find some activity to keep us busy. Saturday mornings would be regimented by collecting from newspaper customers in the morning, paying our bills to Mr. Tangye the branch manager around noon at the garage, and then serving the skinny Saturday edition in the afternoon.

Ninth grade was in the wings and would present brand-new academic challenges.

Separation of Brothers

While I was trying my best to navigate my way through eighth grade, brother Bill was on another educational mission. After graduating from Abington Senior High in 1958 he began attending the Penn State University Ogontz Campus in Abington the following fall. As he admitted years later, he just wasn't ready for college at that time. The requisite drive wasn't there. So, because of academic issues, he left after his freshman year.

Growing up together, Bill always talked about the possibility of a military career, and his experience with ROTC training at Penn State helped to solidify that thought in his mind.

Brother Bill, home after basic training and
before advanced training, around 1960

As mentioned previously, he led many a youthful military mission through Craig Woods with his rag tag team of neighborhood underlings, including myself. So it was no surprise when he enlisted in the army in the summer of 1959. His chosen field was army intelligence.

Bill was more than a brother; he was also a best friend. He moved with an older crowd of course, but we got along well except for occasional sibling disputes. We went to Phillies games together, played slot hockey and joked around famously. Being isolated from the rest of the family on the third floor of our home, we would often continue our verbal banter between our bedrooms after retiring for the night. Dueling puns – one more absurd than the other – would be exchanged, often causing a cacophony of uproarious laughter to erupt. This would continue until we were too tired to carry on, and we'd drop off into slumber.

It was an early August morn when my big brother gathered up a meager supply of clothes to take to basic training. Dad had the 1956 Pontiac revved up and ready to go. As they pulled out of the driveway for the short trip to the Selective Service Board in Jenkintown, Bill turned his head toward me and waved farewell. I cried myself to sleep that night.

—

Soon after induction Bill was sent to Ft. Jackson, South Carolina for basic training. Occasional correspondence would occur between us, but not much time was allowed in his situation to sit down and write a long letter. Isolation from the rest of the world, but bonding between fellow soldiers, was all part of the team discipline. Having gone through ROTC at Penn State, Bill was a natural to be selected as squad leader for his boot camp platoon – being issued an armband with buck sergeant stripes sewn on.

As Bill's eight week ordeal was reaching a conclusion, Dad prepared for a trip south to attend the graduation ceremonies. I was pulled from junior high classes for a few days to join the October excursion. I have vague memories of the trip which included sitting in a grandstand as the graduating class was honored. After the ceremonies we were introduced to Bill's drill instructor, and we got a chance to chat with Bill for a little while, but not much time was allowed since advanced training in his field of endeavor was soon in the offing.

One incident sticks in my mind concerning the ride home from South Carolina. At some point we stopped at a gas station to use their restroom facilities. I was in the back seat of our car and observed a black truck driver walking to the men's room to relieve himself. The door of the restroom stated, "Whites Only." Looking disgusted, he turned to walk away when the white station owner who was standing nearby informed him that he could use the facility despite his race. I suppose that this was a trivial act of kindness that the driver accepted, but I observed the embarrassment etched in his face as this encounter was witnessed by a white youth from the north.

During my brother's training in army intelligence, he was alternately sent to Ft. Dix, New Jersey and Ft. Devon, Massachusetts. At one point we were able to visit him at Ft. Dix on a Friday night. He was only able to talk to us briefly. All was in preparation for a year-long assignment in Turkey; his unit being assigned to intercept Soviet electronic communications during the Cold War. Our mom was concerned about his departure.

—

Between various tours of duty Bill would come home on leave and we would catch up as best we could. The neighborhood girls, including Irene Geiger, Ronnie Donahue and Marge Herrmann were always glad to see him. For his last year of service he was stationed at Ft. Huachuca, Arizona. When his three-year duty was completed, Tuck Hartmann and I took a trip to meet him in Tucson and accompany him on the way home. This will be covered in a later chapter.

Generational Change

In the late summer of 1959, with the final year of education at Huntingdon Junior High about to begin, a sense of change was in the air. The classes were increasingly tailored to get the ninth grade students ready for the more challenging classes in high school. On the political scene president Eisenhower was winding down in his duties as chief executive. Ike, looking tired and old, and having survived a couple of heart attacks, the country was yearning for younger leadership as the Cold War appeared to be reaching a crescendo. As the old guard in the political parties started to reluctantly relinquish power, two relatively young World War II veterans gained prominence in their respective parties. Vice-president and Cold Warrior Richard Nixon sought the Republican nomination with the lukewarm support of Eisenhower, while upstart senator John F. Kennedy, with the youthful looks of a movie star, moved to grab the brass ring for the Democrats' high prize. Amid this backdrop of generational upheaval and transition, we lesser lights continued our educational quest.

My close friendship with John continued, and although we attended few classes together, we saw each other every weekend on Friday evenings and Saturday afternoons after we completed our newspaper duties with The Evening Bulletin. Saturday morning continued to be spent collecting from our customers. We then returned to the branch office in the garage, behind the residence across from the firehouse, to pay our weekly bills. In the afternoon we delivered the skinny Saturday paper and the Sunday comics and advertisement sections to those who subscribed to that edition. Saturday evenings usually consisted of John and I cruising the streets and the school yard on our bicycles, or walking the sidewalks hoping for some pretty girls to emerge from the shadows and fall in love with us. But that school year was rather barren in that regard. So we usually made our way to Doc Davis' drugstore for refreshment, and then returned to my third floor aerie to commiserate about school and the doings in our neighborhood. We still collected Topps baseball cards from the 1959 season, but interest started to wane as thoughts of girls took precedence.

Our neighbor to the rear, Tuck Hartmann, although just a year older than I, was a close friend to my brother Bill, and he felt his absence rather deeply. During this period we began to interact more individually. At some point we strung bell wire (purchased at JAX Hardware) between my third floor bedroom and his room on the second floor of his Osceola Avenue house. On either end of the wire we attached hand-held walkie talkies which worked with the aid of internal magnets. At set times in the evening we would keep in touch by talking to each other for a few minutes on these primitive devices.

On the academic front I was introduced to algebra which was taught by a rookie teacher whom I'll call Mr. Gaines. Despite his best efforts, it was difficult for me to understand the concepts of the subject. Unfortunately, even his best efforts proved lacking because he was constantly taunted by two rather intelligent students who sat at the back of the class and already understood the mathematical discipline in detail. Thus, it was hard to concentrate on his lesson plan since he was interrupted incessantly by the two malcontents. Mr. Gaines was so thoroughly intimidated that he didn't discipline those individuals and handled the situation by nervously pacing the floor and then leaving the room on occasion to get a drink of water from the fountain, or making a mad dash to the lavatory.

It didn't help that I had no confidence in myself relative to algebra's laws. I remember that I scored 12 percent out of a 100 on one test – quite unbelievable. Mr. Gaines retested the low-scoring individuals like myself a few days later. As a result of my more concentrated efforts, I was able to increase my score fivefold, but 60 was still rather pathetic. My barely passing the class with a grade of "D" must have been a result of Mr. Gaines sympathy for me.

Another challenge in ninth grade was the Spanish I class that I attended in preparation for high school. This discipline was taught by the amiable Mr. Schneider. Again I underachieved, barely passing the course, but doing well enough to move onto Spanish II in 10th grade. My only thought was: "No mas, por favor!"

As usual, I was in my comfort zone with English class taught by Mrs. Allen. Somehow I was awakened from my lethargic state when it came to reading books. Each student was issued a copy of Ivanhoe by Sir Walter Scott. The length of the book was rather intimidating, but the story was interesting, so I kept pace with the reading assignment. The character that I recall the most was the young Jewess Rowena, since I somehow felt a bit of sympathy for her situation. In any case I think that I may have pulled a grade of "B"in the course which was something to be proud of for me.

—

As we passed into the new decade of the '60s, the political situation began to heat up with the presidential election on the horizon. The Cold War, which was going strong, became a major issue facing the nation's leadership. On May 4 of 1960, Nikita Khrushchev, the Soviet leader, announced that his country's military brought down an American spy plane over Russia with surface-to-air missiles. The timing couldn't have been much worse since a summit meeting with the Soviets was scheduled for Paris on May 14, which would also include the leaders of France and Great Britain. At first Eisenhower denied that the USA was conducting spy flights over Soviet territory, indicating such flights were for forecasting weather patterns only. This assertion became untenable when Khrushchev produced photos of the captured American pilot, Francis Gary Powers, who had parachuted to the ground. Powers was considered a coward in some quarters since he had been supplied with a needle containing a lethal dose of poison to avoid being captured alive. He chose not to use it.

It was hoped by the Eisenhower administration that a new agreement on limiting nuclear arms could be reached at the summit. The spy incident scuttled those plans when Khrushchev walked out of the meeting just hours after it commenced. The Cold War got colder.

With this backdrop it was up to the presidential candidates to display their "bonafides" in countering the threat of the communist menace emanating from the Soviet Union and Red China. As vice-president, Nixon appeared to have a leg up over his opponent based on his confrontation with Khrushchev at the "Kitchen Debate," which occurred in Moscow in July 1959. In that instance Nixon attended the American National Exhibition where he confronted Khrushchev at the display of state-of-the-art kitchen appliances. In this give-and-take exchange, Nixon more than held his own, displaying forcefulness despite the bluster of the Soviet premier.

Having been brought up in a Republican family, my allegiance was with the vice-president in the upcoming election. My friend John was in the same camp. During the political fervor of the times, John and I visited a Republican campaign trailer that was parked on York Road in Jenkintown. I bought some Nixon buttons, spending 50 cents of my hard-earned money on one pin featuring the likeness of the candidate in full color.

Kennedy, however, presented a more youthful and dynamic persona than Nixon even though they were close in age. JFK's beautiful, enchanting wife Jackie and his young daughter Caroline also offered a refreshing counterpoint to the Nixon family. Before exiting our school bus one day on an afternoon's return trip, I spied a large Kennedy campaign button on the floor between the seats. Although I was a Nixon "man," I couldn't resist claiming the object as my own. I retain the Nixon and Kennedy buttons to this day.

The race would heat up with the presidential debates in the fall, but first I had a memorable summer in the offing.

Summer of 1960

Well, the first summer of the new decade started much like those in recent memory. John and I continued in our paperboys' routines which occupied an hour or so every weekday afternoon. On the home front Mom and Auntie would do their cleaning in the morning after reading the Christian Science Bible Lesson together. In the afternoon, after completing requisite housework, they would hunker down in the den and watch the soap operas on the TV – most notably "The Edge of Night," "The

Days of our Lives," and "General Hospital." The room was inadequately cooled by a noisy window fan that could just about blow you out of your seat. Auntie supplemented this with a handheld paper fan to deal with the perspiration on her face.

A couple of weeks after school was over, summer was officially initiated with the Independence Day holiday. It was a free day for John and me since The Bulletin didn't publish on the Fourth. Now that John was 15, and I was only two months away from that milestone, we no longer walked or rode our bikes in the firehouse parade with the younger children. In preparation for the event, fireman Vince Fisher would be readying his record-playing sound system on a trailer which he pulled with his Chevy panel truck. As soon as the fire siren blasted its report at 9:00 A.M., the annual parade commenced.

The proscribed route of the procession has changed little to this day. It was basically a counter clockwise circumnavigation of McKinley which included a perimeter of the town with the following streets in this order: north on Jenkintown Rd. (In front of the firehouse), left on Huron Ave., left on Cypress Ave., right on Cadwalader Ave., left on Township Line Rd., left on High School Rd., and left on Jenkintown Rd. and back to the firehouse. An Abington Township police car would be at the head of the parade followed by a fireman's color guard. On their heels was a mass of children and parents, walking, riding bikes and waving American flags. Then Vince, trailing the throng, would fire up his makeshift sound system with the musical strains of appropriate Sousa standards. Trucks from the local fire companies including Abington, Rockledge, Elkins Park, Ogontz, Enterprise and Pioneer from Jenkintown – as well as equipment from McKinley – would take up their place in line.

Immediately after the parade ended at the station, the firemen would conduct children's games down at the playground across from the firehouse. There would be races across the field by age group. Then there would be the peanut scramble as the firemen dug into large burlap bags of that tasty legume and flung them high into the air – children scurrying around like ants on a soda spill, filling their paper lunch bags with the treat. The penny scramble would follow and was the most intense activity because cold cash was being tossed to the waiting urchins. (John and I would return in the quiet of the afternoon to search for a few unpicked coins.)

—

Refreshments were served down on the field after all of the children's events. This most notably included cups of birch beer dispensed from stainless steel barrels and Dixie Cups drawn from boxes cooled by dry ice. Inside the lid of the cups would be a collector's photo of some sort that would be revealed by licking off the residual chocolate and vanilla ice cream. It was during the distribution of these treats that John and I encountered two lovely young ladies.

Pat Herrmann and Regina Schorn were hovering around the boxes of ice cream as we were. I'm not sure what started the conversation, but I imagine that the girls uttered the first words since I was bashful to a fault. Slightly built and thin, Pat had dark hair and a light complexion. Regina – evidently having Italian in her blood – was of a fuller figure and had lovely olive tan skin. Initially I was drawn to Pat, but in instances like these it doesn't seem to be the boys that do the picking. It soon became apparent that the pairings would be Pat and John, and Regina and Buddy. As it turned out, that was fine with me and I was soon drawn to Regina's sweet nature.

I'm not now sure how that day progressed, but by afternoon the four of us had congregated on the porch of Pat's home on the west side of Tulpehocken Avenue between Jenkintown and Cypress. Across the street from Pat's house was the home of Regina and her substantial number of siblings. It soon became apparent to me that Pat was the younger sister of Marge Hermann who was acquainted with my brother Bill. I believe that Marge held a bit of affection for him at the time. However, Bill was stationed in Turkey with the Army Security Agency (ASA) that summer.

It's hard to describe the magic of that Fourth and how we were drawn together by fate. But I suppose that in a small town like McKinley these relationships naturally came about. As a group, we were comfortable being around each other. I suppose that it was a casual case of puppy love that endured throughout the summer – the focal point being Pat's porch.

Living in Pat's home with her were her father and maternal grandfather along with Marge. When Pat was very young, her mother passed away, so Marge took on that role as best she could. The two oldest siblings were Al and Jack, but by the time of our meeting they had moved out of the house. Older sister Mary and her husband Landy Howald had recently bought the left side of a twin home at the corner of Cadwalader and Cypress, right down the street from the Burr residence.

Being a Catholic family of that era, the Schorn family was rather prolific. Regina had the following siblings: Jodie, Eddie, Jerry, and Tommy (in order of age), and the youngest, her only sister, Betsy. As it was, most of us interacted to some extent throughout the summer.

When the four of us weren't hanging out on Pat's porch, we'd stroll around McKinley, frequenting fire chief Leary's grocery store across from the barber shop on Jenkintown Road or strolling down to the playground or schoolyard to make use of the swings. The front steps of McKinley school were a favorite place to hang out, talk, and watch the world go by.

Our mutual, innocent relationships continued throughout the summer, but by August John and I wondered if we could up the stakes a bit by proposing that the four of us go to Willow Grove Park one day. Thoughts of riding through the tunnel of love with our female companions sounded rather thrilling. The girls were both in agreement, but we required the final approval of Marge before we could proceed. Sadly our great adventure was squashed in its infancy when Marge exerted her maternal authority.

I remember one early summer evening when John was busily doing something else – possibly away at a Boy Scout function. To pass the time I thought that I'd walk up to Tulpehocken and pass Pat's house. In those days we never used the phone to communicate, nor did we knock on the door to see if a girl was home. As it was, Pat was sitting alone on her porch. Regina was also not around. So, Pat and I just sat and talked for a long while. When I was getting ready to leave, we walked to the sidewalk and talked some more. I looked down into Pat's eyes and told her that I'm sure that John missed her wherever he was, but, I must admit, I was feeling a connection that didn't include John. But being best friends with John, I would never undermine our friendship by pursuing it further, or compromise my relationship with Regina.

—

As the summer rolled on, John proved to be much more industrious than I. It was quite common for carriers in our stable of paperboys to go on vacation with their families. To fill the void, other paperboys would volunteer to temporarily take on another route. As it was, John probably had the second biggest route (Rte. 21) which included houses in the manor – the same route which my brother served years before. But, it seems, John was determined to make more money where he could, and I believe that he served as many as three or four routes at one time while others were on vacation.

I was generally content to deliver my papers for Route 9, and would occasionally, under duress, take on Route 2 which served that portion of the manor closest to the village. When our family went down to Pleasantville, NJ for the week, John gladly delivered my papers for me.

The largest route in our branch during this period was covered by Bruce Moscowitz who lived in Cheltenham. He was the beneficiary of new home development in the Cedar Road area of the branch's domain and had in excess of 90 customers, and he was ambitious in acquiring more. His younger brother Allen had a smaller route and did not display the verve of his older sibling. Our branch captain at the time was a boy named Paul who was probably two years older than I. It was the captain's duty, in addition to serving his own route, to count out the newspapers for the other carriers after they were delivered in bulk to the branch. In addition, the captain filled out a large spreadsheet each week to determine each carrier's bill based on the number of daily and Sunday papers served as well as charges for insurance and magazine subscriptions also offered by The Bulletin. This spreadsheet had to be ready for the manager, Mr. Tangye, so he could collect funds from the carriers on Saturday morning at the branch. The captain also had to be of sufficient stature to control the other carriers and keep them in line, physically and mentally.

I'm not sure of the specific incident, but Paul and Bruce had a heated argument one day, and Paul hurled an ethnic slur at Bruce. Upon hearing of the incident, Bruce's mother angrily confronted Mr. Tangye who summarily fired Paul. Now a void in the captainship had to be filled.

At that time, John and I were the remaining senior paperboys. But I was still surprised that Mr. Tangye offered me the captain's job. As I said, John was more industrious than I, but that trait cost him the position since he was too busy serving multiple routes. I hesitated in accepting at first, because I wasn't sure that I was up to the task. But I relented and accepted. First I had to go to the township-employed doctor to have a physical for working papers, which I did, and successfully passed.

Now I was on The Bulletin's payroll. Each week I received a check for $6.50 with a 20-cent deduction for Social Security (the government got into my pocket for the first time at age 14). Each week I deposited that check into my PSFS savings account that I had opened in fifth grade. Proceeds from the delivery of papers on my route became my spending money.

—

As the summer months lazily moved toward the start of the next school year, John and my relationships with Pat and Regina began to cool somewhat. For one reason or the other, we just weren't seeing each other as much. One incident, I suppose, became the tipping point. It was one late afternoon, after supper I believe, that I wandered down to the front steps of McKinley school. A young Catholic girl whose name I can't recall was walking by. We innocently started a conversation. She lived in a home on Cadwalader Avenue near the corner by the Texaco station. In any event, as we carried on our tete-a-tete, Regina happened by on her bicycle, and catching me in my "indiscretion," gave me a withering stare and continued on her way. I don't know if I ever had occasion to talk to that neighborhood girl again, but that magical summer ended unceremoniously with a pronounced thud.

High School,
Girls,
and
Cars

Into High School

Well, now we're in the big leagues. Abington High School in pure size easily eclipsed the junior high experience. It was the consolidation of the township's three junior high schools: Huntingdon, Abington Jr., and Glenside-Weldon. There would be a much bigger student body to mingle with.

Going into tenth grade I had selected the Business Education curriculum to follow. I figured that this is where my true talents would lie. Not only that, I wouldn't be saddled with the more difficult subjects offered in the college prep classes. Although I wouldn't have to deal with algebra, my guidance counselor felt that I should embark on at least a couple of more challenging subjects such as plane geometry and Spanish II. I really don't think that I had much of a choice. The initial challenge would simply be trying to make sense out of my roster schedule and determining where all the classrooms were located. There were only a few minutes between classes and one often had to mimic the super hero Flash to get from one end of the campus to the other.

Of course each day started with my home room, which was monitored by Mr. Hubley who was also a math teacher as well as an athletic coach. Alphabetic order was the basis for being placed in a particular home room. Our room was 207 and everyone's last name began with a "B." Gary Burke sat in front of me, and we became relatively close friends. Unlike me, he was a college prep student.

Each morning started with announcements over the public address system delivered by students in the radio arts program. This included readings from the scripture which were required by Pennsylvania law. However, there was a challenge to this practice by an Abington student, Ellery Schempp. One day in 1956 during the scriptural readings, he opened the Quran. He was making a statement for the separation of church and state. In addition he refused to stand for the Lord's Prayer and was sent out of the classroom by his teacher. The Schempp family got the ACLU involved with the situation which resulted in the Supreme Court of the United States agreeing to review the case. In late

February of 1963 the justices heard oral arguments, and it was determined, in an 8-1 decision, that mandatory reading of the Bible in public schools was in violation of the establishment clause of the Constitution. The decision was handed down on June 17 of that year. Ellery's sister, Donna Schempp, was a member of our class of 1963.

Once I got into the flow of things such as remembering where my locker was and learning the pad lock's combination (28-2-8), I was ready to take on my new classes. In the area of business education there was typing and bookkeeping. Typing class was taught by Mr. Hantjis and was held in a large room filled with IBM electric typewriters and click-clacking students. Learning the rudiments of the home row — "asdf jkl;" — was essential and the starting point for learning the remainder of the keys. Of course, understanding where the keys were without looking at them was fundamental. One student next to me couldn't take his eyes off of them despite his best efforts. Mr. Hantjis taped an 8 ½ x 11 sheet of paper at the top of his keyboard to mask his hands and the keys under the flimsy obstruction. First lessons consisted of typing words from the home row only, such as fad, sad, dad, and lad; which was somewhat limited because there was only one vowel to work with. In any case, although I was learning the keys without looking at them, I wasn't typing fast enough. So, it wasn't a surprise that I received a failure slip during my very first semester.

Having a mother who could type like a whirlwind, this situation was unacceptable. She responded by buying me a portable Hermes Rocket typewriter for the princely some of 20 dollars. So, every night I would sit down at the dining room table and plink out words on the paper. Since the portable was a manual, I also had to adjust from the easy stroke of an electric to the firm stroke of my Hermes. Mr. Hantjis always impressed upon us to type with a rhythm, and not to go fast and slow. Once I learned that concept I was able to keep up with the class exercises and pull up my grades accordingly. Learning on the manual portable also helped me to adjust to the standard size manuals used during the second half of the year.

Plane geometry presented a greater challenge. There was then a pilot program called "new math," and this class was based on that concept. The text book was a paperback with a maroon cover. Essentially I didn't know "new math" from "old math," so I just went along for the ride. What was intimidating was the fact that I was the only sophomore in the class. All the other students were juniors and seniors. Seated in front of me was a junior named Paul, and to my left was Eric who was a senior. Fortunately, both were friendly toward me despite my tenth grade status.

Eric was a particularly interesting guy since he had been dropped back a grade twice before because of his poor academics, so he should have graduated in 1959. Evidently he had learned his lesson along the way and he just went about doing his work in a knowing and cool manner, tackling geometry with ease. Sporting glasses, he looked a bit like the late Buddy Holly. And he had an ever-present toothpick dangling from his lips. I looked up to him.

Occasionally I would challenge Paul to an arm wrestling match before class. We would often trade wins, but he cheated a bit by wriggling his wrist back and forth during the contests. As for arm wrestling, I won my credentials one day during lunch period. At another dining table in the cafeteria, there was a series of matches going on with the winner moving onto another opponent. I believe all of the participants were juniors and seniors. There was a lull with no one wanting to challenge the winner. I'm not sure what possessed me, but I volunteered to take him on. Being a skinny kid, I suppose that I didn't seem like much of a challenge, but I did have some arm strength which I inherited from my father; I suppose. My opponent was a stocky fellow, and he was ready for me. As we commenced our contest, the crowd of students urged us on. It was touch and go, but I outlasted him and threw his arm to the table. A roar went up from the crowd and I gloried in the moment. Thankfully the lunch period ended and I didn't have to take on any more students.

My English class, taught by Miss Jacobs, was where I felt most at home. She evidently felt that I had some writing talent and encouraged me. I pulled a grade of "A" throughout the year except for the last marking period when I was awarded a "B." That was because I didn't have a verbal book report ready one morning when it was due. I suppose that I just got a little lazy at the end of the year and thought that she wouldn't call on me. Not only did I feel that I let myself down, but that I let Miss Jacobs down as well.

—

The most daunting high school challenge of all was aquatics class. My brother and I were never taught to swim as youngsters so it was with great apprehension that I stepped into the large, domed room with the Olympic size pool. At the one end was a tall exterior wall of glass which overlooked the parking lot. All the boys wore the same dark cloth suits distributed by the school. And the poor girls wore red cloth suits which provided little support or concealment.

The classes were divided into three levels of skill: beginners, intermediate and expert. It was required that you must eventually attain the intermediate class or higher. As I remember, we were first taught to put our face into the water to become accustomed to our soggy surroundings. Then with swimming boards that we held out in front of ourselves we attempted to float. And then we would move up in difficulty to the dead man's float, face down in the water in a prone position. To my amazement I was actually able to stay afloat. One was told by the instructor to relax. Floating on my back was less successful. Despite my best efforts, my legs would begin to sink. I found out later that I had no problem with this situation in salt water.

The rudimentary activities took place in the shallow end. As we learned the various swimming strokes we started with the paddle boards and then put them aside as our skill level increased. As it turned out, I never mastered the crawl stroke, but became reasonably proficient with the side and back strokes. All of this took place in the shallow end of the pool. To be accustomed to the deep end, we were told to jump off of the side of the pool feet first, and then we would bob to the surface where the instructor would hold out a pole for us to grab onto. With great fear I took the plunge and to my amazement I surfaced quickly, flailing and successfully grasping the pole.

To graduate to the intermediate classification, the student had to swim each of the strokes the length of the pool and back. Somehow I managed to do this in my junior year. I would not fail aquatics.

Politics

The 1960 presidential election was looming large on the political horizon. Shortly into the new school year, on the evening of Monday, September 26, the first of the Nixon-Kennedy debates took place in Chicago. Although it was a school night, I believe that I watched the debate on the television with my parents and Auntie. We, all being Republicans, were rooting for the vice-president. Most of what I remember was a discussion on Quemoy and Matsu, islands off of the coast of China of which the Communist and Nationalist governments both claimed ownership. In any case I felt that Nixon did well, although history has indicated that Tricky Dick looked sweaty and pale compared to JFK's suave, sun tanned good looks. I remember that my friend John and I listened to one of the debates on the radio up in my bedroom, either on October 13 or October 21 which were both weekend dates.

I remember John and I running into Pat Hermann one evening as we walked down to Davis' Drugstore, and we kidded with her about the upcoming election since she was a devout Democrat. She and her sister Marge had recently moved in November from their Tulpehocken home, after the death of their father and grandfather, to the home of their sister Mary who lived down the street from our family on Cadwalader Ave.

Our near neighbor, Ray Hamilton, was a Republican Party representative of some note at the time. As usual, when he walked past our house, he checked to see if someone was working out in the yard or sitting on the front porch. If he caught your eye, he didn't miss the chance to tell you that it would be the end of the country if a Catholic like Kennedy were to be elected President. To say the least, Ray tended to be a bit overzealous and prejudiced, but reflected the protestant sentiment of that day.

I don't remember much if politics were discussed in high school during this period, but it was clear that our Spanish teacher, Dominic Lessa, was a strong Kennedy supporter. Mr. Lessa was a product of the Italian-American neighborhoods in Boston if I remember correctly. Evidently he lived there when Kennedy was running for political office. Once he related that he met Kennedy briefly on two occasions separated by a substantial period of time. Lessa was amazed that he remembered Dominic's name in the interim when they again met, displaying JFK's great facility of displaying the personal touch through his formidable memory.

I'm afraid to report that my attention to studying and learning the Spanish language wasn't any greater than my efforts with plane geometry. Again, I barely passed by pulling a "D" in the subject. I remember that I always completed the homework, and I suppose that is what saved me. But, despite the lack of studious behavior on my part, I loved having Mr. Lessa as a teacher. Although he had a fine command of the Spanish language, I felt that his first calling should have been that of a comedian. He looked something like a taller, swarthier Edward Asnor, the actor, and liked to feign a bad guy image. Between imparting his Spanish language credentials with his Boston accent, he would regale his class in stories of his childhood, often causing his students to burst out in laughter. There was one incident that stands out in my mind – one where the laugh turned out to be on our teacher. He told of how he and his boyhood buddies would hang out around the train tracks in the spring and find frogs in the area. They would get their perverse kicks by placing a frog on the track just before a train came by and then watching the poor critter meet its demise as it was squashed below the train's wheels. Then he went on to say how it was special when they found a frog with its baby on its back, because then you could have two executions for the price of one.

After telling this particular tale, Walter Czarnecki, who sat directly in front of me, chimed in and said, "Mr. Lessa, that wasn't a baby frog on the big frog's back, that was the male on the female." Well, the class erupted in a cacophony of uproarious laughter as Mr. Lessa's head turned into a scarlet orb. He quickly returned to his lesson plan, but the laughter wouldn't die down.

Mr. Lessa also ran the after-school detention program where he held military rule over a room full of those students who had misbehaved in some fashion. Fortunately, I never had to attend one of those sessions.

—

As the autumn moved on, the presidential campaigns were active right up to election day, both candidates making visits to strategic communities in a last minute bid to win more votes. On election day my parents and Auntie went to the polling station in the gymnasium of McKinley Elementary School, casting their votes for the Republican ticket. In the evening we watched the election results on TV, but the contest was too close to call and proceeded into the wee hours of the morning. Kennedy led early in the evening with the returns coming in from the large cities in the northeast and midwest, but Nixon started to gain ground from the western rural states as the night progressed. It wasn't until about 3:00 A.M. in the morning that Nixon made a statement suggesting that Kennedy had won. It was thought that Nixon even lost his home state of California, but he finally claimed victory there when all of the absentee votes were tallied several days later. It is amazing that the voter turnout for the election was more than 62% of eligible voters – a high amount compared to modern day tallies.

The morning after the election our family was shocked. Later on there was talk of vote fixing in Chicago behind Mayor Daley which threw Illinois' electoral votes into the Kennedy column. Nixon decided not to contest the results and Kennedy emerged the winner. My mother was so distressed that she subsequently sent a letter to Nixon saying that our family would support a recount. A few weeks later we received a card from the Nixon family thanking us for our support. I still have that card to this day.

—

Inauguration day was cold and blustery. I remember watching it on TV, seeing Kennedy arriving in the limousine with the outgoing president Eisenhower. Holding to the old tradition the outgoing and incoming executives wore black top hats. Standing before Chief Justice Warren, Kennedy took the oath of office while placing his hand on the bible held by his wife Jackie who looked on with admiration. His speech, laced with hope and cold war rhetoric, implored the citizens to "ask not what your country can do for you, but what you can do for your country." Leaning on his New England heritage, he called on the elderly great poet, Robert Frost, to read a poem appropriate for the occasion. Frost struggled with the wind at the podium which ruffled the paper containing the words of his text, and the sunlight which created a glare on the document, making it difficult to read his work. In response, Frost read another poem from memory. It was an important moment for me because I was a big fan of Frost's poetry.

A new era of youthful enthusiasm was being ushered in which was embodied in the new president and his lovely wife. Who knew at that time what a convulsive decade the 1960s would be?

Special Holiday Gifts

In the interim between the presidential election and the inauguration were two of America's most important holidays: Thanksgiving and Christmas. Like the holidays of 1959, the holidays of 1960 were conspicuous by the absence of brother Bill. He was on the other side of the world in Turkey, performing his Cold War duties by listening in on radio messages initiated by the Soviet Union. Here at home the traditions went on, although a bit lonelier. Dad continued the routine of ferrying Nan and Pop Pop, and Aunt Emma and Uncle Ad, to and from the annual festivities. About that time, I assumed the important mantle of filling in as the third player for three-handed Pinochle in the absence of Bill. It would take me awhile to even approach the competence of Uncle Ad and Dad in this cutthroat competition. Having an almost photographic memory, Dad could pretty much tell what cards had been played and which ones were most likely in his competitors' hands. I never saw Pop Pop play cards. He was content to sit quietly in a chair.

Brother Bill surely didn't forget his family though, since a large box was received at our front door a couple of weeks before Christmas. With great anticipation we opened it up, and therein were a portable Philco stereo record player and a score or more of LPs. Genres such as rock, instrumental, and classical were well represented. Two of my favorite rock LPs were the "Elvis is Back" and "Buddy Holly and the Crickets" albums. It was less than two years earlier that Holly was killed, along with The Big Bopper and Richie Valance, in a tragic plane crash in the Midwest. Both Elvis and Buddy were my musical heros.

Classical albums were represented by the likes of Sibelius and Rimsky-Korsakov – "The Russian Easter Overture" being one of my favorite compositions. And there were the jungle sounds of Martin Denny and his orchestra to round out the offerings. It may have been during that Christmas season, or one shortly thereafter, that I received a two-record set of The Nutcracker Ballet from my mother. I still treasure it to this day.

Without much ceremony the stereo was set up in a corner of the living room next to the couch. I made it a habit of playing classical music on Sunday mornings thereafter, when I returned from my paper route and before dutifully heading down to Germantown with the family to attend Sunday school.

Now that I was the ripe old age of 15, gone were toys as Christmas presents, those being replaced by clothes and the like. However, I do remember receiving a car model that year of a Duesenberg. The holiday falling on a Sunday that year, I decided to begin work on it the following Monday. I had everything set up on the card table in the den in the early afternoon – parts, paint and plastic glue. My Philco 500 transistor radio was in place so I could listen to a special event, the NFL Championship game, which began at noon. Evidently the game was also televised on NBC, but I didn't watch it. Maybe I thought that it would distract me from my model building.

The Philadelphia Eagles hadn't won a championship game since 1949. Now they faced the Green Bay Packers at noon at Franklin Field in Philadelphia. The Packers, under coach Vince Lombardi, had won the Western Division championship with their 8-4 regular season record. Winning the East, the Eagles finished with a 10-2 record under Buck Shaw. The low scoring game changed leads several times, the Eagles consistently keeping the Packers from scoring a touchdown until the fourth quarter. In several instances, inside Eagles territory, the Packers went for first down on fourth down and if they simply had converted a few field goals instead, they would probably have won the game. As it was, the Packers were threatening to score on their last possession as time was running out and they were at the Eagles 22 yard line. Quarterback Bart Starr connected with James Taylor on a pass play, and all that stood between Taylor and the end zone was Eagles linebacker Chuck Bednarik who tackled Taylor at the Eagles 10 yard line. Bednarik sat on Taylor until time ran out exclaiming to him, "You can get up now, Taylor. This damn game's over."

That playoff game became the only one that Lombardi ever lost, finishing his career with a 9-1 post-season record. Unfortunately it was the last Eagles championship for decades to come. Anyway, it was a big Christmas present for the city and me that year.

The Year Drags On

As the new year of 1961 got under way, my sophomore experience continued as I tried to acclimate myself to the relatively stressful environment. Typing became less of an issue since I was gaining more proficiency despite our class making the transition to manual typewriters. As the semesters moved on, we learned how to make mimeograph and spirit duplicator masters. Copies made with the spirit duplicator, more commonly known as the Ditto machine, had the distinct pleasing smell of the "spirits" which I recalled fondly from my elementary school days.

Spanish and plane geometry classes continued to be challenges. Although proving geometric formulas, step by step, by the logical application of postulates and theorems, held a certain fascination for me. Of course my poor study habits didn't promote much success.

Another required class outside the realm of business education was biology. Our instructor, Mr. Toplis, was a tall man with a crew cut. He walked around the class with a slightly upturned visage, which may have been the result of too many years smelling the ever-present vapors of formaldehyde that wafted through the lab. I did enjoy viewing live paramecia and amoebas through the microscope as they moved about in a drop of water, but dissecting animals wasn't much to my liking. Thankfully each student was paired with another when it came time to open up earthworms and frogs to expose and identify their innards. My partner took great joy in gleefully channeling Dr. Frankenstein as I looked on.

Once more, sophomores were required to take shop class. The year began under the instruction of a knowledgeable and kindly African-American teacher whose name I don't recall. Sadly, however, he died suddenly of a heart attack one day early in the school year. He was replaced by an older substitute teacher who continued in this position for the remainder of the term. Through his instruction I was able to create a serviceable aluminum letter opener with a clad copper handle.

Precipitation wise, it was an eventful winter with one large storm producing enough snow to close school for three straight days. Evidently the township's snow removing capability wasn't as thorough back then as it is today, because I can remember ruts from the vehicle tires remaining in the streets for quite a few days. Back then virtually all vehicles had rear wheel drive which didn't provide much traction, so chains had to be placed on the tires if you hoped to get around at all. Of course that didn't stop us paperboys from delivering the Evening Bulletin. Sleds weren't of much use, so it was easier to push your bike through the gullies in the street since riding was impossible. I remember that there was a paperboy vacancy in one of the routes in Cheltenham during one storm and I had to accompany the branch manager, Mr. Tangye, on the rounds as his late model Chevrolet got stuck several times along the way. He'd stop and I'd jump out of the car to hand-carry the papers to the doorsteps.

On April 28 my friend John reached an important milestone. He turned 16 years of age which made him eligible for a driver's license. In preparation, he bought a 1951 black Chevy from his sister Helen and her husband Don Shelmire. It was several months, however, before John took and passed his driver's test. We now had wheels as summer approached. It had been a long school year with little or nothing happening on the romantic front for either of us.

—

On the international front, the space race with the Soviet Union was heating up. The United States had been playing catchup since the USSR previously put the Sputnik, the first artificial satellite, in space in October 1957. On April 12, 1961, the United States was beaten to the punch again as cosmonaut Yuri Gagarin circled the earth in a 108-minute flight. We responded by putting astronaut Alan B. Shepard aloft in a suborbital trip on May 5. I remember listening to the event on the radio during Mr. Lessa's Spanish class. It wasn't until February of the next year when we matched the Soviets with the full orbital flight of John Glenn.

—

As the school year ended, my guidance counselor called home to talk to my mother. My business class grades were more than acceptable, but I only pulled a "D" in Spanish II and plane geometry. Although I barely passed the two subjects, the counselor suggested that I go to summer school to pull up my grades which would improve my academic standing if I planned to go to college someday. I couldn't think of anything worse than going to summer school. The mere thought of it was abhorrent to my constitution. Gratefully mom didn't push it, and I had a summer of relative freedom. I believe that John did go to summer school that year for six weeks of algebra, but it didn't hinder our activities much during the vacation months.

John was now driving and I had no problem riding shotgun. Bicycles were only being used for delivering newspapers now. My circa 1957 Roadmaster bike provided minimal transportation. When not in use it stood at the base of the steps by our back porch. By then my handlebars had rusted through and I had to get a reasonable used replacement from Crofty's Cycle Shop for a buck or two. Some of the spokes on the wheels were so loose that the rims became warped and it took a lot of ingenuity to set the axles just right so the wheels wouldn't rub against the frame while riding.

That Fourth of July, John and I made it down to the firehouse activities as in days of yore. During the festivities we made the acquaintance with a girl named Linda Nadjika who lived in Cheltenham Township. She was a rather tall thin, attractive blond with long hair. I remember few of the details, but, evidently, John got her address, so on a subsequent evening we rode up past her house. As luck would have it, Linda was out and about her property and we stopped by to say hello. I remember that she had a nice side yard with a small rectangular pond. In any case we all sat and talked for an hour or so. I was attracted to her, but I think she was a bit more interested in John. There seemed to be a pattern forming in the selection process. In any case we met, in a similar manner, a time or two again. The last encounter was during an afternoon, I believe. Linda had with her a friend name Gail Sharmen who happened to attend Olivet Presbyterian Church with John. The girls proposed that we all should ride over to the Del Ennuis Bowling Alleys in Huntingdon Valley with John providing the transportation.

Linda took the front seat next to John and Gail sat next to me in the back seat. She was an attractive girl – probably two years younger than I – with blond curly hair and nice suntanned legs. Unfortunately we pretty much sat there looking ahead, not speaking too each other. My skills in making a move or initiating scintillating conversation were obviously undeveloped and seriously lacking. To further throw cold water on the whole affair, John and I sat down while the girls bowled and we looked on. I suppose that we were just too cheap and weren't in an appropriate financial situation to pay for ourselves and two others, despite the possibility of future benefits. In any case, that pretty much doomed that relationship and the romantic drought continued.

As the summer moved on I became more established in my role as local branch captain for the Evening Bulletin. In that position one had to maintain a certain level of respect from your fellow carriers so some semblance of control could be kept. I would arrive at the branch a bit after noon and be there when the Bulletin truck driver made his delivery or shortly thereafter. Based on that week's allotment I'd snap the metal wire around the bales with wire cutters and begin to count out each of the 12 carriers' load for the day, writing the route number and amount on the top newspaper of the individual stack.

The carriers would then filter in little-by-little with some dedicated to their task, others grudgingly doing their duties at the behest of their parents. Vibrant adolescent repartee would be exchanged, but nary a curse word would be heard. As branch captain I also had to maintain order in a physical manner at times. I was in no way a bully, being of slim stature, but I was inheriting some adequate muscle tone from my dad. At times, if my authority was being questioned, it would be appropriate to bounce a misbehaving carrier off the branch office's walls – not to cause injury, but to make it known who was boss. However, one had to use discretion when a few carriers were bigger than I, such as Guy Sciola or Steve Daniels, both of whom hailed from the Cheltenham side of Elkins Park. Fortunately neither one was a trouble maker. Steve's brother Brian was more of a wise guy, but of a size that I could handle if necessary.

Some of the carriers held their jobs for a short period, either because they really didn't need the money, or the dedication required in a daily job, even of this limited nature, wore thin quickly. For example, Guy Sciolla's parents owned the popular Sciolla's Supper Club in North Philadelphia which featured popular entertainers such as Bobby Rydell, Fats Domino and Tony Bennett. It was obvious that Guy didn't need the money and he didn't stay in the job for long. Another carrier was Dave Goluboff who was the son of the owner of JAX Hardware Store on Township Line. His tenure was also short-lived.

Other carriers who lived in McKinley included Dwight Ward (a friend of my buddy John), who lived next to the playground on Cadwalder Avenue, and Danny DiPalantino, whose family owned a concrete contracting company on Osceola Avenue across from the same playground.

I would continue in my newspaper delivery career as 1961 marched into my high school junior year.

The Last Family Vacation

The summer of 1961 was special for one notable event. My dad, ever the traveler, was ready to embark on another vacation. Hunkered down over his maps, as in days of yore, he planned a trip to Canada beginning with a drive around the Gaspe peninsula on the east coast. The grand tour would continue along the St. Lawrence River to Quebec City and then move westerly toward Winnipeg, Manitoba. This required quite a few driving miles, but Dad was in his element.

This vacation would be unique in that my brother Bill, serving with the army in Turkey, would not be with us. The passengers would consist of Mom, Auntie, and me. Auntie, at age 71 or so, was only comfortable in the front seat of the family's red 1956 Pontiac. Mom and I would be stuck in the uncomfortable back seat of the two-door vehicle.

I imagine that we embarked early in the morning as was the usual case with Dad. He liked to put in a lot of miles on the first day – usually 600 or more. So it wasn't too long before we were in maritime French Canada starting on our trip around the Gaspe peninsula. A rural two-lane highway wound around the southern half of the peninsula and the going was rather slow. There was little traffic, and the road was peppered with small towns and interspersed signs reading "Ecole." (School). Mom and I would joke and sing silly songs to break the monotony from time to time. At one point, to the harmony of "Mary Had a Little Lamb" she sang: "Mary had a little lamb. The farmer shot it dead. Now she carries it to school between two hunks of bread." Well, that instantly started us laughing. Then Mom chortled another like verse which began: "Mary had a little lamb. The farmer milked it dry." Waiting for a retort from me, I added: "So she carried it to school between two hunks of rye." By that time we were in convulsive laughter with tears streaming down our cheeks. Mom had such a wonderful, and at times irreverent, sense of humor.

I don't remember where we stopped that first night. It was probably a tourist home. The next day we headed up to the town of Perce, on the tip of the peninsula, which had a beautiful view of the ocean. Stopping there at the fishing village, we took advantage of a trip on a small tourist boat on that sun kissed day. The water was rocking by the dock and with the help of the skipper and Dad, Auntie was able to climb aboard with some effort. Beautiful Perce Rock stood out in the harbor – a large monolithic rock with a natural bridge cut through it. Farther out at sea was St. Bonaventure Island which was populated with thousands of sea birds clinging to the rocky cliffs, and those that sailed around, with abandon, in the balmy sea breezes.

At nearly the age of 16, I was in that stage where teenagers didn't normally like hanging out with their parents for too long a period. But being on the cusp of manhood, I was starting to see Dad in a new light and found a measure of male bonding that I never felt before. Without my brother in the mix, we were able to interact more, one-on-one. I suppose I was beginning to relate to Mark Twain's famous quote: "When I was a boy of 14, my father was so ignorant I could hardly stand to have the old man around. But when I got to be 21, I was astonished at how much the old man had learned in seven years." The ages didn't exactly match, but the sentiment did.

Near Perce was the Grand Sablon Hotel which was situated right above the beach overlooking the water. It was decided that we would spend the night there which was fine with me. As I recall, we had supper in their dining room which had a glass wall with a wonderful view of the ocean. However, what impressed me the most were the beautiful French Canadian waitresses in their miniskirts. This revealing fashion was not destined to go south of the border for a few years. The melodious French accents further titillated my senses and accentuated the whole experience for me.

Of course dad was never one to stay in one place for more than a day, so we were set to hit the highway the next morning. To greet the new day Dad and I got up early while the sun was low on the horizon, and we decided to walk along the beach before breakfast. Gulls swooped majestically over the ocean as one of the beautiful waitresses from the night before, back in uniform, strolled along the sand, smoking a cigarette and picking up seashells. It was a surreal scene.

—

As we continued our family odyssey, rounding the tip of the peninsula, we headed west with the St. Lawrence River to our right – a beautiful sight with ships of commerce plying the water in the distance. After a long day of travel we stopped in the little town of Cap-chat where there was a tourist home or small hotel which had some vacant rooms. After we settled in and had something to eat, Dad and I took off on a trek up the road which hugged the coast. The scenery was beautiful along the winding thoroughfare and we spoke easily to each other about unremembered topics, but I surely felt a father-son bonding that I hadn't before.

Next on the itinerary was Quebec City with its European look. The Hotel Frontenak commanded the view. We stopped at the Citadel where the American assault on Canada came to an unauspicious end on New Year's Eve 1776. It seems to me that we intended to take a tour, but didn't for some reason. The fort may have been closed at the time.

I'm rather foggy about further details of the trip until we stopped in Winnipeg, Manitoba on the plains of Canada. I remember that we ate at a restaurant, and I was smitten by a female waitress who may have been a year or two older than I. Teenage emotions of this type can sail high or descend into the depths in mere seconds. But I was ready to stay behind and make my life with her. Although that premise was highly unrealistic for a myriad of reasons, it somehow made sense to my adolescent mind. In any case we were soon on our way again as I lulled into a period of sadness. Life seemed so unfair at times.

As we worked our way back into the states, Dad drove through Chicago on Sunday, August 27, when we heard of a tragedy back home on a radio broadcast. A jet fighter on a training mission from Willow Grove Naval Air Station in Horsham crashed through the roof of the nearby Bargain City USA market while attempting to land on the runway. The pilot was killed and 30 individuals were injured on the ground. Nevertheless, for us it was all systems go, and Dad hunkered down for the final leg home. This summer was soon to be another memory as the new school year loomed on the horizon, and I would reach the significant age of 16.

Manly Pursuits

My birthday was always anticlimactic. Coming on September 7, it coincided with the beginning of the school year. However, having one year of high school under my belt and being rid of most of the college prep courses, I was becoming ensconced in my comfort zone. Outside of the scholastic areas of my life were new beginnings.

First of all was the matter of a driver's license. Turning 16 recently, and having my driver's permit in my possession, I was ready to hit the road. And this was to be a full-blown driver's license with no restrictions. The advent of junior drivers' licenses was soon to come about, but I got in under the wire. Dad was ready to take me out on the road in our 1956 Pontiac and show me the ropes. Surprisingly he was very calm with his instruction, and patient with my learning curve. Since it was early fall, he would take me out while it was still light. After a few weeks of his tutelage, he told me that there wasn't anything else that he could teach me, so I put my effort into learning the traffic laws from the little book that the state provided.

It so happens that my brother came home on leave from the army around that time – probably in the period between completing his tour of duty in Turkey and when he was redeployed to Ft. Huachuca, Arizona. One day it was mutually decided to make the trip down to the Belmont State Police barracks in Philadelphia for me to take the driver's test. Tuck Hartmann, having been happily reunited with Bill again, tagged along with us.

When the time came, I nervously got behind the wheel of the Pontiac at the direction of the state trooper, as he climbed into the passenger seat. Following his directions, I successfully maneuvered around the traffic cones and came to a complete stop at the sign. Next was the space where I had to turn the car around in three moves without hitting the curve. About half way through the exercise, the car stalled, and despite my efforts, I couldn't get it started again. Fortunately the trooper was distracted – laughing his head off while watching someone else taking the test and knocking cones over along the way. During this interim I realized that I had to put the car in neutral to get it started again. The trooper was none the wiser.

After passing the driving part of the test, the trooper told me to park while he asked me some questions. I did well until he asked, "What is the speed limit on an unmarked rural road?" My tentative answer was, "Drive at the limit that the conditions would allow." It was obviously the wrong answer, as he repeated his question in an agitated and louder voice. I knew I was dead. I took a guess and meekly answered, "50 miles per hour." Miraculously I was right. I had successfully passed the driver's test.

Despite the fact that I had a state-authorized card that said that I was permitted to drive along the highways and byways, it didn't indicate that I had the necessary experience. John had been providing the transportation up till now. I didn't have my own automobile, so I had to plead with Dad for the keys so I could take out the old Pontiac for a try. As it was, one Saturday evening John and I decided to make our way to the Del Ennis Bowling Alleys in Huntingdon Valley to play a few games or to see if any pretty girls were eager to meet us. With this man-child behind the wheel I ventured out on the winding curves of Cedar Road. It was a challenge in the dark, but we made it safely to our destination. When it was time to come home and make our way out of the parking lot, I put the car in reverse and turned the wheel to back into the driving lane. Almost immediately I heard a crunch as the Pontiac's left front bumper made a sizeable dent in the door of an adjacent Chrysler which was parked next to us. I guess no one ever told me to first back out straight until the parking space was cleared before turning the wheel.

I was in a panic. What should I do? Ultimately I took the coward's way out and just left the scene, hoping no one got a glimpse of what I did. This was something that I didn't want to report to my parents and John would keep my secret. Well, I lived with a heightened sense of guilt for weeks thereafter, expecting that an Abington patrol car would pull up in front of our house and have an officer take me away in handcuffs. I can't imagine what the driver of the other car thought when he saw the damage. It still haunts me to this day.

—

Another right of passage for a 16-year-old McKinley male was to join the volunteer fire company. John and I decided to make the big move at the same time. Of course we had family connections: John's older brother Fred was a member, as well as my dad and brother Bill. As I remember it, one Tuesday night a month was reserved for a membership meeting, and another was scheduled for fire school.

Indoctrination for John and me was under the tutelage of Captain Frank Devine. Frank was a large amiable man with years of fire fighting experience. Living on Tulpehocken Avenue, he didn't have far to go to serve as a truck driver when a fire call came in. His vocation was that of manager of an MAB paint store in Willow Grove. During that first training session in the truck bay, Frank showed us the difference between 2 ½ inch hose and 1 ½ inch hose. The former was run from the truck to a hydrant near the fire scene, and the latter was pulled from the bed of the truck to fight the fire.

On other less frequent occasions there would be more intensive training at the fire tower on the township lot behind Abington High School. In preparation for class, something combustible, such as an old sofa, was moved into a vacant room of the tower. First, however, fireman Ray Hoffman would scour the folds beneath the cushions, looking for spare change which he would stuff into his pockets – a side benefit. (Ray had married our near neighbor, Jean Mutschler, several years before.) After a fire was started in the concrete-block structure by an experienced fireman, members of the crew would be sent inside in small groups to give them firsthand experience in dealing with the smoke.

Assistant Chief Billy Barr was a "smoke eater" and would lead the charge. He could withstand the dangerous environment for a while without the benefit of a Scott air pack. We new guys were given the same opportunity to breathe the smoke for a minute or two and feel it "burn" our lungs. To help survive in that environment, if we weren't wearing an air pack, we were told to proceed into the building near the floor and breathe the air being drawn in behind the spray of the nozzle. The air packs, if I remember correctly, could operate for 15 minutes or a half an hour depending on the size of the compressed air tank. The smaller tank was usually used by an officer who would make the first determination of the extent of the fire. When the tanks were beginning to run out of compressed air, a bell would sound to alert the fire fighter.

—

McKinley Fire Co. Members 1960
Standing in front:
Fred Bauerle, Billy Barr, Ray Hoffman, Pete Timmins
On fire truck running board:
Bill Burr, Sr. (Dad), Bob Hartmann
On top:
Ed Geissler, Jr.

There was a rather large gap of time for John and me between our initial training and our first fire. But when it came, it was a doozy. The alarm went off one evening during a heavy snowstorm and a house was fully involved on Osceola Avenue past the playground. It was the residence of the West family which included Rollie West, a local Abington High School football hero who had been drafted by the Philadelphia Eagles. I don't remember if Rollie was living there at the time.

It was a difficult fire, and the house was completely engulfed with flames spewing out of the windows. I remember hauling hose while slogging through the snow and helping out as instructed, taking orders from the experienced firefighters, as necessary, while they were engaged in doing the essential work. After many hours, the fire was put out, but the home couldn't be saved. It was a complete loss.

Activities after the fire could take longer than the fire itself. The wet hoses had to be rolled up and returned to the firehouse where they were stretched out in sections to be dried on the floor with its radiant heat. Then dry hose had to be packed back on the beds of the truck in order to be ready for the next fire engagement. Several members would sit up on the bed of the pumpers as hose was fed to them from rolls of hose dispensed from a lazy Susan type device behind the truck. It was essential that the hose was laid in proper serpentine fashion on the bed so it would pull off properly without a hitch when it was time to fight a fire. All members present would be involved in these cleanup activities as they recounted the latest event with a combination of serious discussion and irreverent banter.

—

On meeting nights, the members congregated in the large room in the basement of the building. A table was set up at the end of the room with chairs for the president and secretary. Cigarette smoke created a haze over the low hung ceiling. Although I was a nonsmoker, I probably inhaled the equivalent of a few cigarettes during those sessions.

The president conducted the meeting. I'm not sure who held that position when I first became a member, but it may have been Walt Holden. The perennial secretary was Norm Geisler, and his brother, Ed, Sr., served as treasurer. My dad usually served on the board of directors. Each meeting commenced with Chief Tip Leary giving his report on the fires which were fought since the last monthly session, along with any other pertinent information. Other officers would chime in as necessary during the proceedings. If there were new member applications to process, a vote of acceptance would be taken using a wooden box with a small hole in the top. Each member would place a white ball therein if the member was to be accepted, and the dreaded black ball if he was not.

The firehouse was truly a McKinley social microcosm and male bastion at the center of an active community.

Along the Route

As a result of having a newspaper route, I was able to interact with McKinley neighbors that I wouldn't have had the opportunity to, otherwise. Some of the families included members of the fire company, or friends of my brother Bill. There were also individuals, still unknown to me at the time, that would make profound differences in my life. It was all part of the interactions of a small community.

On Jenkintown Road I served the Hethringtons. As mentioned previously, Mrs. Hethrington ran the cafeteria at McKinley elementary and her husband served there as the janitor. Their son George was a good friend of my brother, and he moved on to become an Abington Township police officer and then a state trooper. His sister Janet was one year older than I.

Bob Croft (owner of the Cycle Shop) and his wife lived on West Avenue with their two daughters, the younger of whom, Gail, was a year younger than I. Other customers on West included the Donahues. John "Corky" Donahue was a close friend of my brother and Tuck Hartmann. Tuck's paternal grandfather also lived on the street – a rather grumpy old soul. The senior Mr. Gillespie, who lived across from the Donahues, worked as a janitor at the fire house, while sons Francis and Mike – both older than I – were Abington policemen.

On Jenkintown Road resided the Dufners. Bill belonged to the fire company, and sister Anne was my age and attended parochial school. The Kelsos, who lived a block away, had a granddaughter, Helen, who was in my high school class.

High School Road included twin homes occupied by the Heiselmoyer and Sefton families. Curt Heiselmoyer – a year or two younger than I – went on to become active in the fire house. The Sefton children included, in descending age: Nancy, Wayne and Joan. Nancy was a year younger than I and attended Abington. Joan was a cute little blond with whom I would interact with at times while delivering my papers. The Morrish family shared twin homes with Mrs. McCormick, mother of Mary and younger sister Marion with whom I was familiar from Tulpehocken Avenue. Frank Morrish was a rather gruff man and captain of McKinley's fire police. His wife Sue was a member of the ladies' auxiliary. Daughter Dale was Joan Sefton's age and also attended Abington, while her younger sister (by 10 years) Barbara, a scrappy impetuous child, was about to attend McKinley elementary.

Jim Gallagher, a member of the fire police, and his wife were next door neighbors to the Morrishes.

Also living on High School Road was the Hogg family. Mrs. Hogg and her two sons, Richard and Sammy, lived in a twin home. Richard was a friend of brother Bill and they were in the same grade at Abington High School. Sammy was a couple of years younger and had an uncanny resemblance to television personality and rock star, Ricky Nelson. Mr. Hogg, by that time, was deceased.

Tony Pisano and his wife Jean lived up the street toward Township Line. Tony was a perennially happy guy and an active member of the fire house. Wife Jean was the oldest daughter of the Donahue clan of Cadwalader Avenue.

Haines Avenue was at the far end of my paper route. Ed Geissler, his wife and daughter lived on the block. Ed was also a member of the fire company and the institution's treasurer. Across the street from the Geisslers was the Casey family, including daughters Nancy and younger daughter Jean. Being my age, Jean had been in my kindergarten class many years before. After that, she attended parochial school. Jean had become Tuck Hartmann's girlfriend, and they would ultimately marry.

Mrs. Kelly who previously worked at the Acme market on Township Line was also a resident of Haines where she live with her husband who was blind. He made money by caning chairs. Often he would be found sitting on the enclosed front porch doing his handiwork when I stopped to collect. Occupying the adjoining twin home were the O'Briens who had two daughters younger than I. Posted on their front door was a sign that said: "Don't knock, Dad's asleep," which presented a difficult situation for me when I collected on Saturdays.

Farther down Haines toward Jenkintown Road was the Speer family which had two blond daughters – one about my age and one a few years younger. Nearby was the family of the Kobeleski sisters who were similar in age to the Speer daughters. I found the older Kobeleski daughter quite attractive, but I never had the nerve to further build a relationship.

Across the street from the Kellys was a family whose daughter I will call Cheryl. She had an impact on my teenage life in the spring of 1962. As I recall, her family had recently moved from Renova in upstate Pennsylvania where her father had recently remarried. Her stepmother was only 28 years old, and I believe Cheryl, at age 14 or so, was impetuous and proved rather rebellious at times.

It was difficult not to form happy relationships with many of these families with whom I would interact over the five plus years that I had my paper route.

Teenager in Love

Academically, the school year was going well. I was pulling all A's and B's in the business courses. Gary Burke from my home room period attended gym class with me. We used to kid around quite a bit, and, under our breath, mock some of the college prep kids. I suppose it was just a bit of jealousy on our part, although some of the prep boys were rather pretentious. They usually dressed smartly while my wardrobe was rather limited. Gary was a much more dedicated student than I, however, and did well in most of his college-oriented classes.

John and I still got together each weekend. In the previous fall, John left the paper carrier life behind when he went to work for Mr. Davis at his drugstore on Township Line. By that time the soda fountain was history and John performed chores around the store and delivered prescriptions for the princely sum of 65 cents per hour. Too lazy to check out other job opportunities, I hung onto the paper route. Besides, I was still pulling down $6.50 a week as branch captain. The biggest problem for me was that school left out at 3:20 each afternoon. By the time I got down to the branch, all the other carriers had picked up their papers and taken off. Fortunately Mr. Tangye, the branch manager, would stop by and count out the newspapers for each route and put them in individual stacks. Unfortunately, Mr. Tangye didn't work on Fridays, so by the time I got there the bundles of newspapers were pawed over by the carriers who counted out their own allotment. Invariably they took more than their routes required, leaving me short of my needs. To make up the difference, I would go to Davis Drugstore and buy the additional copies needed. At five cents a shot, this reduced my profits.

—

As summer eased into spring, I started to notice the girls along the route more, but didn't really give them much heed. I was aware of Dale Morrish because her dad, Frank, was captain of the fire police, and I would see him down at the firehouse from time to time. He and fellow member, Harry Hill, were also representatives to the fireman's relief association.

One spring afternoon, as I began delivery of newspapers at the top of Haines Avenue, the girl Cheryl ran out to me as I rode by on my bicycle, and handed me an envelope. She then scampered back into her house. What was all this about? Her family wasn't a customer so I hadn't paid much attention to her in the past. She was reasonably cute with fair hair and dark brown eyes, but I had no interest in her heretofore. I knew that she attended St. James parochial school.

After I returned home that afternoon, I opened the envelope. Contained inside was basically a questionnaire. How old was I? What were my interests? What was my phone number? I was quite stymied. But I answered her questions anyway. The next day she was right there in front of her house, and I gave her the envelope back. She took it inside as I continued on my way.

I'm not sure when the phone calls began, but she started checking in on me at home. Not being accustomed to such forward behavior by a girl, I was a bit perplexed and nervous. Every time the phone rang I got butterflies in my stomach. But Cheryl persisted, and soon I would stop to talk to her while making my newspaper rounds. It wasn't long, I suppose, before I developed an affection for her. As a pretense for learning how to play chess, she invited me to her house one weekend evening to teach her the basic elements of the game.

So, I was drawn in. I don't know who provided the chess set, but I arrived at her house and we sat down on the couch with the elements of the game on the coffee table. Her parents found refuge in another room while the "instruction" proceeded. I, in my best scholarly fashion, began to teach her the game's basics. She played along for a while in this obvious farce, and set her eyes on me in a seductive way. Somewhere along the line I believed we exchanged kisses. It was by no means like the scene from the movie, "The Thomas Crown Affair," where characters played by Faye Runaway and Steve McQueen played chess while the sexual tension between them accelerated into the expected adult conclusion. This, instead, was meek old Frank trying to make it through the evening.

The relationship grew during that spring, and soon I asked her step mother for permission to take her to the movies. Upon her approval I showed up at Cheryl's door on a Saturday night driving my parents' new 1962 Dodge Dart with push button automatic transmission. Our movie of choice was "State Fair," starring Pat Boone and Ann-Margret, which was playing at the Cheltenham theater. The selection seemed appropriate since I, more or less, related to Pat Boone's character who was a bit of a farm boy nerd visiting the city, while Ann-Margret played a spunky show girl. Despite their obvious differences they managed to have their romantic fling, but you knew that irreconcilable differences would eventually win out. In any case, in preparation for the date, Cheryl had put multicolored sparkles in her hair. While trying to watch the movie, she clung to me while showering me with kisses much to my embarrassment, but I managed to return from my first date alive and in one piece, while having some errant sparkles wind up on my shirt.

Despite the erratic behavior of my new girlfriend, I was sufficiently smitten, but I stayed within the limits of a good boy. On a subsequent evening at her home, while we sat on her couch, she took the Parker pen out of my shirt pocket and placed it in her modest cleavage, asking me to retrieve it. Although tempted, but obviously out of my element, I refused, leaning on my puritanical tendencies. She reluctantly returned the writing instrument to me.

The Big One

As spring melted into summer, John and I spent more time at the firehouse in our spare time. In addition to responding to fires when the siren sounded, we would hang out playing pool upstairs or shuffleboard downstairs in the meeting room. Other young members in our age bracket, such as Eddie Schorn, Allan Gargan, Tuck Hartmann, and the Schneweis brothers would also participate. There was also an influx of new firemen from Rockledge Fire Company, including Paul Conroy, Danny Assal, Jim Sneddon, Bill Foxall, and Ronnie Lipps.

The Girl Scouts often used the facility for meetings on the weekends, and it wasn't uncommon to see active member, Barbara Feick, our old McKinley School classmate, on those occasions. She was always friendly and greeted us with a warm smile.

Most of the fires that we responded to, up to that point, were of little consequence, save the destruction of the West home during the winter. Many of the calls turned out to be false alarms. When there was little rain and the days got hot, there would be field fires to fight from time to time. On one occasion tall dry grass went up in flames on the vacant field off of Cedar and Shelmire Roads, and a fairly large fire had to be dealt with in Lorimer Park. Since that area couldn't be reached by the fire trucks, we had to strap Indian Tanks, which contained several gallons of water, to our backs. By hand pumping a wand that was attached to the tank by a hose, water could be sprayed on the fire. It was a rather unwieldy affair though. Usually field fires could be more effectively fought with brooms.

This relative lull in significant events ended in the early evening of Thursday, June 21, right about the time of the summer solstice. The sound of a thunderous explosion at a manufacturing plant in the fashionable Meadowbrook section of Abington could be heard for miles around. The facility, the Balata Division of Huntingdon Industries, was located at Washington Lane and Old Mill Rd. This conflagration came to be known as the "golf ball factory fire."

By the time McKinley Fire Co. arrived, the facility was completely involved. Many of the area fire companies joined the fight. Black smoke from the flames could be seen 12 miles away in downtown Philadelphia, and area roads were jammed with vehicles. As I remember, two smaller explosions from large naphtha tanks occurred shortly after we arrived. Water was poured onto the flames from a distance because the heat was so intense. A crisscross of hoses from the pumpers was laid throughout the area while firemen fought the blaze from all sides. I was caught up in all of this activity, but it is hard to remember all of the details years later.

What made this fire scene unique were the conditions on the ground beneath us. Balata is the name of a tropical tree which was tapped for a liquid substance that hardened into a rubber-like material. It was used mainly for the outer cover of high end golf balls, although it had a tendency to cut easily if the ball was mis-struck – not very advantageous for duffers. Anyway, the intense heat caused the balata rubber to become a molten river which one had to wade through with great difficulty. The material tenaciously stuck to our boots, the hoses, and other equipment.

The fire was fought into the early morning hours before it was brought under control. But the work had just begun. Since hose had to be drawn off the bed of the pumpers to fight the fire, new hose had to be packed in preparation for future alarms. The hose used at the scene would be rolled up and brought back to the firehouse to be unrolled on the driveway to dry. Unfortunately the balata material wreaked havoc on the hose and it took hours to remove the sticky substance using naphtha – the same substance that caused the explosions – as a solvent. As I recall, food was brought in during the night because we were all famished, and our chores weren't finally completed until the sun rose in the east.

A worker, who was at the golf ball factory when the explosion occurred, suffered significant burns on his body and was taken to Abington Memorial Hospital. Fellow McKinley fireman, Tommy Pearce, was also treated there for exhaustion and smoke inhalation.

I have a recollection of attending school the next day, although it was near the end of the academic year. I probably didn't have more than an hour or so of sleep before going to class. When other students found out that I was there fighting the fire, I got asked hundreds of questions about the situation.

Friday's edition of the Philadelphia Daily News had a full page photo of McKinley's Assistant Chief, Billy Barr, running from the scene with sky-high flames and pillars of smoke in the background. Of course Billy got kidded without mercy by his fellow firefighters. In reality he was just running to get more equipment to fight the fire. Nobody was a braver smoke-eater than Billy.

When I wearily went on my newspaper rounds that afternoon, Cheryl's stepmother stopped me to say that her daughter was concerned about my safety when she became aware of the catastrophic event.

I believe I slept well that night.

A Long Summer

The early summer of 1962 seemed to be primarily focused on Cheryl and the firehouse. Newspaper activities continued as I performed branch captain duties – counting out copies of the Evening Bulletin for the carriers while keeping them in tow. And, of course, I still had my paper route which enabled me to see Cheryl on a fairly regular basis.

Although she was generally affectionate and kind toward me, she displayed a bit of an unseemly streak of trying to make me jealous at times, by flirting with other neighborhood boys in front of me – even my friend John. And I must admit that it affected me negatively, but I soldiered on and still desired to see her more often. At times in the late afternoon I'd sit on our front porch at home, hoping that she would walk by. And when she did, I'd join her. Often she grabbed my arm and put it around her waist as we walked. I felt a little embarrassed by this action, but found it a bit exhilarating.

One day I ran into Pat Herrmann on the street and she incredulously asked me if it was true that I was hanging out with Cheryl. I gave her an evasive answer, but she sensed the truth. Obviously Cheryl didn't have a great reputation among some of her female peers.

Cheryl seemed to be among the missing for several days and I stopped by her house to see her. Answering her door was her stepmother who said that she couldn't come out. Evidently Cheryl was being punished for misbehavior of some sort. Several days later she sneaked a note to me as I was serving my newspapers. The rambling message, in melodramatic tones, essentially said that she was sorry, but we couldn't see each other anymore. She was being grounded and had to move on.

Well, I was devastated and was driven to tears that evening. To make matters worse, I heard Dion's song – A Teenager in Love – on the radio. The lyrics hit home:

> One day I feel so happy
> Next day I feel so sad

> I guess I'll learn
> To take the good with the bad
> 'Cause each night
> I ask the stars up above
> Why must I be a teenager in love?

Fortunately, hanging out at the firehouse provided a diversion for me. When John wasn't working at the drugstore, and I had completed my paper route, we'd often spend time down at the station playing pool or shuffleboard. Chief Tip Leary would often be holed up in his office, but the door was usually open. Several fellow firemen and I would sit around the office while Tip held court. This was where the chief was in his element. McKinley scuttlebutt was discussed in all its lurid detail. For a young guy, it made me feel as though I was part of the adult scene, gaining insight on the greater world outside. And, of course, there was the occasional fire to respond to.

Somewhere along the line Cheryl won her reprieve, and we saw each other on the sly, often hanging out on her porch or in her living room when her stepmother was working. One afternoon she received an invitation from a girlfriend to spend a couple of days down at the Jersey shore. During that summer we shared our love for the music of Elvis Presley's 1961 movie, "Blue Hawaii." Although I hadn't seen the show, we were both familiar with the soundtrack album. While at the shore, Cheryl made a recording on one of those ubiquitous boardwalk machines, singing her version of the Elvis track to me:

> Ku-u-i-po I love you more today
> More today than yesterday
> But I love you less today
> Less than I will tomorrow

She presented this record to me upon her return, which I felt was a really nice gesture, but I had no illusions that she didn't hang out with other boys during her brief seashore vacation.

The Old Studebaker

One summer evening in 1962 our neighbor, Ray Hamilton, stopped by to see Dad. Taking up space in his garage was his departed father's 1936 Studebaker sedan. Old Mr. Hamilton had bought the car new, and Ray was willing to give away the vehicle to me. Dad kindly accepted on my behalf even though the car was not in running condition. It probably hadn't been used for more that a decade.

I don't remember how we managed to move the old car to our property, but it somehow got deposited in our driveway near the garage. The thought of having a means of transportation of my own was exciting, but it was of little import if the engine didn't run. I didn't have a lot of spare money so Dad provided the funds and the labor to get it working. It wasn't long before we made a trip to the Pep Boys store in Abington where Dad purchased a battery, coil and condenser (universal parts since original equipment wasn't available), and spark plugs. And, if the car was going to pass mandatory state inspection, it had to have automatic electric turn signals installed.

So, Dad set upon the tasks at hand, getting all of the parts related to the engine installed. After making sure that there was enough water in the radiator, the ignition key was turned, and, sure enough, the old beast came alive. Next step was installing the turn signals which required drilling holes in the front and rear fenders to accommodate the lights. A signal switch had to be mounted on the steering wheel shaft, and wiring had to be run to a fuse box. As usual, Dad was equal to the task – Jack of all trades.

Since Dad worked occasional nights at the Sunoco gas station on Township Line, he drove the car down there to see if it would pass muster and earn a state inspection sticker. For one thing, it became apparent that the motor was leaking coolant. That was remedied by installing a new freeze plug in the engine block. Additional needs included a new muffler and tail pipe, and the replacement of a cracked pane in the split windshield. The parts for the exhaust system were purchased at Midas

Muffler in Abington and the windshield glass was installed by firehouse member Dave Razzi at his shop in North Hills.

One thing was for sure; the classic vehicle was underpowered compared to more modern standards. The accompanying user manual said that the sedan had 25.35 horsepower. I wasn't about to break any land speed records with this chariot. Of course it was all a moot point anyway if I wasn't proficient driving with a floor-mounted stick shift. I had an idea of the concept, however, since Auntie's 1953 Dodge had fluid drive which was a hybrid of an automatic and manual transmission. Thus prepared, I ventured out one day on my own and managed to drive the car around the block without stalling. I don't remember if I made it past second gear though.

Despite its age, the Studebaker had an innovative feature called a "hill holder." Anyone who has driven a car with a manual transmission knows that it can be tricky taking off from a stopped position on the upward slope of a hill. One must quickly move the left foot from the brake to the clutch pedal and hit the gas before the car starts rolling back down the hill. The hill holder mechanism would cause the clutch pedal, when depressed, to hold down the brake pedal until you applied the gas and eased up on the clutch, thus disengaging the brake.

Another nice feature was the ability to crank open the windshield from the bottom, allowing fresh air to enter the cabin, not a bad idea before the advent of air conditioning for automobiles. So, in any case, I'd have wheels to take me to school occasionally in my senior year when September rolled around. But first there was another adventure in the works to attend to.

———

Go West Young Men

The excitement was building. Brother Bill would be released from the U. S. Army in August 1962. Our family was looking forward to having him home for good after three long years of service. His best friend, Tuck Hartmann, and I had been discussing the situation for a while, and we thought that it would be quite an adventure if we could meet him in Arizona on the day of his release.

So it was that we began planning a trip to Tucson, Arizona, the city close to his base, Ft. Huachuca. After investigating the options for a bit, we decided to make the journey via Trailways Bus Line. Leaving the terminal in Philadelphia, we'd arrive in Tucson about three days later. As I recall, the fare was about $85 apiece, one way.

I remember little about the preparations that we made for the trip: how many clothes we packed, how much money we'd take, etc. Back then credit cards were in little use, so we had to carry sufficient cash. I suppose that I drew funds from my PSFS student account. Neither Tuck nor I had embarked on such a journey before, so it was planned with a mixture of excitement and trepidation. Tuck was only 18 and I would turn 17 in September. Neither one of us had ever been on our own for such an extended adventure. Once we reached Tucson, we'd be in the care of my brother who was only 22 years old, but was hardened by three years in the military.

It was a late summer's afternoon that we made our way down to the bus terminal in Philadelphia. Tuck's girlfriend, Jean, was there to see us off, so I suppose that she may have driven us down. After we boarded and were ready to pull away, feeling a bit emotional, Tuck waved out the window to Jean and said to me, "I love that girl." My ties with Cheryl were rather tenuous by then, so I didn't feel much emotion in that regard.

We settled in for the first leg of the journey which would take us to Pittsburgh, arriving after dark. I can't remember if the bus stopped along the way for the passengers to grab a bite to eat, or not. The layover in Pittsburgh was to be about a half hour. We disembarked and roamed around in the passenger lobby for a while, stretching our legs. When we decided to board again, the bus wasn't where it left us. Panic suddenly set in. Did the bus leave without us and with our luggage? After several frantic moments, we discovered that the bus had only moved to refuel. Hearts beating rapidly, we finally were able to gather ourselves, board again, and continue our odyssey.

—

This was basically one continuous bus trip. We would only stop to have a meal, refuel, or change buses. The biggest adjustment would be trying to sleep on the reclining seats. Boy, did I miss my bed. One had to get used to the constant drone of the buses' motor, the sway of the vehicle, and the acceleration and deceleration along the way. There were no portable listening devices back then, so one had to make do with conversation, looking out the window, or reading. After a restless first night, we pulled into a bus stop in Steubenville, Ohio. There was a small restaurant there and Tuck and I secured a table of our own to have breakfast. Well, that plan went by the wayside quickly when a fellow passenger, a scruffy-looking elderly, bald man, sat down to join us for the meal. We affectionately gave him the moniker, "the old geezer." Of course we didn't refer to him in that manner to his face. In any case, he attempted to bestow his wisdom on us through idle conversation. When our collective meals were completed, he suggested that we shouldn't tip the waitress because "you'll never see her again." Tuck and I ignored his advice and put down a few coins after he left the table.

After our first change of vehicles in an unremembered bland terminal, we had to find new seats. Tuck, being my senior, decided that he would take the coveted window seat so that he could view the scenery along the way, while I had to put up with whatever the vista of the aisle would provide. As it turned out, Tuck selected a defective seat that would recline with the slightest pressure put upon it. It took him a while to situate himself correctly so the seat wouldn't audibly crunch down to the reclining position when not intended. Furthermore, a pretty girl sat in the seat across the aisle from me. To me this scenery was superior to the monotonous view outside of the window. Tuck was enchanted as well, trying to sneak a peak across my seat without looking too obvious. As we traveled along, he chastised me under his breath for not taking advantage of the situation by striking up a conversation with her. I was certainly too bashful for that. By the time that he finally convinced me to trade places with him at a bus stop, she had reached her destination. Besides, he had Jean back home.

If you would like three days of your life to feel more like a week, just spend them around-the-clock on a bus. Sleeping was only sporadic. Along with self-reclining seats was the overacting or underacting air conditioning with varying velocities of air from the overhead vents. We tried to amuse ourselves as best we could. In one instance there was a young native-American woman breast feeding her baby several rows behind us. Surreptitiously, Tuck and I would alternately try to catch a glance of this phenomenon by peering through the narrow space between our seats.

The last leg of the journey was through New Mexico into Arizona. When we boarded that particular bus, it was almost entirely filled with passengers. The only opening available to us was the bench seat at the back of the bus which was situated above the engine compartment. Crammed into the space, Tuck and I shared the seat with a Latino family whose young son swayed into my spot throughout the journey. Not only was the area extremely noisy from the drone of the engine; it was excessively hot as we crossed the western desert.

I believe that it was the early afternoon when we arrived at our final destination in Tucson. It wasn't long before brother Bill met us in the terminal. I was so glad to see him, but I had a terrific head cold from the torturous trip. After the joyful reunion, it wasn't long before Bill drove us to one of his old restaurant haunts for us to partake of supper. Evidently we all checked into a local motel to relax for a bit before we headed to the local motor speedway to watch the sprint cars race under the lights. Bill was a big racing fan and had attended the track frequently with his fellow service members during his stay in Arizona.

After our first good night's sleep in days, we headed out the next morning to visit some of the popular sites as we wended our way home. In Camp Verde, AZ we took in the majestic Montezuma Castle Monument which included ancient Pueblo Indian cliff dwellings. It was quite impressive. The welcoming sign stated, "This is not a castle, and Montezuma never stayed here." We all found that statement rather humorous and oft repeated it during the rest of our journey. Another point of laughter was Bill's early statement concerning the Saguaro cacti. These rather tall plants populated the otherwise barren desert around Tucson. Bill related that they only grew in that area. As it turned out, we saw them frequently even as we traveled farther afield. Of course Tuck and I wouldn't let him forget it.

As we traveled down the highway, I recall listening to two of Elvis Presley's new songs on the car radio – "She's Not You" and "Just Tell Her Jim Said Hello." They turned out to be a couple of my all time favorites. To me, in 1962, Elvis' voice was then at its peak.

The Grand Canyon was another must-see stop along the way. Although I had seen it five years earlier on our family trip out west, it never lost its wondrous appeal. Tuck had never seen it before and he took many photos with his Brownie camera. Neither Bill nor I had a camera with us, a fact that I regret to this day. It may have been the evening after we took in the canyon that we searched for a place to sleep for the night. Eventually we found a vacancy at an establishment which was not quite a motel. The only sleeping quarters were in an old storefront on the main street of the town. It was cheaper than the regular rooms, so that was fine with us.

After the long day, Tuck needed to change the film in his camera. As he began to do so, the back of the camera sprung open before he had a chance to roll the film to the end of the spool. Hurriedly, he scampered into a closet to attend to the situation, trying to keep the light from hitting the film and spoiling it. Bill and I laughed ourselves silly at the scene. Being quite tired, we all eventually fell asleep in our makeshift surroundings. Tuck discovered at the first morning light that his bed was situated in the front window of the store where he could be viewed by the passing public between the shabby curtains. This incident was added to the list of interesting events that we would retell throughout the years.

In the continuing, humorous string of events was an encounter with a rather kookie waitress one evening while dessert was being served to us at a restaurant. Evidently we all ordered apple pie, and after the plates were placed in front of us, the waitress giggled as she looked at the wedge of pie belonging to Bill or Tuck. She reached over and pulled out a human hair that was imbedded in the slice, extracting it with glee as pieces of apple clung to it. With a smile she said, "I don't think that you want that," and returned to the kitchen with the strand dangling from her fingers. I believe that we all enjoyed the baked goods anyway, which we consumed despite their compromised hygienic quality.

The next big tourist attraction in our sights was Rocky Mountain National Park. As we entered the park with Bill behind the wheel in his 1957 Ford Fairlane, the day was nice and sunny. Continuing on the ever-ascending roads through the mountains we witnessed the beautiful snow-capped peaks. In the higher elevations the sun became obscured as clouds moved in, and then it began snowing, right there in the middle of August.

As we continued on the next day, we stopped at a hat store in Estes Park, Colorado. Tuck wanted to buy a cowboy hat and found a suitable Stetson. The following day we heard on the news that a storm came by shortly after we had driven through, and the town was snowed in.

I'm sure that we visited some other attractions after that, but by that time we were all ready to head back home again. Of course as we continued, far from Arizona, Tuck and I would look out of the window and say to Bill, "Oh look, there's a saguaro cactus." Enough with motels, Bill and Tuck took turns driving through the night toward our final destination as I complained that I couldn't fall asleep in the back seat. Of course they both let me have it when I finally woke up after dozing off. Although I had a driver's license by then, I had never driven on a high speed thruway.

When we finally pulled into the driveway at 221 Cadwalader Avenue at the end of our long journey, Mom, Dad and Auntie were all there to happily greet us.

The Last Lap

Here it was. My senior year was right around the corner. When I was in elementary school, the thought of 12 years of scholastic endeavor seemed like an improbable concept.

With my brother out of the army, the family went into adjustment mode. I was no longer the center of attention at home, but Bill and I got along famously. Mom loved cooking for Bill, since he ate almost anything. My limited appetite was always an unwelcome challenge when it came time to devise the daily menu. On the occupation front, it was necessary for my brother to find new employment now that he was back in civilian life. Until he could get his feet on the ground, he took a job as a driver for Abington Cab Co.

Cheryl and I met a few times after I got back from the western trip, but the fire had gone out for me. She was too much of a butterfly for my liking, fluttering from one male interest to another, although she assured me that I was the only one, especially while I was away. The day came when I joined her in a walk down Cadwalader Avenue toward Township Line Road and I told her that I could no longer take her dalliances, and I was ready to move on. Her eyes filled with tears when I told her, but she knew I wasn't wrong. I said goodbye and turned back home, and she continued on her way back to her abode on Haines Avenue. We had never gotten to the point of "going steady," which was the standard of teenage commitment at that time, but it was still a difficult breakup for me.

As the school year began, I had no idea what I would do after graduation. The thought of going to college seemed remote, since I felt that I wasn't equal to the task. My yearbook said that I was going to become an accountant, but that profession seemed like it would be a rather dry, boring life path. There was still the thought of becoming an Evening Bulletin branch manager, and my local manager, Mr. Tangye, encouraged it. He wasn't a college graduate himself. But the thought of having to control a bunch of unruly teenagers on an ongoing basis to make a living, wasn't very palatable either. So, I'd just continue with the business curriculum and see how things would turn out.

It was good to see my friend Gary Burke back in home room class. We joked around incessantly when we got together in the morning before classes and during lunch hour. There was a strange guy named Ed – a sophomore I believe – that used to join us at lunch. Ed wore glasses, had buck teeth and a voracious appetite, though he was slender in build. If you left anything on your lunch tray after completing your meal, he'd scoop it up and consume it. We used to kid the poor soul unmercifully, but he didn't seem to mind. Being oblivious to our actions, he was probably just happy to have some friends of a sort. One day Gary thought that he'd see if Ed would possibly eat something out of the ordinary. Boxes of little pretzel sticks were sold at the lunch counter. When Ed wasn't looking, Gary took about five sticks or so and drew them through his mouth, covering them with saliva. Then he rolled the sticks on the cafeteria floor. When he placed the pretzels on the edge of his tray, Ed looked down, picked them up and eagerly ate them all. Gary and I couldn't contain ourselves and burst into laughter. Ed did have some plans for the future, however, assuring us that one day he was going to build an atomic bomb. One can imagine how that thought would go over in today's environment.

Gary and I also were in the same gym class – another venue for unremembered shenanigans. But it's Mr. Rickenbach's health class that we shared as students that sticks in my mind. During boring parts of class proceedings, such as when subclavian and femoral arteries were being discussed, we would murmur to each other, making jokes to the annoyance of a fellow student. One day Rickenbach caught Gary in the act during one of these episodes. Somehow I got away unscathed. After the class, the teacher took Gary to the front of the class and dressed him down. It so happened that Gary was facing the classroom door from a distance. While he was being berated, I stood there making faces, unbeknownst to Mr. Rickenbach. Trying to contain himself the best that he could, a sly smile would cross Gary's face as he attempted not to laugh out loud. This, of course, infuriated the teacher more. Finally I wandered down the hall a bit so Gary wouldn't be punished too severely.

—

While events were relatively calm in this teenager's life, there was a big confrontation brewing on the international front. On October 9, based on the suspicion that the Soviet Union was building missile silos in Cuba, President Kennedy ordered U-2 reconnaissance flights over the island nation. Over the next two weeks a high stakes chess game was played between the two Cold War adversaries in an attempt to defuse the situation.

Kennedy wasn't going to allow a facility, which could launch nuclear warheads at our nation, to be located so close to our shores. Rather than launching an attack to destroy the silos, Kennedy put in place an embargo on ships entering Cuban waters. Without getting into the details of all that followed, the Soviets ultimately agreed to disassemble the facility if the United States, in turn, would not deploy missiles in Turkey. In any case, it was a fortnight of high tension when the possibility of nuclear war seemed quite imminent.

—

I continued to do well in the business-related curriculum. Bookkeeping II, which included case problems of business accounts, required writing checks and maintaining ledgers, thus preparing students for the real world. Bookkeeping Math dealt with the principles of determining interest payments for loans as well as handling employee payroll. Although there were a half dozen or so adding machines available for use at the back of the classroom, I never utilized them. First of all, there was always a queue of students waiting in line, and second, I was rather proficient at doing the calculations on paper, thanks to the experience of completing manual spreadsheets as an Evening Bulletin branch captain. Robert Miller, the instructor for both classes, helped to make otherwise dry subjects interesting.

Problems of Democracy (POD) class wasn't a favorite of mine. The teacher, Miss Davis, was rather uncompromising and not a very friendly sort. On top of that, the student who sat next to me, John Purcell, would annoy me during the class by punching me in the arm. So that made it a bit difficult to concentrate.

In World Cultures class, taught by Mr. Haynes, an old fellow McKinleyite, Leander Adams, sat next to me. Leander wasn't necessarily known for his scholastic prowess, but he took it upon himself to memorize all of the United States Presidents in order of when they held office. This impressed Mr. Haynes who was famous for uttering the phrase, "How do you like them apples?" A military veteran, Haynes would often relate that he had served in the Marines. As it turns out, he didn't enlist, but was drafted into that branch of the service.

Haynes' classroom was arranged with the desks in the form of a horseshoe with open space in the middle. Directly across from me was Mike Huber with whom I became a casual friend. Mike was nominally a member of the tough guy or "rock" class of students. (These individuals were fairly easy to identify since they carried their school books hoisted under one arm pit.) It was Mike that stood up for me in a small incident with a more notorious student. So it was kind of a feather in the hat of a common guy such as me to have an acquaintance like Mike. We often made signs and gestures across the room to each other of a humorous nature. As an artist, Mike was extremely talented. One day before class started, he quickly drew a picture of a well-endowed, bare-chested woman who was pointing a pistol at the viewer. It had a three-dimensional quality and was quite sensuous. He presented the drawing to me, but I don't know what became of it over the years.

Mr. Haynes made a habit of giving homework with several pages of questions on the current subject with space below for writing the answers in long hand. It became apparent to Mike that the teacher rarely read the answers submitted. So, Mike would write off-the-wall answers such as indicating "Superman" as the name of a prominent figure, or providing a ludicrous description of a historical event. Well, this probably went undetected for a month or so until Haynes actually started reading some of Mike's answers. He wasn't a bit amused. Standing before the class and holding one of Mike's home work assignments, he angrily shared a few of his answers with the class, tearing off one sheet at a time from the stapled offering. It was all we students could do not to break into laughter. As it turned out, Mike got suspended for several days because of his effort. Well, years later after graduation, Mike became famous under the name Michael Buffer, the fight announcer who exclaims, "Is everyone ready to rumble!!!" He's made millions and millions for his effort. I have not.

—

The senior year instructor, who made the most long-term impression on me, was my English teacher, William Gavin. In his late twenties and a former resident of Jersey City, New Jersey, he had an interesting and humorous manner in the way he taught his craft. With his North Jersey accent, he would impart his knowledge while walking back and forth in front of the classroom in a semi-Charlie Chaplain-like manner. He would impart little nuggets of knowledge on how to write properly. For example, it was more effective to demonstrate the nature of a character by describing one of his or her actions, such as, "Mr. Jones strode down the street in haste and kicked a stray dog who happened to be in his path," rather than stating, "Mr. Jones was a mean man."

At the time, Gavin had several pieces published in William Buckley's famous conservative magazine, The National Review. Although he kindled a bit of a fire in me, I was still predominately a mediocre student who pulled a "B." It was one incident, however, that gave me hope. We were given the assignment to write a short story which we were to begin in class. As he walked around the room and observed, I began by writing several sentences. He briefly stopped at my desk and read my words, and then exclaimed to the class that some individuals instinctively have the ability to write. Well, that little bit of encouragement has stayed with me ever since.

A few years later Bill Gavin became a speech writer for Richard Nixon and Ronald Reagan, then subsequently was hired as an aid to a U.S. Senator and the minority leader of the House of Representatives, establishing a long career in politics. As an author he also wrote several nonfiction and fiction books.

—

As late summer turned into fall, another young lady from McKinley would capture my heart, and a long-lasting relationship would be initiated.

Go Long

In the fall, after Bill returned from active duty, the old Sunday afternoon tradition returned. After the family got home from our church in Germantown at about 12:30 or so, Bill and I would change into work clothes of a sort and high tail it down Cadwalader Avenue toward the playground, tossing a football back and forth as we proceeded. My brother would return in his roll as pickup game organizer and quarterback. Being QB was rather natural for him since he had a good arm, but rather lethargic legs.

One-hand touch was the rule for "tackles" since it reduced controversy. Participants included some of the regular McKinley gang of firemen and neighbors such as my friend John, Tuck Hartmann, Bruce Hall, George Hetherington, Richard and Sammy Hogg, Larry and Ray Kanear, Corky Donahue, "Snake" Sneddon, and other locals. Most notably we would knock on the doors of Billy Barr and Donny Shelmire, who both lived on houses across from the field, to see if they would come out and play – at the quarterback position of course. Billy and Donny were the older folk in their late 20s, or early 30s with their own families, so we gave them preference.

While stationed in Turkey, brother Bill had made friends with another soldier, John McGowan whose home was in Philadelphia. John and his brother, Danny, became Sunday afternoon regulars.

By the game rules, it took three pass completions to get a first down. There were no running plays. We all played hard for about two hours or so, or until it started to get dark early in November and December. As I remember, Tuck and Larry had great hands and pulled in a lot of receptions. George Hetherington was like a shape-shifter, who would bob, weave and squirm as he moved down the field with the ball, avoiding the flailing hands of "tacklers" along the way. Danny and I may have been the fastest players on the field and often ran long routes. Both of us, having good hands, often pulled in passes in-stride. However, quite often, we were on opposing teams and covered each other, so it became an ongoing challenge and competition to break up passes thrown to our opponent.

I very rarely went back as quarterback for a play since my arm strength was suspect, but I remember one instance, that may have been a trick play, where Bill, after taking the snap, threw me a lateral pass as he lumbered down the left sideline. My pass to him was perfect and he "sprinted" into the end zone for a touchdown.

Some of the most enjoyable games were played in the snow. The memories of game day are so vivid in my mind. On Monday after the games, my body would be so sore, that I moved around with great difficulty.

—

On the weekends John and I would continue to hang around together, often congregating at the firehouse to play pool or shuffleboard. Utilizing John's Chevy, we'd make our way to the Del Ennis Bowling Alley in Huntingdon Valley to play a few games, or head up to the gigantic Willow Grove bowling alley which was the largest in the world with more than 100 lanes. Meeting girls was always an aim, but never came to fruition since we weren't very proactive. I'd even take out the old Studebaker on occasion.

Some of the local girls tended to mill around the neighborhood with their friends when they weren't in their respective basements dancing to the latest tunes played on their 45s. Now being a member of the firehouse, I had the opportunity to make small talk at times with my paper route customer, Frank Morrish who was captain of the fire police. His daughter Dale – the girl who wore the modified "I Hate Elvis" pin back in 1956, was a year younger than I. She had a casual acquaintance with a High School Road neighbor whom I'll call Lois. Lois had also been a friend of Cheryl's, and I remember once seeing Dale with Lois on Haines Avenue the previous summer. Dale had been babysitting for someone, and she was carrying the infant around in her arms feeding it with a bottle, but I paid little attention to her.

Dale and Lois were complete opposites. As it turned out, Dale was sweet and unassuming while Lois was rather loose, shall I say, in her relationships. It was one Friday or Saturday evening in late fall when I received a short telephone call at home from Lois, I believe, telling me that Dale wanted to speak to me. Well, I heard her in the background, but she was too shy to get on the phone. I don't remember all of the particulars after that, but I would happen to bump into Dale more often on the street, and she was always there to answer her front door on Saturday mornings when I collected for The Bulletin.

When she answered the door, her hair and lipstick were always perfect. I remember the pretty arch of her upper lip and her cute nose. Since childhood she had worn glasses and I loved her in them. Our conversation was casual, easy, and unadorned. All I know is that I was very comfortable with her and their was none of the unnecessary drama that I endured in my relationship with Cheryl.

As it turned out, we began seeing more and more of each other. I'd go to her house on Friday or Saturday nights, and then it became both nights. Unfortunately this put a strain on my relationship with John since almost my whole focus was on Dale. John never complained, although it was a bit heartless on my part I suppose. There weren't too many other girls in the neighborhood that John was interested in at that time.

One weekend I finally got the nerve to ask Dale out for the movies. Playing at the Keswick Theater in Glenside was "Two for a Seesaw" with Robert Mitchum and Shirley MacLaine. So, that Saturday night I picked her up in one of my parent's cars, not my Studebaker, and took her to see the show. I remember that when we returned to the parking lot after the movie, we ran into Tuck and Jean. This became a regular routine and we began going to the movies every Saturday night. Dale would cut out the newspaper announcement for each movie that we saw together and put it in her wallet.

One Saturday evening, as I said goodbye on her front porch, I finally got the nerve to give her a kiss. I practically flew all the way home.

The Winter Chill

My great-uncle, Frank Burr, was beginning to fail at age 92. With this in mind, Dad had taken brother Bill and me to see him one Sunday, before the Thanksgiving holiday, in his little dark bedroom at my paternal grandparents' home in West Philadelphia. As a result of moving slowly into the semi-adulthood of my late teens, along with all the accompanying youthful distractions, I hadn't seen my old friend in quite a while. When Dad, Bill and I entered Uncle Frank's room, he was as jovial and sly as ever with those squinting, smiling eyes. Now that Bill and I were old enough to absorb it, his repartee was a bit racier than it was when I was young. He shared how his "snake" would still impress the local ladies. Near the end of our time sharing funny stories, but sensing that we would never see each other again, he handed me the old tools of his trade – his wood carving tools. I was taken aback, realizing how much he thought of me in bestowing this personal prize upon me. I thanked him profusely and did my best to hold back tears. Final goodbyes were shared shortly thereafter.

Thanksgiving day of 1962 was similar to years past. As had been the custom for many a year, Mom and Auntie prepared the holiday meal with all of the fixings, putting on the finishing touches after returning from our church service. The date, November 22, coincided with brother Bill's birthday, so it was a duel celebration. All the regular participants were there; in addition to the immediate family, Nan and Pop Pop, and Aunt Emma and Uncle Ad made their annual appearances.

It was shortly after Thanksgiving, on December 6, that Uncle Frank passed away. I barely remember the funeral. Later in the month Christmas day dinner was carried out in a similar manner as years past, but Pop Pop wasn't himself. He seemed to be grieving the loss of his older brother. As it turned out, it would be the last time that all of the regular participants would be together for the holidays.

On Sunday, January 6, 1963, one month to the day after Uncle Frank had passed away, Nan phoned Dad at home in the afternoon. Pop Pop, had taken a "spell" and wasn't feeling well. Dad arrived at their home as soon as he could. As Pop Pop was feeling weak, Dad held him close. Before dying in Dad's arms, he whispered, "I can see the angels."

Early in the evening Dad brought Nan to our home to stay overnight. She was trying her best to cope, but she would begin to tearfully remember her husband's last moments. Bill and I had been playing slot hockey in the living room, utilizing the table game that we had received for Christmas, trying to handle the whole situation through this distraction. We abruptly stopped playing as Dad brought Nan through the front door, but she insisted that we should go on with the game and remain cheerful.

The family settled down in the den as best we could, and I can remember the show Bonanza playing on the television. Being a fan of the show, Nan watched, trying to take her mind off of the loss of her lifetime partner as best the situation would allow.

—

My relationship with Dale was on an even keel, and I was seeing her on a regular basis. Having met my brother, she gave him a card for his birthday before Thanksgiving. This, I realized, was a hint for me to buy her a card for her birthday which was four days later. Of course I wasn't stupid enough not to comply.

One day in late January 1963, after Sunday School class at our church in Germantown, a younger female student, who also attended Abington High School in her sophomore year, asked if I would take her to the upcoming "Snow Ball Turnabout" dance – turnabout, since the girl asked the boy. Being caught off guard by this unanticipated invitation, I muttered, "Yes."

This sweet girl, whom I'll call Sheila, had never been on my radar, and I wasn't really attracted to her, but now I was committed. Even though Dale and I weren't going steady, I knew this wouldn't be accepted well by her. As the character William Bendix would say on the TV show, The Life of Riley, "What a revolting development."

When I confronted Dale with the terrible situation, she wasn't happy, but I told her that I was only interested in her, and

I had just been caught in a difficult situation. She accepted my explanation.

Well, I went to the dance, which was held in the high school gym, in early February, going through the motions and trying to act happy as best I could. Sheila's friend and her boyfriend also attended. Her friend was a Hungarian-American girl who managed to emigrate with her family to the United States around the time of the anti-Communist uprising in her native country in 1956.

In the days soon after the dance, I was back in Dale's good graces. As Valentine's Day arrived, I thought that it would be wise to give evidence of my increased commitment to our relationship. After I completed my paper route on that day, I rode my bike down to Davis' Drugstore and purchased a red, heart-shaped box of Whitman's chocolates and then made my way back to her doorstep. She gratefully accepted my gift with a huge smile on her face. As it turned out, her father was as happy as Dale to receive the gift because he loved sweets where she did not. Hey, it's the thought that counts.

Toward the Finish Line

I felt it was about time for me to "lock in" my feelings for Dale and present her with a token of my affections. In the 1960s it was appropriate for a boy to buy his girlfriend a friendship ring to seal the deal. With this in mind, I drove to McCutcheon Jewelers in Jenkintown to make my purchase. Would the depth of my feelings be better expressed with a ring costing $1.98 (sterling silver), or $2.98 (gold-filled). I thought it wise to go with the second option. Dishing out my hard-earned paper route money, I settled for the gold. Now, how would I present her with my gift?

Increasingly, I began driving to school in the old Studebaker rather than taking the bus. In the morning I would pick up Dale on High School Road so we could make the trip together. So it was on the morning of Friday, March 15, 1963 –

the Ides of March I must add – that she met me at the curb of her house and climbed into the old steed. After making a right on Township Line Road, I thought that the appropriate time was approaching. While slowly driving past Poinsettia Cleaners, I took the little box, containing the ring, out of my pocket and pretty much tossed it onto her lap. Despite my presentation inadequacies, she kindly accepted the token with glee and subsequently placed it on her ring finger, left hand. Not knowing her ring size, I had guessed. It turned out to be a bit big, but Dale compensated by wrapping a small band aid around it to close the gap.

That following Sunday was St. Patrick's Day and I walked to her house in the afternoon to spend a bit of time with her. Someone – I suppose her dad – took a picture of us standing at the top of the steps of her front porch. That was the first of many photos of us together.

Dale and I
St. Patty's Day, 1963

As my senior school year was winding down, preparations were being made for the climax of high school. Graduation photos were taken and year books were ordered. I continued to do well in my business subjects and this was recognized by my bookkeeping math teacher, Robert Miller. Near the end of every senior class year, Bloomsburg State College, in Bloomsburg, Pennsylvania held a contest for a selected group of students from participating state high schools, featuring the different business disciplines. Based on my scholastic record, Mr. Miller asked me if I would like to represent the school in business mathematics. I gratefully accepted, but wondered if I was up to the task.

Three other fellow classmates, Kathy Ditmar, Diane Marsh, and Carol Mayhew would also be participating, representing other business subjects. I believe that Kathy's was short hand, but I don't remember which disciplines Diane and Carol competed in.

Typing teacher, Mr. Hantjis, would be driving the four of us the two and a half hours to Bloomsburg where we would be staying at the town's old hotel. It was a small college community in a scenic portion of the state, southwest of Wilkes-Barre. After settling in that afternoon we all went to supper at the hotel restaurant and then congregated in one of the girl's rooms to discuss what to do to pass time in the evening. As I remember, there was only one movie theater in the town, so we decided to attend the show, the title of which is lost in memory. Before we left we began chatting about the various contests which would be held the next day. I related that I'd be tested on various disciplines like determining loan payments based on certain rates, as well as calculating payroll for a hypothetical company. I figured that in the payroll portion of the exam, I'd be supplied with the Social Security rate. However, I wasn't sure of the current rate which, I believe, had been recently increased. Kathy Ditmar said that she knew it and then shared the information with me. As it turned out, it was a good thing that she did.

On the morning of the test, I was ushered into a large classroom with probably 50 other students. Although confident in my abilities, I thought to myself; what are the chances of winning this contest? The test papers were handed out and we all began, pencils in hand. There were no electronic calculators back then, and no desk instruments were provided. When it came time to determine net payroll payments based on salaries and the various deductions, sure enough, the Social Security rate was not provided. Thank you, Kathy. I continued doing the work and completed all of the test questions in the roughly hour and a half provided. All that remained now was to make the group trip back home and await the results.

—

Now that Dale and I were happily going steady, it was only natural that I would ask her to the senior prom. Of course she accepted. Gail Croft – the daughter of Bob Croft, the owner of the bicycle shop on Jenkintown Road, and also my paper route customer – accompanied my friend John to the gala. Before that short trip, Mr. Morrish took several photos of us in our formal finery at Dale's house. I drove the four of us to the May event in my parents' 1962 Dodge Dart. This was before seat belts were standard in automobiles, and it was the custom that the girlfriend would sit close to her boyfriend driver.

The theme of the prom was "Moon River," the then popular song recorded by Andy Williams. We four sat at a table together, and we were joined by Allan Gargan and his girlfriend Pat. Dale and I danced to the wee hours of the morning and then made the way back to the comfortable confines of McKinley.

—

As my senior year wound to its conclusion, I continued to pick up Dale in the Studebaker in the morning for the daily trip to school. It was on a fine late spring day that we were making our way through the back streets of Jenkintown when the old steed lurched to a stop as the engine raced. Here we were, several miles from school without transportation. Dale was a good sport and began the long hike with me, but I'm sure that happy thoughts weren't dancing in her head during this forced march. After about 15 minutes or so, walking down Old York Road, we were spotted by Allan Gargan who was also driving to school that day. Thank goodness. Gratefully, the incident didn't harm my relationship with Dale, a good sign I suppose.

—

We seniors were all gearing up for the final exams, the last hurdle before the end of the long race. One day, before Bookkeeping Math class, Mr. Miller asked me to step outside the classroom to give me some news. I couldn't imagine what it must be. Gleefully, with a wide smile on his face, he congratulated me on winning the Bloomsburg State contest. I was ecstatic. It wasn't long after when the senior class award assembly was held in the gymnasium with the stands filled with students. What was to become my crowning achievement turned into my Charlie Brown moment. Award after award was announced over the public address system; student after student climbed down from the far reaches of the stands to accept their winning token. Well, the assembly finally came to a conclusion and I remained sitting on the bench seat, never having been acknowledged by the teachers or my fellow students.

The following day in Bookkeeping Math class, Mr. Miller apologized for the award mishap and announced my contest win to the class. Receiving applause and cheers from my classmates, I was presented with a gold-filled pendant with the Bloomsburg College seal affixed to it – acknowledgment of my first place win.

At a later school assembly, Abington "A" award certificates were handed out, and my achievement was acknowledged before the whole student body.

—

Some weeks prior to graduation I met with my guidance counselor to discuss my plans for the future. I was convinced that I didn't want to become an Evening Bulletin branch manager. Using some of the business skills that I had learned would be wasted, in my estimation, if I didn't purse a career in that line. The counselor told met that Bell Telephone was looking for applicants to fill some positions, so with that in mind she set up an interview for me.

One school day I took the subway train down to the Bell headquarters at their relatively new office building at One Parkway in center city. After meeting with a representative from human resources, it became apparent that the only job openings were for outside plant linemen – those who climb the telephone poles for repairs and installation. Looking more for an office job where I could utilize my skills, I declined the offer.

In one of our bookkeeping math classes a fellow student, Herman Plenzick, discussed the newly burgeoning field of electronic data processing. Herman had recently attended a presentation on the subject. It sounded interesting to me, although I didn't know what it entailed. About all I knew about the subject was the common IBM punch card that you would see now and then. In any case, Peirce Business School in Philadelphia was beginning a new two-year course called Business Automation Management. It wasn't exactly college, but it appealed to me. I thought that I would check it out before the summer got underway.

—

It was a hot early summer day when the graduation ceremony was held at Abington's football field on Huntingdon Road. Dale and my parents sat in the sweltering stands during the proceedings. Diplomas were, of course, distributed in alphabetical order by surname, so throughout the ceremony my friend, Gary Burke and I were able to keep up a low chatter. As it turned out, it would be the last time that we saw each other. Life took us on different paths.

Dale and I
after my graduation from Abington High

Getting Serious
and
Higher Education

Lost Summer

I don't recall if it was after the school year, or the beginning of summer 1963 when I made an appointment to visit Peirce Business School on 1420 Pine Street in Philadelphia to apply for admission to their Business Automation Management program. In any case it was in the early evening, one day, that I made the trip downtown by bus and subway to take a battery of tests to determine if I would pass muster.

The school representative described the curriculum to me – although I probably had received a brochure previously – and then I took the tests alone in a room. As I recall, the examination wasn't that difficult and I don't believe that it lasted more than an hour. So, based on those results and the grades on my high school transcript, I was notified several weeks later that I was accepted and would begin classes in September.

The tuition for the first year would be $650, and the amount would double the second year when I and my fellow students would be introduced to the specifics of the electronic data processing discipline. Similar to a freshman year in a business college, we would be learning rudiments of accounting, business mathematics, and business law in addition to liberal art classes such as English composition and psychology. The savings in my PSFS passbook account were close to $2,000, based on my paper route earnings, so there would be no problem paying the first year tuition plus textbooks.

Peirce had been established in 1865 with the primary goal of training veterans returning from the great Civil War and paving the way for them to enter the civilian workforce. My dad told me that his father had attended Peirce in the early 20th century, using the business skills learned to help run the family paint store in West Philadelphia which was established by my great-grandfather William H. Burr.

—

Since I wouldn't be 18 years old until the following September, I could have stayed on as a branch captain for The

Evening Bulletin and continued to deliver newspapers on a daily basis. But I felt that I had outgrown the job and decided to quit after graduation. Tom, a fellow carrier and former customer who lived on West Avenue, took over my position as captain. I don't recall his last name, but he lived next door to Bob Croft's family in the adjoining twin home.

My friend John took a slightly different tack than I by being accepted to RCA Technical Institute in Cherry Hill, New Jersey where he would begin classes in the fall. During the summer, John would work full time at Croft's Cycle Shop on Jenkintown Road.

I was virtually unemployed. I did make a stop at the unemployment office in Jenkintown one day to see if they had any summer jobs. A few days later I received a call about coming to a construction site in the borough to work as a laborer. Not being too keen on the idea, I used the excuse that I wouldn't have transportation every day since I didn't have a car of my own. So, I kind of whiled away the hot months for the most part, stopping by to see Dale from time to time during the week.

Of course my mom didn't like me sitting around, and I was getting bored anyway. Late in the summer/early fall, she suggested to Dad that he take me on some of his weekend painting jobs. He'd get me up early Saturday morning and get us prepared for the day, assembling the paint cans and brushes, and hoisting the ladders on the detachable roof rack on the car. Most of the jobs were for individuals who went to our church and lived in the Logan or Oak Lane areas of the city. Teaching me the fine arts of the trade, I was instructed to dip the brush into the paint and then tap it on the inside of the can rather than drawing it across the lip. In this way more paint remained on the brush. Being relegated to painting trim, I used a brush called a sash tool which was tapered and allowed me to make a straight line on the woodwork without having to use painters' tape. Of course dad had plenty of expertise, having worked full time as a painter and paper hanger before returning to work at the Frankford Arsenal.

Each workday we'd take a 15 minute break or so at noon and have a sandwich packed by Mom. And that was it. But I look back with affection on that time working side by side with him and learning some of the techniques of the trade. At the end of the day he'd pay me $20 for my effort.

Most of the summer Mom and Auntie would stay down at the cottage in Pleasantville, New Jersey and Dad would often drive down after work on Friday to spend the weekend. As fall rolled around, I was ready to take on Peirce.

Onto College?

September of 1963 came around quickly and I had to get into the routine of attending Peirce Business School. In order to prepare us for the business world, the male students were required to wear a coat and tie each day. This meant that I had to get moving in the morning and be on my way. Dad was my alarm clock and would come to the top of the third floor landing and yell, "Up and at'em!" If I didn't respond appropriately, he'd bellow again. I can still hear his voice.

Peirce's building was its original – a seven-story structure at the corner of Pine and Carlisle Streets in Philadelphia. I would make my way there most mornings by taking the PTC (Philadelphia Transportation Co.) XA bus from the corner of Cadwalader and Cypress Avenues to the Fern Rock subway station on Nedro Avenue in the far north of Philadelphia. There I'd take the underground train to the Lombard-South station on the Broad Street line.

During my first year at Peirce, the classes for all those enrolled in the general business curriculum would be taught in one room and the teachers of the various subjects would come to us during the different periods throughout the day. I believe that our room was on the second or third floor looking east toward Broad Street. One could walk up the steps to the appropriate floor, or take the elevator which was manually run by an operator. Having a surname beginning with "B," and the seats assigned in alphabetical order, I was situated near the end of the first row near the windows. The desks of the second row were adjoined to the first row, so the seat next to mine was an "H," in the person of Henry "Hank" Hess. We hit it off almost immediately, so I would have a friend and fellow classmate for the whole school year.

Hank lived in Millville, New Jersey and commuted to class daily. His hometown friend, George, also was attending Peirce, but he took a room at the YMCA in center city. The cast of teachers (not professors since it wasn't a college) was an interesting bunch. Some of their names now escape me, but a few stand out. Mrs. Sycamore was an older woman who taught English and spoke with much eloquence as if she were reading lines from a Shakespeare play, looking off into the near distance as though she was imploring her voice to reach the back of an auditorium. Evidently she had some background in acting because she indicated that she had spent time on the stage with the English thespian, Walter Pidgeon. In any case she was often amusing, although she wasn't intending to be so. Of course Hank and I would mutter to each other in low voices, not trying to burst out laughing. I remember that she took it upon herself to read Joseph Conrad's Heart of Darkness to the class over several days, utilizing her signature theatrical flair.

Our accounting instructor was the elderly Mr. Niemand who had an interesting speech pattern, especially where the letter "r" was concerned. For example, he pronounced "January" as "Janiary." This caused me to quietly burst into song one day with the chorus of "Janiary, Febiary, Hune or Huly" to Hank's amusement. However, he was an adequate teacher of the accounting discipline.

Mr. Groff was our business math instructor. He would test his pupils' acuity by audibly reeling off mathematical equations in rapid-fire style, such as: "69 divided by three, times 16, plus 81, minus 23, divided by four, times eight, equals ?" in an almost autistic savant manner. I don't think that I ever came up with the correct answer, losing my way after the third equation, but Hank was almost always up to the challenge, barking out the right answer to my discouragement.

Probably in his mid-70s, Judge Drummond was our business law teacher. Mostly bald and prim while wearing his ever-present bow tie, he would stand at the front of the class often chuckling at his own jokes. Another business education teacher, Mr. Schilling, was similar in age to the judge. Being very hard of hearing it was difficult for him to respond to a student's questions or to hear your answers. Rounding out the pedagogical staff was Mr. Armstrong who taught psychology, although I don't think that he had a background in that discipline.

In the first few months of study it was related to us by the college staff that Peirce was trying to upgrade their curriculum (the one we students were experiencing) so it would be certified as a junior college. By my second year of study the student body was notified that certification was granted and I would graduate with an associate degree in 1965 if I applied myself.

A Country Mourns

By November 1963 I was into the routine at Peirce. The ancient classroom with the creaky wooden floors started to feel like a second home. Lunchtime amenities were limited in the school's cafeteria. There were dispensing machines where one could buy tired sandwiches and small hot cans of Campbell's soup. A step up from this fare could be found at the Horn & Hardart Automat on South Broad Street. Better-looking sandwiches were available in their self-serve, carousel-type dispensers. And there were cafeteria-style offerings as well. Sometimes I would buy a hard roll and a lone hot dog and make a sandwich out of it. My fellow classmate Hank usually brought a sandwich from home, so lunch for me was pretty much a solitary affair.

On the home front, November was rich with two events – brother Bill's birthday on Friday the 22nd followed by Thanksgiving on the 28th. As I recall, mom was making a special meal in Bill's honor of which we would partake in the dining room – a step up from the usual meal-taking in the kitchen. As the school day was coming to a close on the 22nd, Mr. Niemand, our accounting teacher, walked into our classroom to tell us some very distressing news; President Kennedy had been assassinated in Dallas, Texas.

The classroom sat there in stunned silence. This couldn't be. One read of the assassinations of Lincoln and McKinley, but this was a different time in America – a time of hope with a youthful leader. Why did it happen? Who did this? It was too early for answers. All we students could do was make our way home where, hopefully, there would be some semblance of order and love.

As usual I made my way down the steps to the platform of the Lombard-South station on the Broad Street Subway line. Whereas I was now used to the dark dank cavernous environment with the telltale smells of urine, it now took on a more sinister and depressing aura. I don't remember anyone on the platform speaking to one another before the train pulled up. And the passengers on the subway car were just as silent as those waiting on the platform, save an elderly woman who sat across from me, openly weeping.

Upon arriving home I cannot remember if Mom put off having Bill's birthday dinner for a day, or if we partook of the meal that evening in a somber mood. Seeking the most recent news, I walked down to Doc Davis' drugstore to pick up the four-star edition of the Evening Bulletin which also include the late stock prices. Sometime during the evening we all watched TV as Air Force One arrived in Washington, D.C. with the new president aboard, Lyndon B. Johnson, and the remains of Kennedy. The coffin was ceremoniously removed from the plane and Johnson gave a short speech on the tarmac.

Much time was spent during the weekend watching around-the-clock news on the assassination. Lee Harvey Oswald was arrested under suspicion for the murder of Kennedy. Unbelievably, he too was shot and killed by Jack Ruby, a local bar owner, on Sunday morning, the 24th, as Oswald was being moved from his jail cell. The shooting was captured live on TV and shown over and over again.

Monday, the 25th, was designated as a national day of mourning, and citizens were encouraged to attend church services for the occasion. In response, a special service was held at our Christian Science church in Germantown and we all attended as a family.

Much has been written about the assassination and the aftermath, so I won't go into the details of it here, but it was as if the world had been turned upside down, which would usher in a decade of violence and civil unrest.

Another New Year

The Christmas holiday for 1963 was quiet. Mom cooked dinner as usual with the help of Auntie who made her famous pie crusts. Missing from the table for the first time, however, was my paternal grandfather who had passed away earlier in the year. Nan was currently confined to a home in the Oak Lane section of Philadelphia, having never really recovered emotionally from the death of her husband. But, sitting at the table, as in days of yore, were Uncle Ad and Aunt Emma. After dinner, Uncle Ad, Dad, and brother Bill commenced the annual three-handed pinochle game. I, for one, made my way to Dale's house on High School Road to exchange gifts. I missed her.

For New Year's Eve I bought a pair of tickets for Dale and me to take in the Ice Capades show which was to be held at the Arena skating rink in West Philadelphia. On that evening I drove down to Fern Rock station where we hopped on the subway to center city and transferred to the Market Street El which would take us to our destination. I'm sure that my parents were off somewhere for an evening of dancing with a group from church. Otherwise, 1964 was ushered in with little fanfare.

—

Studying at Peirce during the freshman year seemed much like an extension of high school. I plodded along getting half-decent grades, but not feeling motivated to any great extent. Courses related to electronic data processing wouldn't commence until the sophomore year, and I really wasn't sure what it would entail and if I would really be equal to the task. It's safe to say that I was in an academic funk. My friend John was learning vocational skills at the RCA Technical Institute in New

Jersey. After graduation in September 1964, he took a job with IBM in Poughkeepsie, New York as a Test Engineer to test components of their new 360 system. I felt like I was just treading water. In addition, the dark shadow of the military draft hung over my head, although I'd be exempt from service with a II-S student status as long as I was attending college, but that seemed of little comfort. Lyndon Johnson, early in his term after assuming the presidency, was engaging our military more aggressively in Southeast Asia, supporting South Vietnam against insurgencies from the north.

On weekends I visited Dale, continuing our habit of spending Friday evenings in the basement of her house watching TV and stealing kisses during commercials. Barbara, Dale's little sister, would sneak down from time to time to harass us. Almost every Saturday night I'd take Dale to the Keswick Theater in Glenside to catch a movie. Then we'd go back to my house to sit on the couch in the living room and listen to rock and roll music on the Philco portable stereo. As in the past, I'd help my dad on Saturday mornings with any house painting jobs he had in the works.

—

Late winter and early spring were always a time of renewal, especially when you were a baseball fan. My love for the underachieving Phillies was unabated despite their years of futility, never having won a world championship in their long history. Their young, scrappy manager, Gene Mauch, took over the helm in 1960 and the team finished in last place in his first two seasons. In 1962 the team managed to finish over .500 (albeit by one game) for the first time in many a year, but still wound up in 7th place in an eight-team National League. However, the Phils "skyrocketed" to 4th place in 1963, finishing 12 games over .500, so there was reason for optimism in 1964, especially after the team brought up hard-hitting Ritchie Allen from the minor leagues. It would be a season to remember – for the right and wrong reasons.

—

As mentioned previously, my paternal grandmother's health had been deteriorating for a while. Dad would go visit her on a weekly basis at the nursing home and was planning to make a special effort to visit her after work on her 76th birthday which fell on Thursday, April 16. Sadly, however, he got word that she passed away earlier in the day. It so happens that I was up in my third floor room that day when he came home in the early evening, having first visited the nursing facility to make preliminary arrangements with the funeral home. As I looked down from the window facing our side lawn, I saw him quietly strolling about in deep thought, absently looking at the budding trees and shrubs. It came to me that I should go down and try to comfort him, but I think that he desired solitude at that point, so I kept my silent vigil, trying to commune my love as best I could.

—

Dale and I had been going steady for one year on March 15 and our relationship remained strong. Since she was now a senior at Abington High School, it was only natural that she would invite me to her senior prom. Soon after this event, she took part in the graduation ceremony at the school's football stadium on Huntingdon Road. It was a torrid, sunny day, and I sat with her parents and her paternal grandmother in the stands overlooking the field. Mr. Morrish put up an umbrella to ward off the heat from the sun and a parent sitting behind us complained that he couldn't see the field. He quieted down after Dale's father rebuked him. Mr. Morrish was not a man who was slow to anger.

Shortly after graduation, Dale got a full time clerical job with First Pennsylvania Bank on Chestnut Street in the city. Each weekday she would commute downtown via the XA Bus and the Broad Street Subway.

—

After completing my first year at Peirce in late spring, I felt that I needed a more consistent part time job to earn some money. My brother's friend, Richard Hogg, occasionally worked on the weekends for an acquaintance, whom I'll call Kenneth, who ran a florist shop in Elkins Park near the train station. "Flowers by Kenneth" made a good deal of money by providing flower arrangements for big events such as bar mitzvahs. It was one of these affairs where I did my first work for him. My job was to staple decorative leaves on a white trellis which would be placed in a strategic location in the large gathering hall of a country club. Kenneth did all of the fine flower arranging, producing elaborate creations to be placed throughout the facility. Utilizing his large air-conditioned station wagon, we ferried the delicate flowers to the event. Afterwards he even gave me praise for my trellis work.

As spring shifted into summer, I began to work at Kenneth's on a daily basis. There was another worker from the Cheltenham area – several years older than I – who knew all the ropes of the business and performed some of the more artistic forms of floral art such as creating arrangements for sale. One of my main duties was cleaning up after everyone. Kenneth decided, however, that he could use another deliveryman, so the senior worker took me out one day in the florist's VW minibus. Of course the vehicle had a manual stick shift and my only other opportunity of using one was with my old, departed 1936 Studebaker. So, needless to say, it didn't come naturally to me, and their was a significant amount of audible gear grinding. But I did become proficient enough to do the job.

One of the peculiarities of the old Volkswagens was that they didn't have a fuel gauge, so when the vehicle started to sputter at an inopportune time, you had to pull a little lever which would allow you to use the one-gallon reserve tank, giving you about 20 miles to find a gas station. This happened to me on one occasion, but I was fortunate enough not to be in the middle of traffic when it occurred.

A decorative feature on the minibus was the placement of two black, decorative carriage lamps, one of which was placed on each side of the vehicle near the rear. I suppose this was meant to evoke an old world feel. In any case, I managed to drive too close to a street sign one day, dislodging one of the lights, but allowing it to dangle precariously by a couple of electrical wires. When I returned to the flower shop, Kenneth wasn't amused, but the other worker couldn't restrain his mirth.

Despite my misadventures, I continued to make deliveries. Most of Kenneth's clientele seemed to be well-to-do, but that didn't mean that he wouldn't service the poorer folks from time to time. In one instance, he had me make a delivery to an African-American neighbor who lived on Osceola Avenue, the street behind our house. When I knocked on the door, the dear working woman came out, and I gave her the flower arrangement. She said that she didn't order anything. When she called Kenneth to ask about it, he said that he thought that she would like it because it was so beautiful. He said that it wasn't necessary for her to pay for it right now; he'd just put it on her account. Obviously he was just taking advantage of her and I was embarrassed by the situation.

Kenneth's shop shared the same building with a dentist's office, and both utilized a common entrance. Evidently Conrad would display some of his artistic arrangements in the shared vestibule and outside steps. One day, as I was returning from a delivery, the dentist appeared in a mad rage and started to upend the baskets of flowers placed in that area and scatter them around the grounds. Evidently he had an ongoing dispute with Conrad about the situation and could take it no more.

If there weren't enough floral-type activities to keep me busy, Kenneth would find other jobs for me to do. This included refinishing the wood floors with a large orbital sanding machine and then staining them. In addition, he had me paint all of the woodwork. Having done similar painting work with my dad, the results were very presentable. Of course I was doing this for the same $1.25 an hour wages, even though it should have been a higher paying job. I mentioned this to him, and he just shrugged his shoulders and said, "I know."

On July 7 of that summer, I was doing some work on the front steps of the florist shop, and I had a portable radio tuned to the Major League baseball all-star game. It was becoming the Phillies magical season and they were in first place in the National League. Johnny Callison, the Phillies' right fielder, was representing the team for the National League. It was the bottom of the ninth inning and Callison stepped to the plate with two men on base. He hit the first pitch over the right field wall off of Dick Radatz for a walk-off home run to win the contest, earning him the game's MVP award. These heroics came only weeks after Phils' pitcher Jim Bunning's perfect no-hit game against the Mets on Father's Day.

By mid-August the floral business was in a seasonal lull. Conrad, one morning, in an effort to cut his expenses, I suppose, terminated my employment. Knocking the lamp off of the side of the VW minivan probably didn't help my job prospects much, either. It took me by surprise in any case. I tried to hurry home because I knew that Mom and Auntie were heading to the shore that morning, and I thought maybe I'd take advantage of the situation. I was too late, however. As I recall, I didn't have a car and I had to walk the several miles to get back to Cadwalader Ave. The next day I realized I had left my light jacket at the shop, so I called Kenneth to make sure he would put it aside for me. He insisted that it couldn't be found. In the year ahead, Kenneth would call our house several times when he had a big job to do since he needed the extra help. I declined any further offers.

—

Soon after I completed the first year at Peirce in early June, the English department sent a letter home with a list of books that I should read before the second term started in September. For some reason I made my way downtown to visit a bookstore located in the catacombs of the Penn Center train station. I suppose that there weren't any local shops to buy books in the McKinley area. On the list were An American Tragedy by Theodore Dreiser, Billy Budd by Hermann Melville, and For Whom the Bell Tolls by Ernest Hemingway. I purchased them all and brought them home.

Although I still wasn't much of a reader of books, I thought that I'd better get motivated. Hemingway's novel caught my interest, so I started with that. I was aware that he had committed suicide a few years earlier. About all that I knew about him were his exclusive articles in Life Magazine which were centered on bull fighting in Spain. Well, I was captivated by the book's narrative in short order, and had trouble putting the book down. The horror and intrigue of the Spanish Civil War was personified in the character of Robert Jordan who was an American fighting for the Republic's cause against General Franco's Fascists. Also, drawing on my latent feelings of lust, was Jordan's relationship to the psychologically damaged, but beautiful, Maria. It was a poignant love story which described "the act" in an artful, but sensuous, manner. Suspense built throughout the story leading to its tragic conclusion. It remains, to this day, my favorite novel.

The relationship between Dale and me remained strong, but her mother felt that we were getting too serious, and we should take the opportunity to date other individuals. So, one summer day we discussed the situation, and decided, reluctantly, that maybe this was the best course of action. Dale handed me her friendship ring and we talked for a while. Her only stipulation was that I promise not to date a specific individual who lived nearby. It probably wasn't more than 15 minutes or so when we realized that this was a bad idea, despite her mother's imperative. In no time, the ring went back on and we hugged and kissed amidst a few tears.

—

During the dog days of summer 1964, there was an incident halfway around the world which would set the stage for a decade of international upheaval. On August 2, the USS Maddox, a destroyer deployed in the Gulf of Tonkin in Southeast Asia, was attacked by a North Vietnamese torpedo boat in international waters. This would set the stage for a congressional resolution escalating our involvement in military actions against North Vietnam in support of the South. What was not known to the American public at that time was our country's previous, ongoing support of South Vietnamese raids along the North's coast which were orchestrated by the Defense Department. Essentially the attack on the Maddox became an excuse to go to war. Being of draft age, but currently protected by a student deferral, this could have implications for me down the road.

More happily, however, the Phillies continued their winning ways, entering September in first place in the National League while beating up on the league's two new teams, the New York Mets and the Houston Colt 45s. In any case, I was ready to start the new term at Peirce and see what this electronic data processing stuff was all about.

A Pivotal School Year

It was September again, and I was back at Peirce getting ready for my second year of study. On our first day of orientation I ran into Hank Hess, but he wouldn't be around for long, having decided that his course of proposed study didn't appeal to him. He had other plans, and I wasn't to see him again for a number of decades.

Unlike my previous year of study, I would be moving from classroom to classroom, following the teachers rather than the teachers coming to me and my classmates. The morning sessions consisted of normal business management courses such as marketing, statistics, and office management. Liberal art classes such as English composition, public speaking, and applied psychology, were also in the mix.

Afternoons were spent in the renovated basement of the school which was air conditioned to provide a suitable environment for the electronic data processing (EDP) machines. There were perhaps 16 individuals enrolled in this particular field of study who were divided into two groups – glass walls dividing the classrooms. This was to be the first year of the Business Automation Management curriculum. Now that Peirce had become accredited as a junior college, I would receive an associate degree at the end of the school year if all went well.

Initial EDP studies covered the basics, such as the Hollerith Code on the ubiquitous IBM punch card – understanding the 80 rows of 12 positions and how punched holes in those positions related to coded numbers, letters and special characters. Using data written on coding sheets, we were taught how to transcribe information onto the IBM cards via the card punching machine. Case studies were developed by the teachers – most notably Mr. Meitzler – where account numbers and monetary data were punched onto specific fields. (Mr.

Meitzler had this unique ability to catch flies in the air and throw them onto a hard surface to kill them) The first machine that we learned to use was the card sorter. For example, if you wanted the cards to be in order by three different fields such as account, date and dollars, one would sort the cards three separate times in reverse hierarchical order. During the noisy process, cards were electronically read and deposited in various stackers. One had to be certain to pick up the processed cards in the right order. The machines were prone to jams and the cards would get mangled in their various mechanical components.

After becoming proficient in the use of the sorter, we were taught how to program more sophisticated machines like the collator, which was used to merge two stacks of cards, followed by the 407 accounting machine, which read the processed cards and printed business reports on continuous form paper. Programming was accomplished by manipulating replaceable wires on slotted panels which were inserted into the 407. The position of the wires in various slots determined how the data was processed and how it would appear on the printed reports. It required logic on the programmer's part, and I soon found that I had the aptitude to accomplish these tasks – many of them relatively difficult.

As the first semester wore on, we were assigned case problems to solve through sorting, collating and processing specific data to accomplish required results. I was equal to the task and felt a bit emboldened by my progress.

Not having Hank Hess around any more as a friend and fellow classmate, there was a bit of loneliness, I suppose. But this void became filled by my association with Jim Moyer. Jim was nominally a Mennonite who lived in Perkasie in the far Philadelphia suburbs, so he had a long commute every day. He, as well as I, seemed to have the knack for the data processing discipline. As a result, we became friends. Being a high achiever, he became an example to me. His goal was to get top grades in all of his subjects, be it EDP or those of a traditional nature. The situation made me more competitive. It was as if a maturity light finally went on in my head and I became driven to study more diligently and succeed.

—

During that first month of school in September 1964, the Phillies continued their dominance of the National League. As of the 21st of the month, they had been in first place since July 17. On the 21st, with only 12 games to play in the season, the Phils were ahead of the Reds and Cardinals in the standings by six and a half games, and the Giants by seven. All looked good in Mudville. In the top of the sixth inning of the game against the Reds that night, the dangerous Frank Robinson came to the plate with Chico Ruiz on third base. Inexplicably, Ruiz stole home. It was the only run scored in the game, and the Phils were on their way to a 10-game losing streak.

In statistics class during that streak, professor Millar used formulas to determine the likelihood of the Phils blowing the pennant. We were assured along the way that it wasn't a strong possibility. Fans all across Philadelphia, however, were getting a sinking feeling that the Phils may blow it again. Here was the team that hadn't gotten into the World Series since 1950, when they were swept in four games by the hated Yankees. Despite Millar's calculated statistical analysis, the Phils defied all convention and lost the pennant to the St. Louis Cardinals, landing in a tie for second place with the Cincinnati Reds.

During the 10 game losing streak, manager Gene Mauch used his two pitching aces, Jim Bunning and Chris Short, on two days rest. When he finally gave them their required breather, the Phils won the last two games of the season, but by then it was too late. Having won the pennant, the Cardinals went on to be triumphant in the World Series against the Yankees. The whole situation put Philadelphia fans in a state of shock and disgust that wouldn't subside for another decade or more.

—

On the political scene, Mid-autumn saw the election of President Lyndon B. Johnson as president for a full term. It had been a racially charged Democratic nominating convention during the summer in Atlantic City, New Jersey. African-American representatives protested an all-white delegation being seated for Mississippi. Johnson, however, easily beat his

Republican adversary, Barry Goldwater in November. Coming from a Republican family, I favored Johnson nonetheless since Goldwater seemed a bit too extreme in his conservative views. He was against national civil rights legislation, and felt that the federal government should be small government. At the Republican National Convention in San Francisco, he uttered the famous words in his acceptance speech: "extremism in the defense of liberty is no vice!" Being a military hawk, he was for escalation of the war in Vietnam. Although I was now 19, I couldn't cast a vote in the election anyway, since the voting age for national elections was still 21.

—

As the Christmas holidays approached in 1964, Dale and I were still going strong in our relationship. Looking for a gift to show my love, I thought that it would be appropriate to buy her a hope chest. Shopping with my mother at Marbett's Furniture Store in Glenside, I picked out a maple cedar chest of colonial design. On Christmas day, dad helped me get it into the den back home, and I filled it with additional small gifts and topped it all off with a big red bow on the lid of the chest. In the early afternoon I picked Dale up from her house on High School Road and brought her back to celebrate the day. Leading her into the room containing her special present, she broke down in tears of happiness when she saw what I bought her. (This very chest is located at the base of our bed today, and I have often cracked my knees inadvertently on the sharp corners of its lid.)

A new year was right around the corner, and events in 1965 would be critical in determining my future employment prospects.

Professions

Although the world of data processing was showing promise, and I was finding my niche in that discipline, the literary world whispered to me from the not so far reaches of my mind.

It was the inspiration of my American Literature professor, Frank Pennypacker, which pointed me in this direction. As we progressed through the reading list of the previous summer, I found class discussions on the various works thought-provoking. And the analysis of poetry, especially that by Robert Frost, was capturing my imagination. The year 1965 was starting off on the right foot.

Mr. Pennypacker's words of encouragement, like those of my high school English teacher William Gavin, gave me hope that I could be a writer someday. Receiving positive feedback from the essays and short stories that I wrote for the class, this feeling was reinforced. I was pulling an "A" in the subject.

Public speaking class was more of a challenge for me. It wasn't easy getting up in front of your peers and delivering a coherent talk on a subject while blood was rushing through your veins and your knees were a-knockin'. Having a basic interest in science, I chose the topic of Einstein's Theory of Relativity. Not having a deep knowledge of the facts, I tried to give an overview of the theory, such as how the speed of light was the only constant in the universe, traveling at 186,282 miles per second. And, if you tried to reach that speed, you would turn into energy. Strangely enough, once I stood before the class and gave my spiel, the nervousness abated and I got through the ordeal while using my notes only sparingly.

—

On the social scene, everything seemed to be falling into place. Jim Moyer and I were becoming close friends, and I began interacting more with other students in the BAM curriculum. These individuals included the Detweiler twins – David and Dennis –, and Dan Slemmer, among others. I was starting to feel the pull of the world outside of McKinley.

As February rolled around, word went out that Peirce would be sponsoring a Queen of Hearts dance for Valentine's Day. Of course I invited Dale, and she accepted. The affair was held in a large room on one of the upper floors of the Bellvue-Stratford Hotel on South Broad Street in Philadelphia – the future site of the infamous Legionnaire's Disease scare in 1976. But that disastrous event was years in the future.

For the evening, Dale wore a beautiful dark pink dress, and I a suit and tie. President of the college, Thomas May Peirce, was in attendance with his wife. I don't remember, at all, the music that was played. But I do remember paying 50 cents for a six ½ ounce bottle of Coke, the price of which I thought was rather exorbitant.

—

The second, and final semester at Peirce, was dominated by the study of computer programming in the school lab. I knew little or nothing about computers as did my fellow classmates. Whereas large corporations, until those recent times, handled customer billing by a phalanx of clerks sitting at desks with adding machines and paper ledgers, the number of accounts that had to be processed monthly was growing exponentially and it was becoming too great a task for raw manpower alone. Smaller companies could still get by with only punch cards and accounting machines, but they didn't have the speed and agility to handle the complex logic required by large corporations. General purpose computers could be programmed to process data in an almost infinite manner, depending on the instructions given to the system. Peirce was one of the few institutions at that time to offer courses for this technical discipline.

Our training centered on a fixed word-length computer called the Monrobot. This machine was first offered to companies in May 1960 by the Monroe Calculating Machine Division of Litton Industries. The whole system was placed in an "L" shaped desk configuration containing the central processing unit (CPU), a punched card reader, a paper tape reader/writer, and an electric typewriter for reports. The electronic memory was housed on a rotating magnetic drum which contained 1,024 (1K) words of 32 bits each. This pales in comparison to today's desk-top computers which often have one trillion bytes of memory. But, for all its limitations, programming the Monrobot was similar to programming the large scale IBM computers of the day.

January into March we were taught all of the fine points of the Monrobot by our instructor, Mary Picado. We were given 15 programs to write over that period. It was challenging, but very interesting, and Ms Picado kept our feet to the fire. Each night I'd sit at my desk in my third floor bedroom on Cadwalader Avenue, analyzing each case study. Then I'd draw flowcharts depicting the step by step logic which would manipulate the input data to produce the desired results. Utilizing that logic, I'd put down the specific Monrobot machine instructions on coding sheets to be transcribed to punch cards the following day in class. I had never studied this hard before, being engrossed in the problem solving.

Sitting at the Monrobot console (actually an electric typewriter) in class, I'd load the program on punch cards into memory and then process the data input – from either additional punch cards, the typewriter, or paper tape. As March came to an end, I had completed all of the 15 case problems successfully. Jim Moyer and I were running neck in neck in the academic sweepstakes.

Hopeful Spring

Spring was here, and hope was in the air. Studies at Peirce Junior College were going well, and I was still ensconced in the McKinley community.

Brother Bill and I still lived at home, partaking of Mom's home-cooked meals every evening. Becoming involved in the insurance industry, Bill was now working for Underwriter's Salvage Company. Our neighbor and friend, Tuck Hartmann, was up in New York attending Rochester Institute of Technology (RIT) while pursuing an Associate Degree in Graphic Design. This was his first school year at that institution with the goal of graduating in the spring of 1966. My friend John was making a career for himself at IBM in Poughkeepsie, New York.

Always one to play the field, Bill dated a number of different girls, in and about McKinley, and girls who were acquaintances of members of our church. I, on the other hand, was a one-girl man, happy with my sweet Dale. Continuing her employment at First Pennsylvania Bank in the city, I'd see her each weekend night, watching TV or going to the movies. In the absence of Tuck, Bill would often go out one night each weekend with other friends from McKinley and environs such as Corky Donahue, George Hetherington, Tommy Gatter, and Teddy Culp. That tight-knit group would often frequent the automotive race tracks in the area during the warmer weather.

Bill, Dad, and I were still active in McKinley Fire Department, running to fires when the siren sounded day or night. However, now that school studies were foremost in my mind, there were times that I didn't answer the call in the middle of the night, especially if I knew that there would be an important test scheduled the following day. Dad was perennially elected for terms on the board of directors, and Bill was becoming more involved in the firehouse government as well, eventually becoming president. Tip Leary continued as chief, being unopposed for that position in yearly elections.

Ever the organizer, Bill would become manager of the fire department's softball team. I'd give my best shot at second base where I was an erratic fielder. Being an effective singles hitter, however, I usually batted first in the lineup. In another sports related activity, the two of us would play paddle ball on the courts of Alverthorpe Park located on Forrest Avenue. At home, the ping pong table was always set up in the basement where we would often play a game after supper, or take each other on in a game of slot hockey on the card table set up in the livingroom. We enjoyed each other's company and the competition.

Firehouse Crew after winning a trophy in parade (1965)
First Row:
Bobby Schneeweis, Ed Schorn, ?, Al Grimshaw, ?, ?, Ed Geissler, Jr.
Top Row:
?, Ed Geissler, Sr., Joey Thomas, ?, Tip Leary, Me, Tom Hartmann,
Bill Burr (Bro), Ray Rickard

—

It wasn't all study at Peirce. There had been a class trip to the 1964/65 World's Fair at Flushing Meadows, New York. It was a beautiful warm spring day, and I visited the various sites with my fellow classmates. The Hall of Presidents sticks in my mind where automatons such as that of Abe Lincoln moved spookily and gave a speech. We all stopped for refreshments at the Lowenbrau Beer Garden. Being a teetotaler I didn't partake of the suds like my classmates, but settled for a root beer instead. The waitresses were beautiful, sporting ample cleavage and, remarkably, unshaven legs.

Also, late in the spring, a bunch of my classmates and their girlfriends, including me and Dale, attended a Phillies game at old Connie Mack Stadium at 21st and Lehigh in North Philadelphia. But, despite these friendly distractions, studies at

Peirce were becoming more critical as the school year was coming to a close and work prospects had to be considered.

—

Peirce was advertised as always being available to help their students find employment, even years after graduation. I for one didn't want to wait years. On April 14 I received a letter inviting June graduates to attend a meeting with the placement director where we would talk about topics such as "application forms, resumes, work training programs, salary ranges, job hunting, interviewing techniques, and how to size up a job offer." I have no recollection of the session, but I do remember formulating a resume shortly thereafter. When the need for references came up, my English professor, Mr. Pennypacker came to mind. Having a good rapport, and knowing that I did very well in the subject, I asked him, after class one day, if I could list his name. He replied that he surely would, but cautioned me that I had too creative a mind to become merely a computer programmer. I meekly replied, "but writing programs is creative." But I understood what he meant and it troubled me somewhat.

—

Shortly after meeting with the placement director, certain of the students taking the EDP curriculum, were scheduled to meet with representatives of The Bell Telephone Company of Pennsylvania to be interviewed for possible job opportunities. Having substantially exhausted the pool of in-house candidates from craft jobs to positions in computer programming, they were extending their search to prospective Peirce graduates. During the third week, or so, of April, I and several other candidates were interviewed by two Bell directors. Howard Dreisler managed the programming system support group at Bell. The company's internal EDP programming school was also under his purview. Mr. Dreisler had a rather direct approach, asking a lot of technical questions while not accepting evasive answers and giving no quarter. I'm sure that he was aware, however, that I was doing very well in the EDP curriculum.

The other interview was conducted by Ray Smith, the director of college recruiting. He was a young man of about 27 years of age, so he was obviously on the fast track for promotion, having already attained a director position. As I recall, he smoked a pipe and was very genial. His purpose, I suppose, was to see if I had potential managerial, as well as technical, talent. Mr. Smith, by the way, later became CEO of Bell Atlantic a few years after the breaking up of AT&T and the Bell System in the 1980s.

On April 27 I received a letter at home from Bell from their General Personnel Supervisor, stating:

> Dear Mr. Burr:
>
> > Mr. Smith has told me how much he enjoyed meeting you.
> >
> > We would like very much to have you visit our Company to further discuss employment possibilities on Friday, May 7, 1965. Please be in my office at 8:30 a.m. on the 14th floor of the above address (One Parkway, Philadelphia). If you have any questions, please call Mr. Smith on
> > . . . . .
> >
> > We look forward to seeing you.

The following week I received another letter from Bell, dated May 10, that I was being offered a job in their Philadelphia Programming Department at a starting salary of $500 per month. This offer was contingent upon my receiving a Business Automation Management degree and passing the company physical. I had until May 18 to give them my decision.

Well, I was warily ecstatic. Mom was quite proud of me for receiving such a generous offer for a mere 19-year-old. Gnawing at me, however, were Professor Pennypacker's words. The opportunity of working for an established company which offered lifetime employment was hard to discount, but I realized that this was quite a commitment. One afternoon after receiving the letter, I remember walking the downtown streets of Philadelphia in a bit of a daze, wondering if I should accept a position which would tie me to the corporate world for years to come. The lure of the prospects and the money, however, were too much, and I accepted the position.

Other Peirce candidates who were offered programming positions were my friend Jim Moyer, Dick Cummins, Bill Herr, and Jack Pensabene. All of us passed the company physical and were told we would begin employment on June 14, 1965 – Flag Day.

—

As graduation at Peirce drew near, the institution was also celebrating its 100th anniversary. On a sunny afternoon, students of Peirce assembled in front of the building on 1420 Pine Street where several speeches appropriate for the occasion were offered by various dignitaries including Philadelphia City Council President, Paul D'Ortona.

The first ceremony for associate degree graduates in Peirce's history was held at the University of Pennsylvania's Irvine Auditorium. After the proceedings, Jim Moyer and I planned our next interim step.

Employment
then
Call to Duty

One Last Fling

It was great getting a meaningful job right out of college, but it didn't offer much time for a respite before we launched on a career. My fellow classmate and friend, Jim Moyer, felt the same way. The question was: What could we do on such short notice?

My family's house (glorified shack?) in Pleasantville, New Jersey was surely not a vacation haven, but one couldn't beat the price. I approached my parents with the idea of the two of us spending a few days at the house, and they quickly assented. Not having a car of my own, Jim agreed to provide the transportation. So after a leisurely ride to Pleasantville one sunny June morning, we settled in.

Neither one of us was flush with cash, but we were able to manage. Poor Jim was in a compromised mental state, since the girl that he dated throughout much of his days at Peirce unceremoniously broke off the relationship recently. So, being on the rebound, he was attracted to some of the young women we encountered along the way – especially a waitress that served us at a restaurant on the boardwalk in Atlantic City. But I, being loyal to Dale, put a bit of a damper on the proceedings. In any case, all went well as we went about relaxing the best we could.

I provided direction to several of our family's old haunts, bathing at Ventnor's beach and walking the boardwalks of Atlantic City and Ocean City. Not having a lot of spending money, we couldn't eat at restaurants on a regular basis. One evening, back at the house, we were starving. In the pantry we found a large can of Chef Boyardee meat ravioli. I think that we boiled the can in a pan of water and then poured it out. Surely not a gourmet meal, but our hunger was satiated nonetheless, although there was a lot left over.

—

The particulars of that first day of work at Bell Telephone don't come to mind, but I know that it was primarily concerned with orientation. During that first week we would meet with various department heads in their sizable offices. Situated in his 12th floor abode at One Parkway, with a beautiful unobstructed view of the Philadelphia Art Museum in the distance, was Ian Robinson. As General Accounting Supervisor, he commanded respect, sitting behind his large desk as our entourage entered for a visit. Having a long career in the Bell System, he offered his learned view of the company and how we would become an integral part of the organization, providing essential data processing services. Being originally from Georgia, I believe, he delivered his good-old-boy spiel with a marked southern accent.

Our group of new employees did not include only Peirce graduates, however. In addition to the "Peirce five" were two male associate degree graduates from Penn State – whose names I can't recall –, two female four-year college graduates, Irene Bolton and Pam Smith, and a former vocational bell employee, Joe O'Donnell. As a commentary on the times, it took the female trainees four years of college to reach the same employment status of us two-year males from Peirce, although the company gave the women a slight advantage in salary treatment.

During that first week of orientation we also visited other Bell sites in the city to give us an overview of the company's vast communication operations. At Ninth and Race Streets we observed "the frame" where rooms full of switching equipment were maintained.

Down Arch Street at the 1835 location, was the Philadelphia Revenue Accounting Center (RAC) where customer bills were processed. We got our first glance of the large scale IBM 7074 computer with its bank of drives with whirling magnetic tapes. It could take up to a day to process a cycle of customer bills. IBM 1401 medium scale, or slower, computers were used to transfer stacks of customer input punch cards to magnetic tape which would be processed by the 7074. Output tapes from the 7074 went back to the 1401 computers to print telephone bills to be mailed to customers.

In another room very large reels of wide paper tape – maybe three feet in diameter – registered long distance toll calls. When a customer initiated a call, information was automatically punched into the slow-moving tape. More holes were punched when the customer completed the call. When a roll was full, it was converted to magnetic tape where it would later be processed on the 7074 in a separate toll processing cycle.

Three other regional RACs were located in Harrisburg, Greensburg, and Conshohocken, Pennsylvania.

Now the real test would come. In our second week on the job, we relative neophytes would undergo training that would entail programming the large scale IBM 7074 computer.

The Long Grind

During the second week of our new employment at Bell Telephone in the summer of 1965, we attended class at an IBM facility which I believe was on Market Street in Philadelphia. Teaching us the ins and outs of programming the 7074 computer was Jim Shea. Shea was an amiable bear of a man who methodically took us through the instruction set of the 7074. Although he was no-nonsense, he had a sense of humor.

First we learned the internal architecture o f t h e 7 0 7 4 which was a fixed word length computer which housed ten thousand words that could be used to hold either instructions or data. Each word could hold either 10 digits or five alphanumeric characters. So, in essence, the 7074 had the capacity of up to 100,000 bytes of information in a computer that took up much of a room. There are thousands of times that capacity in a modern day thumb drive that can be carried on a key chain.

For the remainder of the two weeks we coded case problems using the Autocoder instruction set to manipulate, move and calculate data. All mathematic work had to be accomplished through one of three specialized computer registers, the results of which were stored in the regular memory words.

In any case, the discipline came rather easily to me since what I had learned at Peirce on the Monrobot was similar enough. The only problem was that we didn't have a 7074 computer to test our programs because time on the system was too restrictive. I believe that Irene, Pam and the two male students from Penn State had previously used the FORTRAN language in college which was used mainly for scientific calculations. It appeared that Irene and Pam had no problem keeping up with the pace, but the Penn State boys seemed to be having trouble adjusting. Although Joe O'Donnell had no previous programmer training, he seemed to take the lessons in stride.

—

The following weeks of training were conducted in Bell's One Parkway building on the second floor in Conference Room 2B. Each day I would commute from McKinley via PTC's XA bus and the Broad Street Subway. Occasionally, if brother Bill was going to a fire loss with Underwriter's Salvage, and his route was close to Fern Rock Station, he'd leave me off there during his morning drive, thus saving me the bus fare and some of the hassle of the trip.

At One Parkway we all sat at a long table in the conference room while two members of the Bell computer training center – Bob Stackhouse and Carol Lewis (he was a man) – put us through our paces. Unfortunately the first week or so was just a repeat of what we learned at the IBM facility – quite boring. But, subsequently, we were given a case problem to code which entailed customer billing and reporting. It was at this time, I believe, that the employment of the Penn State boys was terminated.

During the training period up to this point, a budding romance was occurring between Jim Moyer and Irene Bolton. Jim was on the rebound from his lost love at Peirce, and was easy prey for Irene. It appeared to be a true match, however.

All of us trainees began working studiously on the case problems, first putting our logic down on paper in the form of flow charts. The next step was to begin writing the program in Autocoder language on IBM coding sheets. After pages and pages of code were completed, the next step was the laborious process of desk-checking. Much like writing a work of literature, one would go over the logic and instructions time and time again, making sure everything was correct. Despite our best efforts, many errors would not come to light until the programs were actually tested on the computer. During this period, fellow alumnus Dick Cummins sat across the conference table from me, utilizing an easel-like contraption to hold up his flowcharts while coding the program. One day I could take no more, and I swept my hand under the easel, knocking it over. It was all in good fun, and the rest of the class laughed heartily at poor Dick's expense. Dick and I would become close friends over the years, however.

As we all completed coding our case problems in the allotted time, the coding sheets were sent out to NORTRON Associates, a vendor who would transcribe the information onto punch cards. When the cards were returned to us, more desk-checking ensued. One day we all walked the few blocks down to 1835 Arch Street, home of the Philadelphia RAC. Our instructors were able to acquire enough 1401 computer processing time to read each trainee's program decks to produce a magnetic tape which would be used as the first step in testing our programs. Now the real work would begin.

—

Bob Stackhouse and Carol Lewis were making all of the necessary preparations for testing our programs during the second weekend in August 1965. The only place that computer time could be found was at the RAC in Greensburg, east of Pittsburgh in western Pennsylvania. Two company cars were loaded with all the work of the past few weeks – punch cards, mag tapes, logic sheets, etc. I was assigned to the car driven by Bob Stackhouse. Our journey began on Friday morning August 13. In any case, it was more than a six-hour trip when necessary stops along the way were included.

During most of the trip, I was stuck in the back seat with Joe O'Donnell in the middle and Dick Cummins and me on either side. Joe had a pack of Pinochle playing cards, and we may have played a bit of the three-handed variety in the back seat. Having a very technical mind, Joe showed us what the highest possible score would be in a hand of four-handed partners' play – anything to keep us occupied.

Around midway across the state on the PA Turnpike, our driver, Bob Stackhouse, flicked his spent cigarette out the window. Not having air-conditioning, all of the vehicle's windows were open. Several miles down the road, smoke began emanating from the rear windows. Evidently the ejected cigarette landed under the back seat, unbeknownst to us passengers. It was necessary to pull over to the shoulder of the highway and find the errant butt before the car went up in flames with us in it. In short order it was found and a catastrophe was averted with only a bit of bench seat material scorched.

As we neared Greensburg, we stopped for supper at a restaurant. I can't remember what I ordered, but I recall that Joe had a fish dish since he was an observant Catholic and it was Friday.

—

After partaking of supper our group checked into a motel near the computer center. As the evening progressed, a few of us congregated in one of the men's motel rooms to play four-handed Pinochle. I participated, but can't remember who my partner was, but the other three players were Joe O'Donnell, Dick Cummins, and Bill Herr. Six packs of beer were obtained somewhere along the line, and I, being a nondrinker myself, got the opportunity to watch my card-playing mates slowly succumb to slurred speech, the tossing of bent playing guards, and hurled epithets. Thankfully no fights broke out and we all settled down for a night's sleep before the next day's moment of truth in the computer room.

The Testing Begins

Bright and early Saturday morning, we trainees gathered in the computer room to have our programs assembled and compiled in order to make individual test tapes. The assembly process converted the 7074 Autocoder source code to machine code while the compiler pulled in necessary data input software and put it all in an executable format while producing an IBM card deck to initiate the process. An additional tape was produced which contained the program listing which would be printed out on the 1401 computer. The listing was essential in working out "bugs" in the program when testing began.

Sometime in late morning we began, one-by-one, testing our programs with accounting data provided on tape. Nobody had successful results the first time around, but that was to be expected because there is so much room for error. As for me, my program came to a screeching halt quite early in the process. Upon examination of the results, something like the exclusion of a comma in a record definition word, caused me a huge headache which would take me hours to correct.

Once a program was compiled it was necessary to patch the program with corrections in machine object code. In my case I had to create multiple patch cards on a keypunch machine. Situated in a keypunch unit with multiple machines which would be humming with activity during a normal work day, I was basically all alone trying to master the machine at the same time as I was making my corrections. Sequestered from the rest of the trainees in the computer room, I sat in solitude punching away at my employment fate.

—

Late in the afternoon I was able to make another test run with my program using the patches that I had created on the punch cards. I was now successful in processing the input tape, but now I had program logic problems that needed to be corrected. But we were moving into late evening, and I would have to wait until Sunday morning to continue the testing of my program. Jim and Irene had, by that point, successful test runs, so they could "enjoy" their evening as they saw fit. I, for one, had a cloud hovering over my head which would remain until all went well. Fitful sleep was the best I could muster.

Bright and early I was back at the computer room, trying to determine the errors in my program. Dick Cummins and I were in the same boat, working feverishly to find a solution. As it turned out, only several instructions required alteration and I finally reached end-of-job (EOJ) successfully. It was a great relief.

As the afternoon wore on, only Bill Herr was yet to reach an affirmative test result. But, eventually, he too made the grade.

At some point in the afternoon I called home to tell my parents that I did well and I'd be home again in the evening. I was surprised when Mom told me that brother Bill became engaged to Anne Gargan that weekend. There was a lot going on in our world.

Now it was just a matter of all of us Bell employees making the long six-hour drive home.

Work Assignments

All the members of our programming class were quite tired after the arduous weekend of testing. I for one hadn't caught up sufficiently on my sleep. But nonetheless, here we were.

Sometime in the morning back at One Parkway we were given our work assignments. Bob Stackhouse and Carol Lewis must have consulted during the testing weekend to recommend who should go where. Jim Moyer and I were assigned to the EDP Standard group. At that time these were the top assignments for the class, with Jim edging me out for the most coveted position. Dick Cummins was appointed to the Interdepartmental Programming group which was the next most important job. The remaining members of our class received assignments in various Customer Record & Billing (CRB) groups.

Jim and my immediate second-level supervisor was Howard Trappler who reported to our District Manager, Howard Dreisler.

Jim was given the responsibility of maintaining the operating system for the 7074 computer and coordination of large scale program updates from the various EDP groups. As for me, they didn't have room for a desk in the Standards group, so I was moved temporarily to a vacant seat in another group next to Howard George, a guy who looked a bit like a hefty Clark Kent. With no specific assignment yet, Mr. Trappler gave me a computer program listing to study. I was bored out of my mind. This went on for a couple of weeks. The high point of the day was when the coffee cart came around in the morning and I got a carton of milk and a donut.

Mr. Trappler finally came up with a non-programming job for me. I was assigned the task of writing a standard for the use of the Simplex Time Clock which was utilized in the computer rooms to register the duration of a computer operation. To get an understanding of the process I interviewed the manager of the Philadelphia computer room, Bill Lyon. Soon I was putting it all down on paper with illustrations of the time card and how it was used. Howard was quite pleased with the result and sent me a short note praising me on a job well done. That positive feedback was very important to me. I still have that note filed somewhere today.

—

As summer turned to fall, the specter of military service was hanging over my head. I still had not heard of a change in my draft status from 2S (student) to 1A (eligible for draft). But for the time being I was satisfied to remain in a state of denial. On the work front, the introduction of the new IBM System 360 was coming to Bell. Unlike the 7074, the 360 was a variable length computer (the instructions weren't of a fixed length) which used Assembler Language Programming (ALP). Since Jim Moyer was the top trainee in our group, he was sent to ALP class to learn the new language so it could be supported in Standards. I was then thrust into Jim's old job of maintaining the 7074 operating system. In this capacity I set up the periodic FLIER (Find Load and Initiate Executive Routine) updates which created the newest versions of the various computer programs for production use.

—

Dale and I were still serious in our relationship. Usually one day a week I'd walk to her place of employment on Chestnut Street and have lunch with her in the First Pennsylvania Bank cafeteria. On other days I'd have lunch in the Bell cafeteria at

One Parkway with Jim Moyer and Dick Cummins. We'd walk around center city during the noon hour.

I don't remember much about the Christmas holiday of 1965, but as for the New Year, Dale and I were invited to celebrate the holiday eve with Jim and Irene at her house in Delaware County, staying there overnight. Neither Dale nor I was very keen on the idea, but I didn't want to hurt Jim and Irene's feelings. In the early evening we went to a local movie house to see "The Glass Bottom Boat" starring Doris Day and Rod Taylor – surely not a classic. Later in the evening we played ping pong in the basement of Irene's house and retired soon after celebrating the new year.

The next day Dale and I made it into town by some means that I don't recall, but I remember being on Broad Street for a short while as the Mummers paraded down the thoroughfare. From there we took the subway for our connection back to McKinley.

—

Not long after the new year of 1966 was upon us, Jim got the first call from the Draft Board to report for a physical and subsequent military duty. Being a Mennonite, however, he could register as a conscientious objector and be able to avoid being drafted as long as he performed public service for two years. In short order he was able to obtain a job with the medical facility at New York University (NYU) in New York City in their programming department. At some point before leaving, he married Irene Bolton and they began life together in the Big Apple.

Shortly thereafter, Dick Cummins followed Jim's lead and secured a job at Temple University Medical Center in Philadelphia as a programmer. As a Christadelphian, he too was a conscientious objector. Then there was one. I was the only male from the class who was destined for military service.

—

On the heels of the exit of Jim and Dick, I was given the charge of learning COBOL (Common Business Oriented Language), a high-level programming language, to be used at some point on the new IBM 360. A COBOL assembler was not yet available on the 360, however, but there was a test version for the 7074. A new application programming group was being formed that would be using COBOL for their systems, so those involved were beginning to use the 7074 version to learn the language. I was to become the Standards support person for that effort. There was no formal class available at that time for learning the language, so I had to teach myself from a self-instruction book. I was getting comfortable in my new surroundings, but that ever present elephant was in the room.

A Greeting and a Wedding

As the new year of 1966 introduced itself, Dale and I marked time. The specter of the draft hung over me like Damocles' Sword.

One weekend, for entertainment, and as a diversion, we traveled down to the Cherry Hill Mall in New Jersey to do a bit of shopping. It was the only large shopping mall in the area at that time. As we roamed the aisles of various establishments, we wound up in a toy store. Setting my eyes upon a Ouija board, I thought that it might be fun to purchase one, not that I ever believed in fortune telling. When we got to Dale's home later that evening, we gave it a try.

I don't remember the specifics, but we laid the board out and positioned the planchette upon it with our fingers on either side. Foremost in my mind was whether I was going to be drafted soon. The planchette crept across the board, seeming to have a mind of its own. In any case, it spelled out a response that indicated that I'd be saying goodbye to civilian life soon. Subconsciously, I suppose, we were directing the results.

As late winter moved into early spring, plans were underway for brother Bill's wedding to Anne Gargan. Saturday, May 14 was the date set for the big occasion, it being the same as our parents' wedding day 27 years earlier. The ceremony would be at St. James Catholic Church in Elkins Park, followed by a celebration dinner at the Schwarzwald Inn in the Olney section of Philadelphia. Generational transitions were taking place in good old McKinley.

—

Well, the inevitable occurred when I received a letter from the Selective Service System in mid-April. With a sinking feeling in my stomach, I slowly opened the envelope and read the message from the President of the United States:

To Frank A. Burr

Greeting:

You are hereby ordered for induction into the Armed Forces of the United States, and to report at:

LOCAL BOARD NO. 106
533 GREENWOOD AVE.
JENKINTOWN, PA 19046

on May 23, 1966 at 6:15 A. M.
for forwarding to an Armed Forces Induction Station.

—

The die had been cast, and I had a little over a month to prepare for the big change in my life. I'd be leaving all that I knew since my youth. I'd be thrust into a new world of uncertainty and chance, where most big decisions would be made for me, without regard to my personal feelings. I'd be torn from the arms of my loving Dale for who-knows-how-long? My promising career at Bell Telephone would be put on hold.

The next morning at my office on the 12th Floor of One Parkway, I gave a copy of my draft notice to my boss, Ted Marschal. He expressed a true regret that I'd be leaving, knowing what possibly lay before me, since he too had served in the army.

Arrangements were made for my leave of absence. Fortunately, by law, I would resume work at Bell when I returned from duty in two years, having any regular increases in pay applied. And I would be due a severance amount of two-week's pay since I had been employed at Bell for three weeks short of a full year, otherwise I would have received three months' salary. I simply got hosed. Another Bell programmer, Angelo Palumbi, started employment about a month before I did and was also drafted. He bought a VW Beetle with his three-month windfall.

—

Rightfully so, preparations for Bill's wedding took precedence over my military draft situation as mid-May got closer. Rehearsal for the ceremony took place at St. James RC Church some days before the big day, followed by a dinner for the wedding party and friends. I was a bit disappointed that Dale wasn't invited since she was a real part of my life by that time.

The weekend prior to the rehearsal, a low-key bachelor party was thrown for Bill. Attending was I, Richard Hogg, George Hetherington, and Bill's other friends, Teddy Culp and Tommy Gatter. After a drive to center city Philadelphia, we had supper at the Pub Tiki on Walnut Street near Rittenhouse Square. Post-meal, we all went to a Midtown movie house to see "The Silencers," a spy spoof featuring Dean Martin as Matt Helm with his sexy co-star, Stella Stevens. What we guys probably remember most about that movie was the scene where Ms. Stevens – playing a possible enemy spy – leaves Martin in a Mercury station wagon during a thunderstorm. As she tries to escape, she falls in a mud puddle, getting her low-cut dress thoroughly drenched as she stumbles to get up. It was quite a sight to see.

—

I don't remember many of the details of my brother Bill's wedding even though I was best man. Father Grace presided at the ceremony at St. James Church. Being noticeably nervous, Bill fumbled a bit with the wedding ring that he placed on Anne's hand, but other than that all went smoothly. After the traditional tossing of rice at the new couple as they left the church, we were all soon on our way to the Schwarzwald Inn for the post-wedding meal.

The guest list included those from my father's side of the family – Aunt Helen, her husband Clarence, and cousins Gerry, Sid, and Jimmy with their spouses. My uncle Bud Wernett was the only representative from Mom's side of the family. I believe Uncle Bud had stayed overnight at our house, having driven up from Camden, New Jersey.

Sitting at the long head table with the wedding party, toasts were offered before the meal began. I suppose that I gave a short spiel of some sort, but the whole matter escapes me. As I sat there trying to enjoy the festivities, my upcoming induction in the U.S. Army weighed heavy on my mind.

After dinner the band struck up a tune and I was soon on the floor dancing with Anne's cousin, Carol Jean Stevens, the bridesmaid. The dashing Uncle Bud, who was an excellent dancer, chose my Dale as her partner for a number of dances. But he could do no wrong in my book, and I always cherished any chance to be around him.

—

Bill and Anne stole away after the party wound down. In secrecy, I was chosen to drive the newlyweds back to McKinley, but there was a bit of deception and misdirection going on since Bill didn't want his car to become the victim of his friends George Hetherington and Teddy Culp who would have surely "decorated" it in a rather unfashionable manner. So earlier on their wedding day, Bill got permission from friend Mary Herrmann Howald, older sister of Pat and Marge, to park his car in Mary's garage at the corner of Cadwalader and Osceola Avenues. Subsequently they were ab e to escape McKinley unscathed as they headed to the Pocono Mountains for their honeymoon.

Bill & Anne's Wedding Day

Wedding Party on side lawn at home
May 14, 1966
Mr. Gargan, Carol Jean Stevens, Mrs. Gargan
Bill, Anne, Mom, Me & Dad

Dale and I outside St. James Church

The Longest Day

As draft day crept closer, I tried to put my affairs in order, saying goodbye to my workmates at Bell, packing the essential civilian clothes that I would need before being issued a GI uniform. The weekend before induction Monday, Bill and Anne came home from their honeymoon and set up home in their apartment on Hofnagle Street in Northeast Philadelphia. Bill stopped by to wish me well. Not only was it to be a great transition for me, the whole Burr household would be upended. In a little over a week's time, brother Bill and I would be gone. I believe that my mom took it the hardest, her two sons ostensibly leaving home for good.

After attending church on Sunday, the 22nd, I proceeded to Dale's house on High School Road. I draw a blank after that until we both arrived at my home to visit the family before saying goodbye to each other. I have a black and white Polaroid photo that I snapped of Dale that afternoon, smiling while sitting demurely on a tree stump on the side yard. She's wearing a loose gingham-type top over white slacks. It was a tearful goodbye.

—

On Monday morning, the 23rd, Dad checked to see if I was awake around 5:00 A.M. He need not have bothered. I was already stirring – totally preoccupied with the apprehension of the unknown.

I suppose I managed to choke down a breakfast of some sort before I hopped in the passenger seat of the old 1962 Dodge Dart, having bid a sad adieu to Mom and Auntie. Dad would take me for the short drive to Jenkintown.

What was so unsettling was the fact that I was leaving my boyhood home – my comfort zone – for the first time. Sure, I went on many family vacations over the years, but I never went to camp; never stayed overnight anywhere away from family members except when I attended the business education contest in Bloomsburg, PA in my senior year of high school.

Dad slowly backed out of the long driveway of our Cadwalader Avenue home and proceeded down the street past my old school on the right, McKinley Elementary. Pausing at the stop sign at the intersection of Jenkintown Road, I took a final look at McKinley Firehouse where I had been an active member since my days in high school. Proceeding north on Jenkintown Road we passed the Village and the Manor, the homes of the more affluent members of the community.

As we neared the intersection of Washington Lane, I gazed at the fairways of the Old York Road Country Club – an oft-traveled thoroughfare of my boyhood when walking to the old Hiway Theater or the Hobby Shop in Jenkintown.

Turning left on York Road (PA Route 611) we traveled the short block to Greenwood Avenue where Dad made a right, passing by the Woolworth's 5 & 10 where I had spent many hours walking the aisles in my youth.

The draft board building loomed ahead on the right. Near the curb, a handful of fellow, dejected draftees, with faraway looks in their eyes, waited in anticipation for the doors to open. I suppose dad uttered a quick, "Take care son," before I joined the growing mass. There's a hole in my memory from that point until we arrived, via bus, at the reception center at 401 North Broad Street in Philadelphia.

—

Having stopped by the 401 location months before, in consideration of possibly enlisting and finding an MOS that would utilize my programming skills, I now put my hope in the uncertain fate that awaited me. Before long all we potential recruits were being herded along half-naked, taking physicals – being poked and prodded by the army's physicians and nurses. Although I felt like an anonymous hunk of skinny meat, I did strike up a friendship with a fellow recruit, Tom Marshall. Misery loves company. Some of the tests that were performed on us were by a female nurse whose hair tended to fall across her eyes, which she managed by flicking her head back to put the wily strands back in place. Thus she acquired the moniker of "Sally Flick" by the two of us.

The day dragged on and on, and I no longer remember all of the details. We were all given tickets to partake of the lunchtime fare in the cafeteria. Later in the afternoon, those that were up to snuff, as far as the army was concerned, were lined up in rows and administered the oath which would make us property of the United States government for the next two years – God willing.

Around closing time for most of the Philadelphia businesses, we were unceremoniously herded out the front door onto Broad Street. This was a ritual that I had witnessed a number of times in the past, when leaving work in the evening at Bell Telephone's One Parkway headquarters, which faced Arch Street. As we turned south on Broad and made a right on Arch, I now knew that I would become part of the spectacle, and hoped dearly that nobody that I had worked with would observe me in this woeful parade. Fortunately, none did.

Our destination was 30th Street Station, where we would later embark on a special train that would take us to an interim stop at Union Station in Washington, D.C., but first we were treated to supper at a restaurant at 30th Street where we actually ordered from menus. It would be the best food that I would experience in the months to come. There were even cloth napkins at each place setting.

Later on we boarded the dedicated recruit train. No one of any note in authority would accompany us. A short-in-stature inductee by the name of Charles Fries was instructed to watch over us by a sergeant, he being chosen because he had experienced a year of ROTC training in college. He appeared to be scared witless by the responsibility placed on him. He was duly ignored by his fellow, would-be soldiers, and I felt a bit sorry for him.

As the train pulled out of the station and into the night, I was beginning to face the unknown, uncertain what would lie ahead. Letting myself become mesmerized by the swaying of the cars and the metronome cadence of the wheels traveling along the tracks, I mentally bid farewell to all that I held dear: my dear home of McKinley; the city of Philadelphia; my family; and my dear girlfriend Dale.

THE END

Epilogue

My childhood in McKinley seems idyllic in retrospect. There are so many fond memories – a bit similar to living in the fictional town of Mayberry depicted in the 1950s Andy Griffith Show. Growing pains were always a part of the equation, but having a loving family and religious faith helped to overcome adversities, building some measure of character in the author. Friends and acquaintances also played a major role in my development.

After being inducted in the army in May 1966, I endured basic training at Ft. Benning, Georgia where, upon graduation, I became a member of the resident 139th Military Police Company. Forty of us, right out of basic training, were placed in that unit. But my service with that group was short-lived since I received orders to join the 152nd MP Platoon of the 199th Infantry Brigade, then forming in Benning, in October 1966. We were to be deployed in November of that year to Vietnam. When first I was assigned to the 139th, and assuming I'd be stationed at Benning for the extent of my two-year term, Dale and I planned to get married in the spring of 1967. This new development altered our plans.

Shortly before overseas deployment, our unit was given a seven-day leave to spend at home. Dale and I decided to alter our wedding plans and get married during that week . While I could do little in Georgia to help in the planning, other than getting the reluctant permission from my commanding officer to get married, Dale put everything in motion. Being only 19 years old at the time, she would need permission from her parents. Her dad was initially against it, then Dale reminded him that he did the same thing, marrying her mother shortly before being sent overseas to fight in World War II. After getting a physical from a doctor in the area, to make sure that I didn't have a socially transmitted disease (no problem there), Dale and I, and our fathers, went to Norristown to get our marriage license.

A simple ceremony was planned for the evening of Veterans Day, November 11, 1966, at the chapel at Willow Grove Naval Air Base. We were married by a navy chaplain as brother Bill stood in as best man and Dale's friend, Maria, acted as bridesmaid. Afterwards, a reception was held at my parents' house in McKinley. Sneaking out after an hour or so, we headed to the Howard Johnson Motel in Willow Grove to spend our first night together before heading to Atlantic City, New Jersey to enjoy our honeymoon as best we could under the conditions.

Prior to my coming home on leave, Dale was invited to live on the third floor of my home on Cadwalader Avenue, where she would reside during the duration of my assignment abroad. She did a wonderful job, turning my brother's and my old bedrooms into a comfortable apartment. We spent our last, and tearful, evening there before my leaving the next morning for a flight back to Ft. Benning. Dad, Mom, and Auntie sadly saw me off – Mom's eyes puffed from obvious crying.

From Ft. Benning, The 199th members were flown to Oakland, California where we boarded the USNS D. I. Sultan for the two and a half week voyage to Vietnam across the Pacific Ocean. Upon arrival in country our MP unit was given base camp security duties for the 199th at Long Binh, VN. I spent my time there initially on guard duty at the various camp checkpoints, but later I was appointed clerk of the Provost Marshal, typing reports for our platoon leader, 1st Lt. Salvatore Chidichimo and the detective (CID) Mr. Hudson. The typing skills that I learned at Abington High School came in handy. Gratefully I returned home on October 5, 1967, several months before the violent TET Offensive which began the following January. Everyone was so glad to see me home safely, but the attention of the family quickly shifted when Bill and Anne gave birth to my parents first grandchild, my niece Victoria Anne Burr, on the 7th. Till this day I still tease Vicki about upstaging my homecoming.

I spent my last seven months of military duty at Ft. Monroe, Virginia where Dale joined me in living in an apartment off-base. On May 22, 1968, we made our way home to McKinley in our 1965 VW Beetle, and lived in our Cadwalader apartment until June 1969 when we purchased a home in the Willow Grove section of Abington, not far from the old amusement park, where we still reside.

After my return from the military, I continued my career at Bell Telephone as an information technology professional, achieving a second level manager position. Although I felt that I performed well in that capacity, the unique demands of the corporate life were taking their mental toll on me. With that in mind, and in order to maintain some measure of sanity, I retired after 30 years service at age 50. In a complete about face, I then became a school crossing guard for 12 years. In 2002 I began writing a weekly opinion column for a local publication, **The Trend**. It was the best job that I ever had, giving me the opportunity to put down my thoughts in print, and happily interfacing with readers. When the publication changed management in 2007, freelance writers, like me, were let go. I then wrote a monthly column for a 55+ plus publication, **In Your Prime**, for two plus years until that paper ceased to exist. In 2007 I self-published a book of poems and essays entitled Common Thoughts.

—

My Mom passed away in 1989, and my Dad survived to the age of 91 in 2005. Dad continued to live in my boyhood home until 1999 when he remarried and moved to a retirement facility in Lancaster, PA. Auntie continued to live with my parents until she passed away in 1980 at the age of 92. Dad remained a member of the McKinley Fire Co. until he moved to Lancaster. Dale and I have spent more than 50 years of marriage together, as have my brother Bill and Anne. Our son Andy, and daughter-in-law Vincie, have three sons: Tyler, Noah, and Sean. The Burr name should live on in the future.

Most years I still make it a point to return to McKinley on the Fourth of July to attend the festivities promoted by the fire company. Little has changed in the annual parade since I was a child. Usually before the celebration begins, I walk around the neighborhood and travel back in time in my mind – picturing myself playing in the side yard with our dog Teddy, or riding down the street with my old friend John on our bicycles and stopping at Doc Davis' Drugstore to have a treat at the soda fountain. Old friend Tom Hartmann has traveled up to McKinley several times over the last two decades to walk around the old neighborhood with me and reminisce. We've even had lunch at the former Square Deal Market which became the McKinley Market in later years

Although my heart is still in McKinley, I don't think that I could live there anymore, since, in my mind, it is locked in the time of the 1950s and 60s. And that special feeling is something I never want to spoil.

Frank (Buddy) Burr - 2018

Acknowledgments

It took me about five years or so, of off-and-on writing, to complete this memoir. It was very cathartic, but not always easy. So many distractions tend to interfere, and I don't always employ the necessary discipline to set aside time for writing. My wife Dale has been tacitly supportive although she can't figure out why I have wanted to bare my soul, so to speak, with the possibility of embarrassing myself and others. But it has been my intent from the beginning to be fair and explain past situations through the youthful eyes of someone who basically doesn't exist anymore.

I've shared my writings along the way with my niece, Victoria Burr Miller, who has been diligent in providing useful suggestions and has advised me, where appropriate, on grammar and sentence structure. Being a part time teacher and tutor, she has brought the expertise that I needed.

My lifetime friend, John Bauerle, who lives in the Poughkeepsie, NY area received draft chapters as I relived our boyhood years in McKinley. He has kept me honest with my recollections and let me know, diplomatically, when we haven't agreed on some of the facts. Being the author, however, I made the final decision when there were perceived discrepancies. Although I usually see him only at high school reunions now, we frequently keep in touch and the personal bonds have never been broken.

On occasion I have also shared some of my drafts, or have sought to verify recollections, with Thomas "Tuck" Hartmann and Patricia Herrmann Conroy. Brother Bill and his wife Anne have also helped me get the facts straight when necessary.

At a meeting of the McKinley Civic Association in April 2009, Joyce Tighe (former owner of McKinley Market) and Marge Herrmann Sexton provided a list of McKinley Businesses which existed through the years. This was very helpful in my research.

I'd also would like to thank Sheri Elfman-Bonnanno who got me started as a freelance writer by hiring me to do a column for The **Trend Mid-Week.**

Two of my teachers of yore have influenced me through encouragement in years past. Frank Pennypacker, the American Literature teacher in my sophomore year at Peirce College, felt that I had potential writing talent, and suggested that I should follow that course rather than pursue the less artistic field of becoming a computer programmer. He has long passed, and I didn't heed him at the time, but his words have achieved some measure of fruition after these many years.

Then there is my senior year English teacher, William F. Gavin, from Abington High School who uttered a simple encouraging phrase as he looked over my shoulder while I was working on an assignment in class. A few years later, after ending his teaching jobs, he pursued a career in politics, becoming a speech writer for Richard Nixon and Ronald Reagan, as well as an aide to House Minority Leader, Bob Michael, and U.S. Senator James Buckley. As good fortune would have it, I tracked him down about four years ago, writing to him at his home outside Washington, D.C. I let him know how I valued his simple words of encouragement a half century before. He didn't remember me or that particular incident, which didn't surprise me because of my less than stellar academic standing in high school. However, he was happy to interact with me and share his insights on writing a memoir. And I cherish the signed copy of his book, **Street Corner Conservative**, which he so graciously sent me. He passed away about a year and a half after I had made contact with him, but I cherished that re-connection albeit its relatively short duration.

83728906R00141

Made in the USA
Middletown, DE
14 August 2018